PRAISE FOR
KID CAROLINA

"Heidi Schnakenberg writes with passion and energy in *Kid Carolina*. This woman knows her facts, and she presents them with clear, straightforward ease. Ms. Schnakenberg weaves a compelling narrative that provokes and entertains throughout, and more than once I found myself gasping at the events in the story." —Keith Powell, actor, *30 Rock*

"A page-turner! A juicy and intriguing account of Dick Reynolds's life and legacy."
—Nadia Yakoob, former editor-in-chief of the
Georgetown Immigration Law Journal

"A life up in smoke, with plenty of heat, passion, and scandal along the way. Heidi Schnakenberg's lively chronicle of riches-gone-wrong proves that money may not buy happiness, but it sure makes for a good read."

—Deborah Davis, author of
Gilded: How Newport Became America's Richest Resort

"R.J. Reynolds Jr. had way too much money and left the type of legacy that I find oddly intriguing and reprehensible—an unbelievable life of debauchery, vanity, sorrow, adventure, and philanthropy. But this biography is more than a comprehensive account of a tycoon's accomplishments and mistakes. Schnakenberg's adept storytelling gets the blood flowing through the complicated heart of "Dick." *Kid Carolina* seizes the reader with a tale of passion, longing, and uncertainty. Of course there is an influential legacy here, but there is also bona fide life pulsing through every page."
—Mattox Roesch, author of
Sometimes We're Always Real Same-Same

"An immersive, sprawling saga of scionhood, tobacco, manslaughter, and love. Unlike his contemporary Howard Hughes, precious little has been known about the outsized life of enigmatic tycoon R.J. Reynolds Jr. . . . until now. This fascinating tale is rescued from the dustbin of history by Heidi Schnakenberg's extraordinary, clear-eyed *Kid Carolina*. The legendary cigarette magnate's best and worst days are resurrected with an excess of evocative detail, viewed from a psychologically astute perspective with a palpable empathy for all involved. Even if you're a non-smoker, *Kid Carolina* burns long and satisfies deeply, like only the best cancer-sticks . . . but without any of the risk."

—Steven Bagatourian, screenwriter of *American Gun* and Independent Spirit Award nominee, Best Feature Film

KID
CAROLINA

R. J. REYNOLDS JR.,
A TOBACCO FORTUNE, *and the* MYSTERIOUS DEATH
of a SOUTHERN ICON

HEIDI SCHNAKENBERG

CENTER STREET

New York Boston Nashville

Center Street
Hachette Book Group
237 Park Avenue
New York, NY 10017

www.centerstreet.com

Center Street is a division of Hachette Book Group, Inc.
The Center Street name and logo are trademarks of Hachette Book Group, Inc.

Printed in the United States of America

First Edition: March 2010
10 9 8 7 6 5 4 3 2 1

Library of Congress Cataloging-in-Publication Data

Schnakenberg, Heidi.
    Kid Carolina: R. J. Reynolds Jr., a tobacco fortune, and the mysterious death of a Southern icon / Heidi Schnakenberg.— 1st ed.
        p. cm.
    Summary: "An intimate look at the dramatic, tumultuous life and mysterious death of Dick Reynolds—tobacco fortune heir, business tycoon, cultural obsession, and true American icon"—Provided by the publisher
    Includes bibliographical references.
    ISBN 978-1-59995-103-4
  1. Reynolds, R. J. (Richard Joshua), 1906–1964.   2. Reynolds, R. J. (Richard Joshua), 1850–1918—Family.   3. Businessmen—United States—Biography.   4. Heirs—North Carolina—Biography.
5. R. J. Reynolds Tobacco Company.   6. Philanthropists—United States—Biography.   7. Politicians—North Carolina—Biography.
8. North Carolina—Biography.   9. Winston-Salem (N.C.)—Biography.
10. Sapelo Island (Ga.)—Biography.   I. Title.

CT275.R497S36 2010
975.6'043092—dc22   2009027899

For Karl

CONTENTS

CONTENTS

R. J. REYNOLDS JR. CHRONOLOGY

April 4, 1906	Born in Winston-Salem
July 29, 1918	R.J. Sr. dies
1921	Katharine marries J. Edward Johnston
1921–1923	Attends school (Reynolda, Woodbury Forest, Virginia; Tome School, Maryland; Culver Military Academy, Indiana)
May 24, 1924	Katharine Reynolds Johnston dies
1924–1925	Attends North Carolina State University
1925–1927	Obtains pilot's license from Orville Wright, founds airline companies in New York
May–Nov. 1929	Drunk driving accident in London, trial, and incarceration
July 6, 1932	Z. Smith Reynolds dies
Jan. 1, 1933	Marries Elizabeth Dillard
Dec. 7, 1933	Birth of first son, R. J. Reynolds III
1934	Comes into full inheritance, builds Devotion
1934	Purchases Sapelo Island
July 31, 1936	Birth of second son, John Dillard Reynolds

1937–1939	Yacht racing
July 19, 1938	Birth of third son, Zachary Taylor Reynolds
Jan. 27, 1940	Birth of fourth son, William Neal Reynolds
Jan. 4, 1941	Appointed treasurer of Democratic National Committee
May 12, 1941	Becomes mayor of Winston-Salem
June 1942	Finishes Z. Smith Reynolds Airport; joins the Navy
1942–1945	Navy service in World War II
Jan. 1, 1946	Divorces Elizabeth Dillard
Aug. 7, 1946	Marries Marianne O'Brien
July 13, 1947	Birth of fifth son, Michael Randolph Reynolds
Dec. 2, 1948	Birth of sixth son, Patrick Cleveland Reynolds
1951–1952	Builds *Aries* in England
Aug. 7, 1952	Divorces Marianne O'Brien
Aug. 8, 1952	Marries Muriel Marston Greenough
1953	Mary Katharine Babcock dies
May 16, 1960	Divorces Muriel Marston Greenough
March 15, 1961	Marries Annemarie Schmitt
May 1962	Second divorce from Muriel Marston Greenough
May 1963	Settlement with Muriel Marston Greenough
July 10, 1963	Second marriage to Annemarie Schmitt
Dec. 14, 1964	Dies
Dec. 17, 1964	Birth of seventh child, first daughter, Irene Sabina Reynolds

INTRODUCTION

I was first introduced to Jeanette Scotton, a Southern trans-
plant and family friend, at a wedding in South Carolina in
2001. A few years later she approached me because she heard
I had a penchant for nonfiction drama and she had something to
show me.

As I sat down in her parents' cozy Midwest farmhouse, she
pulled out stacks of manuscripts, newspaper clippings, letters, archives, estate documents, photos, diaries, court filings, old, dusty
magazines, private investigation materials, and a suitcase etched
with the monogram MRM. This suitcase had belonged to Muriel
Reynolds, the third wife of R. J. "Dick" Reynolds Jr., the late heir
of the RJR Tobacco dynasty. Jeanette had acquired the suitcase
and its contents from Muriel's best friend, Humphrey Hutchins,
who was compiling a book for Muriel that he never completed.

As I sorted through the papers, Jeanette told me she had to be
careful because, well, she was convinced she had been haunted
by a ghost who paced her Georgia balcony at night. In the South,
legend has it that a well-documented electromagnetic charge
attracts the human spirit in Savannah and Georgia's coastal
islands. Jeanette felt sure she was being haunted by the ghost of
Muriel, who was encouraging someone to tell the story.

I was struck by the detail and enormity of the story of

R. J. Reynolds Jr., as told from Muriel's point of view. I was well acquainted with the RJR Tobacco Company, but I didn't know much about the family. Dick Reynolds's personal life captivated me, and I was intrigued by his love of the sea—his constant desire to escape. I imagined how the pressures of Dick's life and his alcohol-induced misery led him to simply want to run, or in his case, sail. It was interesting to see that this great man was not so different from anyone else—seeking love and freedom, but often disappointing others and hurting himself in the process.

Dick's story and mysterious end reminded me of many other tales of the wealthy who ran themselves into a circle of destruction and controversy, like the Kennedy, Onassis, Ford, and Niarchos families, who were also struck with untimely deaths in the midst of unimaginable wealth.

The dynasty from which Dick came is, without question, one of the most famous tobacco empires in America and the Southeast, where the Reynoldses and their products—Camels, Winstons, Kools, and Reynolds Wrap, to name a few, are household names. The power and influence of the Reynolds family is most deeply felt in North Carolina, where R. J. Reynolds Sr. is considered the forefather and patron of the city of Winston-Salem, and the majority of the population is employed by Reynolds establishments or organizations made possible by the vision of R.J. Sr. and his descendants. Every corner is touched by the family—from the city's premier museum, Reynolda House Museum of American Art, to city parks such as Tanglewood and Reynolds Park. Winston-Salem's Z. Smith Reynolds Airport and Wake Forest University were established by the Reynoldses, and the Baptist Hospital, once heavily subsidized by Reynolds money, is the city's largest employer. Towering over the skyline is the twenty-two-story RJR Tobacco building—the first Southern skyscraper, and the model for New York's Empire State Building.

In the 1930s, the Reynolds heirs were considered the wealthiest in the country and dominated the newsreels with the nearby Dukes. As the twentieth century roared on, young Dick Reynolds shared the reputation of the quintessential daredevil-playboy heir with the likes of young billionaire Howard Hughes.

However, Dick was more than a successor to the family riches. He was a Southern icon in his own right, and a pioneer in business, engineering, politics, and philanthropy. He served as treasurer of the Democratic National Committee and developed numerous industries across America. He earned his pilot's license from Orville Wright as a teenager and developed aviation at Long Island's Curtiss Field after Charles Lindbergh's transatlantic flight. But his greatest love wasn't tobacco, aviation, or even the stock market—it was the open water. Dick became an expert yachtsman—an accomplishment that was as personal as it was ambitious, and his precious boats shaped a life that was as successful as it was tumultuous.

Dick thrived on the highs of every new, wild endeavor, only to crash and burn into drastic declines. At home, he would often run from his obligations and toss opportunities for bonding with his sons into a blue-green ocean somewhere off the coast of a foreign land. His yachts were first, and his family was second. Muriel once said, "If I was drowning and Dick's boat was sinking, he'd save the boat first."

But Dick's nautical getaways couldn't save him from the physical effects of alcoholism, emphysema, or the dramatic events of his last years, until he finally met his entangled end in a question mark.

~ ⋅ ~

As I scrounged for further details of Dick's life and death, I read the Associated Press archives, the *Atlanta Journal*, the *Winston-Salem Journal*, the *New York Times*, the *Los Angeles Times*, and *Time* magazine anytime Dick Reynolds's name popped up from the 1920s to the 1960s. His life was closely followed by the press from his teens until his last divorce. After he married his fourth wife,

Annemarie, his name and legacy all but disappeared from the news and his death was little more than a footnote. My journeys took me all over the country, from California to New York, and to North Carolina, Florida, and Georgia many times over. I had Dick's steps retraced in Europe and my team visited his final resting place in Switzerland. My research team spent hours going through court documents, newspaper archives, and libraries in five states and three countries. We talked with family members, friends, former employees, acquaintances, and descendants of people who knew Dick at the height of his fame. I visited with staff at Reynolds residences, Reynolds institutions and businesses, and Reynolds tourist attractions, and with residents in North Carolina and Georgia who knew the family. What I learned most about Dick was that he was very popular and loved, and is still greatly missed by many who never quite got over his early death. I also learned that his descendants never got over the pain of the loss of their father.

Informed by this exclusive material and exhaustive documentary research, *Kid Carolina* provides a window into the intimate personal life of the scion, astute businessman, and sailing genius. This story is not only a tale of Dick's great accomplishments and fame; it is also a love story about Dick and Muriel—an intricate documentation of the passion and troubles Dick shared with his most controversial wife, who matched him in both intellect and temperament and with whom he shared his life story. *Kid Carolina* reveals how R. J. Reynolds Jr. shaped and influenced American life and shows the ways in which his personal choices corrupted a once promising life and family.

Until now, Dick's life has never been given this kind of personal attention—he has always been chronicled in the shadow of his father. In the pages ahead you'll read a portrait of the side of an icon that has never been seen before, and witness the unraveling of the firstborn son of R. J. Reynolds and heir to one of the world's greatest tobacco fortunes.

KID
CAROLINA

"We cannot control the winds,
but we can always adjust our sails."
—R. J. Reynolds Jr.

CHAPTER I

The Patriarch

1850–1906

Richard Joshua Reynolds Sr., founder of the family tobacco fortune, was born on July 28, 1850, in Critz County, Virginia, where his parents, Hardin and Nancy Reynolds, had settled after their marriage in 1843. As a youngster, R.J.'s father had participated in an auction and won a bid to expand on his family's remote homestead at the foot of Virginia's No Business Mountain and in the shadows of the Blue Ridge and North Carolina mountain ranges. The 717-acre property, located between the North and South Mayo Rivers, which they fondly named Rock Spring Plantation, was part of Hardin's huge, eight-thousand-acre local land ownership, and the humble house sat in the middle of the great estate. To maintain the vast plantation, much of which was used to grow tobacco, the Reynoldses owned dozens of slaves.

In the 1840s, the Reynolds family rebuilt, expanded, and remodeled their modest yet aristocratic house as their brood grew. The two-story brick home included several bedrooms, a dining room, a parlor with a fireplace, a central hall, and solid chestnut wood flooring throughout. A brick cookhouse sat apart, connected by a covered pathway. They had luxuries that few farmers in the area dreamed of—soft beds, a brick milk house, a log ice house, and silver flatware. They even had their own rosewood piano, books, and photographs, which few other farmers could afford.

The house was surrounded by an iron fence and a simple garden. When family members passed away, they were buried in a small cemetery in the backyard. A tree-lined, mile-long road led from the remote homestead's main gate to the tiny village of Critz.

From 1844 onward, Hardin and Nancy produced a family of sixteen children, but only eight survived childhood, and Richard Joshua "R.J." was the second oldest son. Some of Hardin and Nancy's children died in infancy from disease and later from a smallpox outbreak during the Civil War. All of the lost children were buried in the estate's graveyard.

After the Civil War, the Reynoldses were nearly broke. The family's eighty-eight slaves were freed and their cattle pillaged, but thankfully the house was left standing. Young R.J. managed to save the family's horses during the war as well—he hid them deep in the woods when the Northern troops descended. The family might have been helped by a little good luck, too. Nancy had retained an old silver coin, which had been handed down to her by her father. It was called the "Joshua Coin"—a square, seventeenth-century Peruvian silver piece that Nancy's grandfather had procured during the French and Indian War. Joshua Cox Sr. had worn the coin around his neck, believing it saved his life during the war. Since then, the coin was thought to bring good luck to those who rubbed it on a piece of gold. The Joshua Coin had to be passed down to male heirs with the name

"Joshua." Naturally, R.J. inherited the coin as a young man and carried it with him wherever he went.

During the fighting, Hardin managed to continue farming tobacco in the hidden areas of the acreage—away from the prying eyes of Southern officials who forbade farmers from growing nonnecessities during the war. They were to grow only food in support of the troops, but Hardin knew he would face economic ruin if he ceased tobacco production entirely. When the war ended, Hardin quickly put his boys and remaining horses to work farming the tobacco plantation again.

The days of Reconstruction were tough for plantation owners in the South. Their land could be taken from them unless they stated that they agreed with the abolition of slavery and the terms of the Civil War. Hardin didn't hesitate to proclaim that the Civil War was right and just, and he successfully safeguarded his land from Union forces.

Whether Hardin believed what he said or whether he simply wanted to protect his land, no one knew for sure.

A Businessman Is Born

As the Reynolds family resumed tobacco farming, Hardin's boys, including R.J. Sr., who had severe dyslexia and dropped out of college early in his academic career, took wagonloads of tobacco to markets in numerous neighboring states, including Tennessee, Kentucky, and North Carolina. One town in North Carolina called Salem caught young R.J.'s eye. Salem was a predominantly Moravian town, originally settled by Czechs, Austrians, and Germans in the 1700s, with a cultural center square big enough for the county market, and with its soon-to-be developed rail line, it was a prime location for tobacco sales. Many of the wealthy Moravians, who had built some of Salem's most beautiful old homes, loved tobacco as much as any other Southerner.

In R.J.'s early selling days, the Moravians had also established a rare women's college in Salem, which two of R.J.'s sisters later attended. The female students lived on campus and kept their own horses, which was unheard of in those days. The college was a testament to the progressiveness of Salem—a trait that R.J. admired and further attracted him to the region. The shared values of R.J. and the Moravians would soon turn into a lifelong business and civic partnership. In years to come, the Moravians would not only buy Reynolds tobacco products, they would eventually work directly for R.J. The Reynoldses considered the Moravians responsible for their early success and later worked to preserve as many of the original Moravian buildings in Salem as possible, as well as the museums and the old Salem town square where they got their start. And by the time R.J. was middle-aged, he served as host to numerous receptions for the female graduates of the progressive Salem Female Academy he had admired for so many years.

While still a teenager, R.J. Sr. hauled overflowing wagons of tobacco to town all over the country and became one of the best bargainers at market. Sometimes selling could be tough in the Reconstruction era, and on at least one occasion R.J. returned to Critz after a sale with wagonloads of textiles, animal skins, furniture, and other household goods—anything he could barter—but no cash. The family was livid. In response, R.J. sold some of the bartered supplies for a bigger profit than he would have earned from selling tobacco. He was never questioned again.

By age twenty-five, R.J. had gained extensive experience as a tobacco seller and he was hungry to venture out on his own. He became convinced tobacco would flourish in a town with a rail line and accessible labor. He talked to his father about selling his interest in Rock Spring Plantation early and moving to Salem to build his own tobacco factory. Hardin was supportive and gave him $10,000 in exchange for his forfeited interest in the family farm. With that, R.J. left Rock Spring for good in 1874.

Young R.J. eagerly set out for Salem on horseback to start his business. Out of respect for the wishes of the townspeople of Salem, R.J. opened up his first tobacco factory about a mile away on Depot Street in Winston, and invested $7,500 on his first purchase of flat plug (pressed cake) chewing tobacco. To make the plug, the tobacco was sweetened and pressed into sheets, then cut into thick strips and rolls that resembled beef jerky. The strips and rolls were sold directly to consumers and chewers would bite off the tobacco directly from the roll.

R.J. came to love the smell and sound of his factory at work, and he lived and worked in his personal office above his factories for most of his life. Today, one of R.J.'s old factories still stands, along with the rail line that trailed through it.

R.J. at Work

Young R.J. was a tall and handsome man—six foot, four inches—and although he spoke with a stammer, he was thoughtful, confident, and intriguing to the town's ladies. In spite of the attention he received from women in Winston, R.J. stayed intensely focused on his work—a trend that would keep him from settling down for decades to come.

, As an employer, R.J. was known for his fairness, his self-control, and his industrialist attitude. He felt that any man could make a million dollars honestly. R.J. was a hard worker and expected the same of his employees; he was always at his office early and worked alongside his employees all day, six days a week. He kept to this schedule even after he became a millionaire.

For years, R.J. had distinguished himself through the use of bright leaf twist and flat plug chewing tobacco with saccharin flavoring. After decades of success, R.J. eventually made the departure to burley smoking tobacco. One of R.J.'s most popular twentieth-century products was the burley-based, light-air-cured-leaf pipe and smoking tobacco—a brand he called Prince Albert. He launched the brand in 1907 with an aggressive advertising campaign and it quickly became a hit.

By the turn of the century, R.J. was rumored to have single-handedly created thirty to fifty millionaires in North Carolina, and he employed three hundred people in his factories and another two hundred in his administrative offices. As his products soared in popularity, the tobacco company became a stockholder's dream. R.J. was excellent at keeping many of his self-made millionaires involved in reinvesting, and he was kind to and generous with everyone who worked for him. One of R.J.'s most ingenious moves was to offer his labor force stock options as well, which created an unmatched sense of employee and investor allegiance to RJR Tobacco.

R.J. was equally generous with his own family. Not only did he take his two younger brothers, Walter and Will, in under his wing at the tobacco factory in Winston, he took in his ailing mother, Nancy Jane, in 1893 and extended his bachelor years even longer so he could care for her until her death in 1903. When four of his young nieces lost their mother in 1900, he brought the girls and his brother-in-law to his large Victorian house on Fifth Street in Winston-Salem. R.J. had lived in the Merchant Hotel for years before he moved into the new home in 1893. The towering, turreted Queen Anne home with the welcoming wraparound porch was the largest in town. Soon, Fifth Street was lined with homes of the city's wealthy, self-made men and was regarded as "Millionaire's Row." R.J. also co-founded the country estates of Roaring Gap with his brother Will so he and his family could have a mountain retreat.

More family members, in-laws, and nieces and nephews followed. Across the street lived one of his favorite nephews,

Richard S. Reynolds, who was the son of R.J.'s brother Abram. He had worked at RJR since 1902 when R.J. persuaded him to quit law school and come work in the tobacco factory. From then onward, they were more like father and son than uncle and nephew. Richard S. was a bright entrepreneur, and because of his intimacy with R.J., he believed he'd eventually inherit a stake in the tobacco company he helped build.

R.J. Finds Love

When R.J. was in his fifties, he was still a bachelor, and was still caring for his elderly mother on Fifth Street. When he was fifty-three years old, she passed away, and R.J. began to consider, for the first time, settling down and marrying. At the same time, his cousin from his mother's side of the family, Zachary Taylor Smith of Mount Airy, North Carolina, wrote a letter to R.J. discussing his daughter, Katharine, who had returned from college with an independent spirit and wanted to work for a living instead of being married off, at least for a few years. At the time, she was teaching painting classes in Mount Airy after graduating from North Carolina's Normal School and Sullins College in Virginia.

R.J. agreed to hire her as a secretary, and invited her on a trip to New York to transcribe his dictations. In Winston-Salem, his nieces oriented Katharine and trained her for her new position. Katharine worked at the factory for nearly six months when R.J. held a contest and offered a thousand dollars to anyone in his staff who could produce the best advertising design for the next marketing campaign. R.J. was most impressed by Katharine's design and awarded her the prize. He famously joked that he'd have to marry Katharine to get his money back.

Maybe it wasn't much of a joke, because shortly after, R.J. began courting her. R.J. had spent dozens of years on his own, and he already felt that it was time to finally find a partner. While he dearly loved his company and the life he led, it had not been without its loneliness. Just a year later, R.J. proposed to his twenty-five-year-old cousin, who was thirty years his junior. She accepted, and they set a date to marry.

After their morning wedding on February 27, 1905, in her father's rose-filled parlor, they traveled to Europe on a four-month honeymoon, and conceived their first child shortly after their return. In Winston-Salem, Katharine rushed to prepare the Fifth Avenue townhouse for the baby's arrival. In fact, Katharine had plans to completely remodel the home and garden over the next few years with the help of Philadelphia designers Hunt, Wilkinson, & Company. No expense would be spared for their growing family.

On April 4, 1906, exactly nine months after Katharine and R.J. Sr.'s return from Europe, a beautiful, nine-pound baby boy was born. R.J. Sr. was elated by his firstborn son's arrival and Katharine showered him with attention and affection. He would be named Richard Joshua Reynolds Jr. That also meant he would one day inherit his father's ancestral Joshua Coin.

While little R.J. Jr., nicknamed "Dick" like his father, was still a newborn, R.J. and Katharine took him on vacations and signed their holiday postcards in their son's name. The charming jest was also symbolic—after decades of hard work and bachelordom, the tobacco visionary finally had an heir who would one day represent him. As R.J. Sr.'s boundless energy turned toward fatherhood, the future of his legacy lay in the form of this little boy. RJR Tobacco finally had its first blood successor. R.J.'s years of fortune building had come full circle.

CHAPTER 2

Favorite Son

1906–1918

In five short years, three more siblings came along—Mary in 1908, Nancy in 1910, and Smith in 1911—but Dick was clearly his father's favorite. Dick was a bright, well-behaved child, most of the time. R.J. Sr. had expectations for Dick and could be strict, but he also treated him with an unconditional, grandfatherly love as well.

By the time Nancy was born, R.J. and Katharine had enlisted the help of a German nurse, Miss Henrietta van den Berg, to take care of both Nancy and Katharine, who had a long struggle with heart problems. Katharine's mysterious heart problems were later thought to be caused by undiagnosed rheumatic fever. Because of her weak circulatory system, Katharine was advised to have no more children after Nancy's birth in 1910. When she had Zachary Smith just a year later, doctors told her this had to be her last child—her heart would fail if she had any more.

Between Katharine's health and R.J.'s schedule, the children were usually with Miss van den Berg most of the time. Dick said that the nurse spoiled and favored Nancy, whom she had taken care of since her birth, and treated the rest of them more harshly. The older he got, the more Dick and Miss van den Berg, whom they called "Bum," didn't get along. Dick often left his siblings in the nursery and went off to play by himself in his own room— a turret bedroom that he'd moved into when he was five. He later told his wife Muriel that he was terrified the first night he slept there alone in a huge double bed. But he eventually learned to love the big bed, which was so high that he could crawl under it and play with his toys for hours alone whenever Bum got on his nerves. It was the first sign of Dick's loner spirit.

One of Dick's fondest early memories of his own personal hideaway was of the time the morning angels sang to him. In the dark just before dawn one day, little Dick was startled awake by a chorus singing outside his window. He thought he'd gone to heaven and was hearing angels. In reality, it was early Easter Sunday, and a crowd of Moravians were walking up the street, singing in praise of Jesus' resurrection. The Moravians made the pilgrimage down Winston-Salem's streets every year, singing on their way to Easter Sunday services, which were always held before the sun came up and had been a tradition since 1773. Dick loved the beautiful music and chanting, and he watched them out his window, his little, wide-eyed face cupped in his hands.

Dick's Idyllic Early Childhood

When Dick got a little older, old R.J. took him down to the tobacco factory every morning in a horse-drawn carriage. Of course, the horses were named Prince and Albert. On the way, R.J. talked to Dick about the tobacco company and explained to him what he would do that day. Father would take the time to explain to son how things worked, which inspired Dick's interest

in engineering. When Dick was just four years old, he was genuinely delighted when his father described to him the mundane
details of how the water pumps on their estates functioned.

Dick loved these precious moments with his father. When
they reached the factory, R.J. plopped Dick in the front seat with
the driver and ordered him to take the boy home to his mother.
Dick loved "taking Dad to work" each day. And every night,
R.J. spent time with the children, no matter how tired he was.

The Reynoldses often spent the summers going to Mount
Airy to visit Katharine's side of the family, as well as Atlantic
City, Florida, and the Thousand Islands near the Canadian border. Often, the family traveled in a caravan of children, luggage,
and nurses, and the journeys would take several days and nights,
but that was part of the fun. Dick and his siblings enjoyed the
ride the most.

Richard S. Reynolds

As R.J.'s growing family expanded, his nephew, Richard S., had
become increasingly restless at the tobacco company. Richard
was admittedly wary of R.J.'s shifting priorities, and he had his
own growing family on his mind. He had a son, Richard S.
Reynolds II, born right after Dick, and Richard considered the
idea that it might not be in his or his family's best interest to stay
in Winston-Salem with his uncle. R.J. was close to his nephew
and couldn't understand his change of heart. R.J. felt the company would only grow and expand, and Richard would have
plenty of opportunity to fulfill his own ambitions. R.J. appreciated that Richard had devoted his life to the tobacco company,
and he would be handsomely rewarded for it.

But Richard S. insisted that he wanted to start his own company. R.J. knew how hard it could be to start a new business, so
he offered to loan him several thousand dollars and advised him

to go into tinfoil. R.J. would guarantee to purchase his packaging paper from Richard for RJR Tobacco's production needs. Richard S. didn't take him up on the offer right away, uncertain if he was interested in tinfoil. According to local legend, R.J. sent him to Europe to learn more about the trade as a preliminary step. Richard S. stuck with R.J. a while longer, but Winston-Salem seemed too small for two barons, or at least too small for Richard S.'s ego.

In February of 1912, Richard S. made the decision to leave Winston-Salem for good. He packed up his family and moved to Bristol, Tennessee, to start an entirely new business with his father, Abram Reynolds, who had recently discovered industrial sand and gravel mines on one of his properties. Richard S. had plans to process the "silica sand" and mix it with household cleaners, which would be much easier and cheaper to produce than tinfoil. Richard S. formed the Reynolds Company after his arrival. Both R.J. and Dick were very sad when Richard's family left—R.J. still thought of Richard as a son and protégé, and Dick cherished his neighbor and cousin, Richard S. Reynolds II.

RJR Tobacco Flourishes

By the time the country was in the middle of World War I, R.J.'s famous Camel cigarettes were selling in the hundreds of thousands to soldiers and civilians at home and abroad, and R.J. was the largest employer in all of North Carolina. The decision to place the unique Turkish cigarettes on the market in 1913 was a risky and expensive one. They were the first prepackaged and prerolled cigarettes, and the bright and flue-cured (dried indoors with the heat of a furnace) burley leaf blend had a mild taste and palatable, dark scent. R.J.'s brother Walter came up with the innovative idea of creating prepackaged cigarettes. R.J.

launched a full-scale marketing scheme, now considered the birth of modern cigarette advertising, and solicited the town's wealthiest investors to take the risk with him, to great effect. R.J.'s Prince Alberts were already the most popular pipe and cigarette tobacco in the country and now, because of the avalanche of Camels being shipped all over the world, Camel would outsell its own brands. Soon Camel was a household name.

The plan was a great triumph for RJR Tobacco, which continued to thrive. R.J.'s success was not without long battles, though. At the turn of the century, he stood to lose his company to another North Carolina man, David Duke, the dominant seller of smokable, roll-your-own cigarettes. Duke was one of the first tobacco manufacturers to buy an automatic cigarette roller, called the Bonsack machine, which helped to launch the first prerolled cigarette. But smokers preferred to roll their own, and the idea didn't catch on until RJR's well-advertised prepackaged Camel phenomenon. Although RJR was always one of the country's most competitive tobacco companies, R.J. had gone deeply into debt after rapidly expanding his factories and acquiring his brother Abram's tobacco company. Abram had become a born-again Christian and renounced tobacco, alcohol, and other vices, and wanted out of the industry. By the 1880s R.J. faced stiff competition from David Duke's newly formed tobacco trust, the American Tobacco Company (ATC). It was a conglomerate of five merged, publicly traded tobacco companies that soon bought out most of the country's smaller tobacco companies, including manufacturers of both smoking tobacco and plug chewing tobacco. After the formation of ATC, R.J. went from making massive profits to barely breaking even. The trust was extremely unpopular—religious groups used it as an example of the evils of tobacco and pushed to outlaw its use. Doctors began reporting health problems associated with tobacco, and lawmakers and farmers alike fought Duke. In fact,

RJR Tobacco was vulnerable to the same groups, and before the launch of Camel, the North Carolina legislature was considering a bill that would outlaw all manufacturing of cigarettes in the state. The bill didn't pass. R.J. escaped much of the community's scrutiny because few realized how closely tied he was to Duke. R.J. had maintained the perception that he was a smaller player in the controversial tobacco industry.

In the 1890s, R.J. met Duke in New York City at his Fifth Avenue offices to discuss a possible trade agreement. R.J. was in need of extra capital and Duke was his only hope. Duke agreed to buy up large portions of Reynolds stock—$3 million worth—under one of ATC's 1898 subsidiaries in New Jersey, the Continental Tobacco Company. Duke would then own two thirds of RJR, and he agreed to stay out of R.J.'s plug market. But the collaborative agreement ran the risk of becoming another one of Duke's monopolizing schemes.

Though R.J. agreed to this arrangement, he realized how easily he could be devoured by Duke. Publicly, he portrayed himself as a rebellious underdog to Duke's ATC, and once said, "If Buck Duke tries to swallow me he'll have a bellyache the balance of his life." Privately, R.J. knew he needed to be clever in his efforts to retain control of his company. He quietly bought out other small North Carolina–based tobacco companies and offered stock options to former and present employees to gradually regain his independence. He used the added capital from ATC to maintain his plug and other chewing tobacco brands, upgrade his facilities, and continue the expansion of his business.

In 1904, President Teddy Roosevelt's administration began investigating the ATC's activities using the 1890 Sherman Antitrust Act. The government filed suit in 1907. R.J. was saved by a 1908 Supreme Court antitrust ruling against Duke and subsequent 1911 appeal in a U.S. Circuit Court that upheld the ruling.

Duke was forced to break up his companies, much to Roosevelt's delight. Because of the success of R.J.'s Prince Albert, he was able to survive after he was back on his own. On November 16, 1911, RJR Tobacco was once again a free, independent company.

Just a few years later, the added sales boost from the war and the growing popularity of Reynolds's Camel cigarettes catapulted RJR Tobacco's sales into the billions. Ten years after the launch of Camel, the cigarette brand would dominate almost 50 percent of the market, and the company's stock soared to new heights.

Dick's Early Business Ventures

Meanwhile, R.J. trained Dick to do small chores and to work for a living. Dick was required to feed his own white leghorn chickens and rabbits and clean up after them, and help his father around the yard. R.J. once joked to his wife, "Tell Dick and Mary that their chickens crow so loud that I will have to eat them to keep from being disturbed early in the morning." Dick said that although many assumed he never saw a day's work in his life, his father did teach him how to work. R.J. knew his children risked being spoiled by their money and he sought to mitigate that.

Under his father's tutelage and attention, it didn't take long for Dick's independent personality and stubbornness to take shape. He wasn't afraid of his father and even kicked him in the shins once when R.J. tried to discipline him. On another occasion, Dick packed a small wagon with ham and biscuits, and ran away from home, determined to start out on his own. He was found almost three miles down the road, headed for the mountains. The little loner had turned into an escape artist.

Among his closest childhood friends Dick counted Gordon Gray, the son of R.J.'s partner, Bowman Gray, who went on to become a major executive himself at RJR Tobacco; Bill Sharpe; and Bosley Crowther, with whom he started up his first official business venture—the *Three Cent Pup*. It was a weekly newspaper that the boys founded in the summer of 1917 when Dick was eleven years old, with Sharpe and Crowther as contributing writers. The boys delivered the newspapers to subscribers and charged three cents per copy. One of their last papers, the holiday edition for Christmas of 1917, sold out.

Although the paper shut down, Dick's venture kicked off the writing careers of several friends. Sharpe eventually wrote for the city's main newspaper, *The Sentinel,* and Crowther became the premier film critic for the *New York Times.*

Katharine Builds Reynolda

When Dick was still nine years old, Katharine had started work on a new country estate that she had been planning for at least two years—again sparing no expense in the process. According to Katharine, her thousand-acre estate would include a modest summer cottage—a "bungalow"—located a few miles outside Winston-Salem. R.J. let Katharine manage the construction of the entire estate and allowed Katharine's name to be listed on all the property deeds.

Some sources say R.J. was supportive of all of Katharine's plans, while others suggest he was annoyed by the grand scale of the home and the use of so much good land for expansive gardens and recreation. Although he was wealthy, R.J. was known to be relatively conservative in his spending, and Katharine had more expensive tastes. While the extent of R.J.'s disapproval is uncertain, Katharine did express concern and worry in some of her letters that she had gone far over budget. Nevertheless, construction went on.

Apart from the sixty-four-room bungalow, gardens, a church,

and numerous farm and utility buildings, the estate included a man-made lake, stocked with black bass and trout, and complete with a dam, arched spillway, and waterfall. Near the lake was an outdoor pool for the children and tennis courts and a nine-hole golf course for the adults. Katharine's giant bungalow and gardens were developed by some of the country's best architects, designers, and landscape artists at the time, including Thomas W. Sears and Charles Barton Keen. The centerpiece of the bungalow's interior was a grand, cantilevered gallery that served as the entrance hall. Flemish tapestries hung from the walls, large Oriental carpets covered the floors, and the home was furnished with custom-made furniture from John Wanamaker. Katharine ordered new silver and china for the Adam Revival dining room and a large Aeolian organ was installed in the living room, with its 590 pipes climbing up through three levels of the house.

Outside, cedar trees, cherry trees, and daffodils were planted all over the acreage, and behind the house sat a seemingly endless line of buildings as far as the eye could see—a greenhouse, vineyards, food garden, cottages, dairy farm buildings, blacksmith shops, post offices, staff housing, outhouses, stables, garages, and barns. Next to the house was a sunken formal garden that was marked by wisteria-covered, white-columned pergolas and water lily ponds, and symmetrical slate pathways cut through the dozens of exotic species of flowers and plants.

The farm was almost as romantic—Shropshire sheep, Tamworth swine, and Percheron horses dotted the landscape. The main entrance to the farm village was marked by a stone drinking fountain for workers and animals alike. Artisan wells serviced the fountain and the entire farm—thirty thousand gallons of fresh water a day were pumped throughout the estate. Reynolda—as Katherine dubbed the estate—also had a coal-fired heating system, and its own telephone and electricity lines.

At the time, the estate was the largest and most extravagant

of any private home in Winston-Salem by far. The acreage
boasted R.J.'s wealth in a way his lifelong friends and neighbors
had never seen before. As the construction came to a close, those
who knew R.J. from the time of his first arrival in the Salem
markets marveled at what this tobacco-farming Appalachian
had produced.

In 1914, the first building, Reynolda Presbyterian Church,
opened. But Katharine was in ill health and unable to completely enjoy it. She had become pregnant again, and in early
1914, she was rushed to Johns Hopkins Hospital in Baltimore.
The pregnancy had caused her to have a heart attack and doctors
warned her that carrying the child to term could kill her. Katharine made the difficult decision to terminate the pregnancy. The
message was clear; no more children for Katharine.

Over the course of the next few years, construction at Reynolda was delayed due to a shortage of supplies during World War
I, but by the time Dick turned eleven, the house was almost
complete and ready for move-in day. In the spring of 1917, R.J.
Sr. had become so inexplicably sick from a mysterious stomach
pain that he could no longer get by on the advice of local country
doctors, who were unequipped to diagnose his health problems.
Although R.J. was a heavy drinker and had smoked his own
brands for decades, no one knew exactly what was wrong with
him. R.J. traveled to Johns Hopkins Hospital for a few months
in the fall of 1917, and consulted with doctors, who also were
unable to give him answers. The best they could do was treat
him for his stomach pain. While he rested, doctors asked Katharine to refrain from discussing any business with R.J., because
he was very ill and the added stress would disrupt his recovery.
Upon hearing this news, executives at RJR Tobacco knew R.J.'s
condition was grave. He always had the energy to talk business.
In reaction, the company purchased one million bonds—the
largest single subscription of bonds ever at the time.

Fearing there was nothing more they could do for him except provide him with medicine to ease the pain, doctors sent R.J. home for the following Christmas.

Dick Learns the Tobacco Trade at His Father's Bedside

As construction came to a close that Christmas on the vast acreage on the western edge of Winston-Salem that Katharine would call Reynolda, R.J. knew his days were dangerously numbered. Some say he would have preferred to go back to the Fifth Street house in which he felt comfortable, but he didn't want to disappoint his wife. His familiar furniture was brought to Reynolda, and the library was reorganized so he could sleep there — he had to remain on the main level because he couldn't get up the stairs to the master bedroom. Once R.J. was settled in, he quietly languished in the splendid new home.

R.J. had one brief reprieve from illness in February 1918 and was allowed to ride along in a rabbit hunt with young Dick and other family members. But the reprieve didn't last long. By spring, he had to be moved to the larger Jefferson Hospital in Philadelphia.

Dick and his mother joined his father in Philadelphia and stayed in the hospital with him. After an unsuccessful operation, R.J. prepared a new will and talked to his wife about his wishes for the company after he was gone. As R.J. lay sick and weak, Dick stayed by his bedside as much as possible. R.J. used the little strength he had to lecture Dick about the structure and operations of the tobacco business and explain to him what was expected of him when he became a young man. R.J. openly accepted the fact that he was dying, and focused on preserving the legacy he would leave behind. R.J. worried about leaving his children without a father, but he knew he was out of time.

Dick and Katharine continued to stay at the hospital with R.J. Dick sometimes went out in Philadelphia alone, buying books and going to the movies by himself, while his mother was occupied with R.J. With the looming possibility that he could lose his father soon, Dick felt both insecure and uncertain, and the need to be mature and grown up at the same time.

Later in his adult life, Dick always revisited those days in Philadelphia whenever he faced a decision. He rarely made a business move without considering what his father would do. In times of crisis, Dick would lie in bed and quietly go over the things his father used to tell him before taking any action.

Death of a Legend

In July of 1918, R.J. was released from Jefferson Hospital and sent home on a train. On July 29, the day after his sixty-eighth birthday, he died.

R.J.'s death was a shock to young Dick. His mother's sorrow was unbearable, and his little brother and sisters seemed lost. Dick felt immensely lonely, unsure of how to grieve.

The funeral for R.J. on July 31 shut down the city of Winston-Salem. The town was draped in black bunting, and the streets were lined with people who wished to pay their respects to the "biggest blood" in Winston-Salem.

R.J. was adored by the city—not just for the jobs he brought to North Carolina, but for his generous treatment of his employees and his philanthropy. Taking his wife's advice, R.J. was one of the first employers in America to implement a nine-to-five workday and five-day workweek and to offer employees paid benefits, including health care, vacation time, and on-site child care. Dick recalled overhearing his mother persuade R.J. that good food was vital to the health of his employees, and he listened. He was one of the first employers to provide hot lunches and drinking fountains at work, and he built the sixty-room Reynolds Inn for young female employees who had flocked to the city to work in the factory. R.J. joined the City Council in 1884, subsidized the first black hospital in the South, started a savings and loan bank, protected Winston-Salem's rail lines, built hundreds of sanitary housing units for his employees, and worked hard to uplift women and minorities and to provide opportunities for them—a legacy that continues to this day. Ever since R.J. rode into that town, he earned the respect and friendship of the community and anyone who worked for him. He was a meritocrat—a fortune builder, a genius at his trade, and an ethical industrialist who made his thirty million honestly.

Twelve-year-old Dick was a pallbearer at his father's funeral. With his Uncle William Neal by his side, he watched his father's body be lowered into the ground in the small cemetery of Winston-Salem.

Dick's Uncle Will, a quiet man, was clearly suffering from the loss. Having joined R.J. when both brothers were in their twenties, he'd spent his whole life with R.J. in the tobacco factory. But Will also had business on his mind. RJR Tobacco would have to go on seamlessly without its founder, and he and Vice President Bowman Gray wanted to take over RJR Tobacco permanently.

A pall of sorrow was cast over Reynolda. Dick immediately felt the absence of his father's attention—his death left a void in Dick's life that would never be filled.

CHAPTER 3

Life after R.J.

1918–1924

Katharine dressed in black for a year. When she couldn't sleep at night, she would go down to the reception hall of Reynolda and softly play the aeolian organ to ease her soul. Nor did she give Dick much time to mourn, but leaned on him for support. Dick was expected to be the man of the house almost immediately. He sometimes felt as if the whole town was looking to him to decide what the Reynolds family would do next.

All the way out in Reynolda, Dick missed the companionship of boys his own age. The country was lonely and too far away from his neighborhood friends on Fifth Street. Sometimes Dick often wandered off alone in the woods near the sixteen-acre Lake Katharine and played with a toy sailboat his mother bought him. Dick pondered the construction of the boat and dreamed of owning his own one day. He often sought refuge in that little boat—a habit he would nurture over a lifetime.

Katharine eventually coped with her widowhood by participating in numerous philanthropic projects, throwing herself into her favorite organization—the YWCA—and busily constructing Winston-Salem's R. J. Reynolds High School and R. J. Reynolds Auditorium in her husband's memory.

The fall after R.J.'s death, twelve-year-old Dick wanted to go to boarding school somewhere far away where he could get away from the sadness of Reynolda. Exactly where Dick went to school that fall is uncertain. It appears that he first briefly attended classes at Katharine's Reynolda school, then went to public school in Winston-Salem. After a semester there, he most likely transferred to Woodbury Forest in Virginia, and then later transferred to the Tome School in Maryland. He appears to have finally finished his studies at the Culver Military Academy in Indiana.

Dick did, however, have his reasons for school hopping. In Winston-Salem, he often overheard people comparing him to his father, and quietly predicting that Dick would never be the man his father was, no matter how well he turned out. This confused and hurt Dick at a time when his world was already turned upside down. These rumblings stuck with him, and made him want to run from the burden of being a Reynolds.

To make matters worse, the goings-on at Reynolda were soon to become unbearable to Dick, and he was having a hard time concentrating on his studies.

Katharine Falls in Love

Less than a year after R.J.'s death, Dick noticed his mother spending more time with the Reynolda school's newly hired, twenty-five-year-old headmaster, Edward "Ed" Johnston. Johnston was a World War I veteran from a respectable South Carolina family. He was highly educated and an excellent teacher, but Dick didn't trust him. Johnston was comparatively poor, and the more Dick caught Katharine and Ed in intimate conversation, the more Dick wondered what his motives were.

Everyone knew Katharine would eventually remarry. She was still young, and after R.J.'s death she was the most eligible bachelorette in town. Johnston was handsome and much younger than Katharine, but his social status was no match for hers. He was the last person Winston-Salem society imagined for Katharine.

Katharine fell madly in love with Johnston anyway. Prior to telling Dick, Katharine wrote a letter to a friend, telling her that she was more nervous about telling Dick about her new lover than her own parents. It turned out that she was right to be nervous. When Katharine finally told Dick, he was mortified. How could his mother do this to him? To his father? He felt personally betrayed. Dick resented his mother's affection for someone who wasn't half the man R.J. was. Of all the admirers his mother had among upstanding businessmen about town, she had settled for a common schoolteacher.

Katharine was tormented by Dick's reaction. When he realized he was hurting his mother, he tried to be supportive after he got over the initial shock. Dick considered that maybe his father would have wanted Katharine to find someone and not be lonely, and that Dick should be more generous. But Dick still couldn't stand the young man. To make matters worse, his siblings loved Johnston and showered him with affection. It made Dick sick to his stomach.

As Johnston spent more time at Reynolda, Dick stayed away as often as he could. He spent the next summer working through the school holiday or going to camp so he wouldn't have to be at home. At first, he asked to stay with Uncle Will and worked at the tobacco company for seventy cents a day. His job was working in the stemming room, and he later learned how to operate the cigarette machine on his own. Anything, even gritty factory work, was better than putting up with Johnston.

The following year, Dick had by then transferred to Tome and came home to Reynolda for spring break in March of 1921. He still had no kind words for Johnston and avoided him as much as possible. In June of 1921, Katharine announced that she and Ed Johnston were getting married. Dick refused to attend their wedding ceremony, which was held in the living room of Reynolda. His Uncle Will didn't go either. When they departed for their two-month honeymoon the next morning, Dick was so upset Miss van den Berg had to spend a lot of time with him, trying to calm his anger. In spite of the fact that Miss van den Berg reported Nancy's and Mary's joy at the union, Katharine was deeply disturbed by Dick's emotional outrage. Again, Dick stayed often with Will and worked in the tobacco factory to take his mind off things. By then he was putting in a forty-five-hour workweek.

Katharine decided it was time to send Dick to Greenbriar Summer Camp in West Virginia. When she and Ed returned from their honeymoon, they visited Dick there, in an attempt to heal the tensions between them. Dick tried hard to be understanding, but they still felt the strain. It didn't help that Dick wasn't feeling well either. He'd already developed breathing problems and a bad cough, and a Winston-Salem doctor told Katharine that both Dick and Smith might have genetic lung problems. The doctor advised her to send Dick to a better climate—perhaps a boarding school in Arizona instead of a school in the East, but for unknown reasons, that never did happen. Katharine seemed to believe that Dick's problem was a sinus condition, and eventually Dick had surgery on his nose and sinuses. But the operation only seemed to exacerbate Dick's breathing problems. The older he got, the worse his breathing problems would become.

At Reynolda, the three younger children were usually in the care of Miss van den Berg, while Katharine moved out of the house and enjoyed her new husband in one of the estate's smaller cottages. Katharine and Ed were gone a lot. Katharine traveled to New York, Washington, and Baltimore regularly, often tending to business and sometimes just to get away from the prying eyes of Winston-Salem society. However, even Mary and Nancy, who were happy for Katharine and Ed, had grown weary of their increasingly absentee mother. Dick found fewer and fewer reasons to go home, and his resentment toward his stepfather and mother grew once again. He felt Katharine had coldly abandoned them all when she moved out, and that feeling would only intensify as her relationship with Johnston deepened.

At the same time, Katharine's heart condition and circulatory problems had continued to ail her, and she was often in and out of doctor's offices. From time to time, Dick emphatically reminded Ed that his mother had a serious heart problem and to see to it that she didn't get pregnant. Ed promised Dick that wouldn't happen.

In 1922, Ed and Katharine bought an apartment in New York and brought the younger children with them, and Mary, Nancy, and Smith were placed in private school there. The move happened because Katharine had found out that she was pregnant, and she knew she would require the care of the best doctors. In spite of the huge health risks, she was thrilled by the pregnancy. Dick, on the other hand, was terribly worried when he heard the news.

By the spring of 1922, the whole family, minus Dick, moved to the Plaza hotel where Katharine rested in comfort before her delivery. On May 1, 1922, with Miss van den Berg attending, Katharine gave birth to a premature baby girl who died shortly thereafter. Again, doctors warned Katharine not to get pregnant. It wasn't safe for her or her unborn child. Katharine was disappointed. Dick was furious. Once more, he berated Ed for letting her get pregnant. Ed swore he understood, but told Dick it was Katharine who wanted another child, not he.

Katharine moved the entire family back to Reynolda. Dick joined them there for the summer and continued to work in the tobacco factory. By August, he agreed to go on a vacation with Katharine and Ed, mainly to please his mother. Dick was worried about her health and wanted to see her happy, so he tried yet again to be supportive.

Escape to Sea

In the summer of 1923, Dick again returned to Winston-Salem. But his summer vacation plans were sidetracked when he caught his mother and Ed in an intimate moment. Still worried about his mother's health, Dick became enraged. This time he punched Ed in the face. His tolerance of his mother's reckless relationship with Ed had worn thin, and he would no longer stick around anymore to watch it. In a move that would become his lifelong motif, he fled.

Dick caught a train to New York and jumped on a freighter, the *Finland*, which was set to sail to Hamburg, Germany. He hid his identity from the captain and crew, who hired the able-bodied boy as a grunt. The rowdy crew dubbed him "Kid Carolina." He was seventeen years old when he first tasted the freedom of the open sea.

When she finally tracked him down, Katharine let him stay with the proviso that the captain keep an eye on him. Dick fell in love with the ocean and stayed onboard for three months working as a seaman, cleaning the toilets and in general doing whatever remedial tasks the crew asked of him. The crewmen didn't have the faintest idea who was living in their midst, and Dick was delighted by the dirtiest language he'd ever heard in his life and the most unrefined table manners he'd ever seen.

After hearing from Katharine Reynolds, the captain asked the crew to be more mindful of the young man, and they toned down the crudeness of their conversations. Dick was disappointed at their sudden civilized behavior. He didn't realize until he was much older that his mother had communicated with them, and he simply thought all the life had gone out of the crew.

Dick couldn't have been happier living the simple, ordinary life, which was more entertaining to him than a million social dinners. Still a teenager, Dick had already found a way to run from his life and the pressure of being a Reynolds. Young Dick, aka Kid Carolina, had found his perfect escape.

Punishing Katharine

At RJR Tobacco, Uncle Will oversaw a 20 percent growth spurt as a result of wartime sales. For several years afterward, the company would grow by 20 percent annually, massively increasing the value of the estate R.J. left behind.

If R.J. Sr. had had his wishes, Katharine would have been a much bigger part of the company than she was. R.J. trusted Katharine with his business and wanted her to be involved in the board's decisions. She tried to appoint finance officers that R.J. wanted on the board right after he died, and she faced stiff resistance from Bowman Gray before her wishes were finally granted.

Uncle Will tried to be more respectful and kept Katharine involved in the goings-on at RJR Tobacco. But when Katharine met Ed, she knew she had to keep the affair a secret from Will or his willingness to work with her would end. Katharine quietly increased her holdings in 1920, valued at $500 per share, not only to ensure her own financial security but to ensure her influence in the company. Still keeping the affair a secret, Katharine managed to persuade Will to offer Ed a job at a tobacco factory outside Winston-Salem. Once he had a job, Katharine bought Ed a block of controlling shares in the company. Only after she had completed these steps did she make the announcement that she and Ed were getting married.

Will was unimpressed with Ed, and his presence at the factory became awkward and uncomfortable after Katherine announced the engagement. Bowman Gray didn't like Ed either and had no respect for what he felt was his lack of business sense. When Ed announced that he would leave the company, they were happy to let him go.

But Katharine still hadn't given up on staying involved, and she even asked Will if Ed could join the board of directors. Will refused. The goodwill between Katharine and Uncle Will was waning.

Since R.J.'s death, federal taxes had also soared in order to pay for the war, and once R.J.'s will was domiciled, there was little cash left to pay the taxes that Katharine owed on the estate. Will suggested that Katharine sell her controlling tobacco shares to pay the taxes, which would effectively shut her out of the business for good. But Katharine was smarter than that, and instead she went to the Baltimore Bank and Trust Company and obtained a loan. Then she used her accumulated capital and income from her stock dividends and interest to repay the note. The estate had almost no debt just a few years after R.J.'s death, and Katharine had wisely retained her financial influence on the company.

Meanwhile, Richard S. Reynolds came back into the picture. His cleanser company failed when his products were deemed unnecessary during the war, and since his uncle's death he considered the advice he had given him years earlier. He decided he would get into the tinfoil business as he had been trained. Just a year after R.J.'s death, R.S. opened up U.S. Foil in Louisville, Kentucky. He went to Uncle Will to obtain the loan that R.J. had once promised him. Uncle Will honored the request and agreed to buy all the foil for RJR's tobacco packaging from R.S.

Although Will proved to be a less willing and savvy partner to R.S. than R.J. and they eventually ceased doing business together, R.S. had mastered aluminum production. He eventually expanded U.S. Foil, renamed it Reynolds Metals Company, and moved his headquarters to Richmond, Virginia—which would later be the home of Reynolds Wrap.

Orphans

In the winter of 1924, when Dick returned from school for a week in February, he learned that his mother was pregnant again. He also heard the distressing news that his mother said she wanted to have a baby with Ed "even if it killed her." In Dick's mind, Ed wasn't off the hook. He said that if Ed really loved her, he would have abstained from intimacy with her entirely.

On March 14, Katharine moved to New York's Harbor Hospital to stay on bed rest until the baby was due. She must have known that her life was at serious risk because she rewrote her will at the time to include Ed and her unborn baby, and she bought more shares of RJR Tobacco, increasing her controlling interest.

At the age of forty-four, Katharine gave birth to a boy on May 20, 1924. Surprisingly, the baby, J. Edward Johnston Jr., was healthy, and Ed and Katharine were overjoyed. However, Katharine remained bedridden, and Miss van den Berg joined her in New York to care for her.

About three days after the delivery, a blood clot burst in Katharine's brain, killing her instantly.

Dick was at Reynolda when he heard the news. He was overcome with heartbreak, fury, and a sense of powerlessness.

By the time he saw Ed, all he felt was rage. It was all he could do to refrain from lunging at him. Dick had predicted this would happen if his mother got pregnant, and he held Johnston responsible for her death. He entertained thoughts that Ed deliberately let his mother die so he could get his hands on her fortune. Dick was convinced that Ed never sincerely loved his mother. He couldn't bear to look at him.

Dick was now an orphan at age eighteen.

After Katharine

Katharine's funeral procession was one of the largest Winston-Salem had ever seen. Even more stunning than the outpouring of grief was the vision of the Reynolds children burying yet another parent in a span of only six years. Now the children had no parents and no one they could count on, except for each other, and the overflowing treasure chest at the Baltimore Bank and Trust Company.

Before Katharine had died, she set up a trust for the children at the bank, which would also serve as the children's financial guardian. Upon her death, Katharine's assets, including the very lucrative RJR stock, were to be placed in a trust and divided among all the children, Ed Johnston, and her unborn baby. They would gradually receive yearly allowances worth hundreds of thousands of dollars, and then come into the rest of their inheritances as they turned twenty-eight. The trust would administer the children's inheritances.

When R.J. died, his will stated that his estate, which comprised about $11 million in RJR stock as well as all his real estate and investment holdings, should be divided in five equal parts for each of the children and Katharine. Although R.J. had been dead for only six years, the value of his estate had grown to $35 million and produced dividends of $300,000 annually

Ten years later, when Dick would inherit his portion of these funds, Katharine and R.J.'s estate was worth over $150 million. The soaring dollar amount of their future inheritance made the Reynolds kids the equivalent of billionaires at the time. Katharine's investments ensured Dick's coronation as a quintessential filthy-rich heir to his father's massive fortune—a benefactor of circumstance.

In Winston-Salem, Ed found himself facing hostility and quiet disdain over Katharine's death, and there were few congratulations for his new baby boy. Not even Nancy's and Mary's adoration of Ed could withstand the pain of the loss of their mother. Katharine was beloved for her philanthropy, and as tributes to her were paid all over town Ed found that Katharine's children weren't the only ones who blamed him and his newborn for Katharine's death. Ed wanted to take his son and leave for his hometown of Baltimore, but Uncle Will, who assisted with the administration of Katharine's estate, demanded that Ed stay long enough so the town wouldn't suspect any discontent within the family. Johnston did as he was told and followed Will's orders until the estate was settled.

Years later, Johnston eventually transferred the responsibilities of the children to their cousin-in-law, Robert E. Lassiter, who was a longtime friend of R.J.'s and an executive at the tobacco company, and left town. He later remarried, fulfilled his wish to move back to Baltimore in 1928, and lived off Katharine's money for the rest of his life. He never managed to escape Katharine's shadow.

At first, Dick wouldn't acknowledge the baby, J. Edward Johnston, as his brother, and tried to forget the whole thing happened. Instead, he ran away from home again—this time hopping on a cruise headed for South America with his cousins for a few weeks.

CHAPTER 4

Crashing with the Stock Market

1924–1929

After Katharine's death, there was the small matter of raising the four orphans. Uncle Will, along with Ed Johnston as a figurehead, was named their guardian in Katharine's will. With respect to R.J. Sr.'s wishes, they administered the Baltimore Bank and Trust Company funds to the children slowly and gradually. The children would initially receive $10,000 to $15,000 per year in allowance. When they went off to college, they would receive $50,000. At twenty-one they would receive $100,000, and at twenty-eight they would receive their full inheritance. R.J. added another provision to encourage them to work—for each dollar they earned on their own, the estate would give them two dollars more.

Instead of moving into Reynolda himself with the children or taking them back to his enormous Tanglewood estate, the childless Will left them in Reynolda and hired distant cousins and would be guardians, Robert Lassiter and his wife, to move into Reynolda and look after the children. Will was a good man, but his decision not to take in the children himself left many perplexed. His wife, Kate, was the daughter of a prominent banking family in Winston-Salem and had been married to Will since 1884. She was a generous woman who often worked with Katharine on their numerous philanthropic projects and was well respected in town, but she wasn't keen on raising the young family herself. All four of them, ages eleven to eighteen, were basically on their own.

Dick was grateful to the Lassiters for offering to help, but it was clear from the beginning that Dick would be the head of the household and the only father figure his younger siblings would have from that time forward. And it was obvious to Will, the Lassiters, and Ed Johnston that it would be best to let Dick do what he wanted.

After returning home from the cruise in South America, Dick toured Europe for the first time with his sisters for the rest of the summer. What would be Dick's lifelong affection for Europe was sparked on that trip. He traveled France and Spain on a bicycle and stayed in youth hostels like any other normal kid. He memorized many of the country roads and was endlessly curious about each landmark he visited.

College Adventures

When Dick came back in the fall, he registered at North Carolina State University at Raleigh, enrolling in mechanical engineering classes and joining the football team. He apparently never told his family where he went.

About four months into the semester, and after the family finally figured out where he was, his Aunt Kate decided to pay him a visit. Unsure of where he was staying, she spoke to the dean and asked where her nephew R. J. Reynolds Jr. was living. Dick had escaped the attention of the dean, who didn't even know he was in school there. The dean politely said to Kate, "Ma'am, you must be mistaken. Surely if R. J. Reynolds Jr. was here, I would know about it." She insisted that her nephew had been attending for quite some time already and asked to look through the list of Reynoldses. She found Dick's name and pointed it out to the dean—he was living right there on campus.

The dean excitedly spread word of this when he found out, telling everyone that *the* R. J. Reynolds Jr. was attending *his* school. Newspapers picked it up and soon the whole town knew about Dick's enrollment. Before, Dick hadn't been asked to join any fraternities; now they were knocking at his door. He got distracted by all the attention and eventually dropped out of school after only two semesters. Although he never did gradu-ate from college, Dick later became a generous donor to NC State and joined the board of trustees of the University of North Carolina.

Armed with his healthy yearly allowance of thousands of dollars, Dick moved to New York in 1925 and shuttled back and forth between the city and Winston-Salem over the sum-mer. He dated a beautiful local girl named Ella Cannon (of Can-non Towels fame), in Winston, and used his generous allowance to indulge in his next great curiosity: aviation. For Dick, this would mean nothing less than flying with the world's best pio-neer aviators and building his own airline.

The Aviator

In 1925, Dick took flying lessons from Lewis McGinnis at Cur-tiss Flying School in Long Island. With his new skills, he prac-ticed stunt flying and would fly to Winston-Salem and land right on the lawn of Reynolda, taxi to the front of the house, and offer his sisters a ride. Back in New York, he would obtain one of the first official pilot's licenses in the United States. Orville Wright had just become the newly elected chairman of the Aero Club of America and the Fédération Aéronautique Internationale, and Dick applied for a license at the same time. Many of the official pilot's licenses in the early 1920s would bear Wright's signature, and Dick was lucky enough to be a part of that exclusive list of recipients. The license was so precious to Dick that rather than show it off, he kept it locked in a safe.

Dick was seriously bitten by the aviation bug. He went back to Europe, took up an apartment in St. John's Wood in London, bought a plane for himself, and spent the next year flying as often as he could. He took intensive courses in commercial flying in France, Germany, England, and Italy. While there, he also explored his love of sailing.

In between commercial airline courses, Dick bought his first sailboat and acquired an English girlfriend named Pat, who followed him wherever he went. He picked up two crewmen, both two decades his senior, who were badly in need of work. One was a Navy sailor named Captain Phelps; the other was a sweet old man called "Honey" who knew the English coast like the back of his hand. Over the course of their route down the European coast, Captain Phelps taught Dick everything he knew about sailing.

Honey had little formal navigation education, but he had a good sense of the sea. Instinctively, Honey managed to steer the boat anywhere they wanted to go. On one occasion they hit a storm in the Mediterranean, and Pat was thrown across the boat and injured. They were all up to their armpits in water but managed to survive and had to sail all night with the ship full of water. With Honey at the bridge, they made it safely through the night. Dick never doubted Honey's navigation skills or the sturdiness of the sailboat again.

Dick loved the boat so much, and the memories of his first

sailing experiences that were associated with it, that he kept it for the rest of his life. The old boat symbolized Dick's adaptability and his willingness to withstand extreme discomfort and danger for the sake of sailing, proving he was more than a soft, spoiled heir. But his strength when confronting such risky adventures would later contrast sharply with his weakness in the face of personal responsibility.

~ · ~

Dick returned to New York in 1926, and recruited his younger brother, Smith, to Long Island's Curtiss Field to work on planes with him for a new company he'd formed called Ireland Amphibian. The company was named for George Ireland, the builder of the fly boat aircraft that his company maintained. In 1926, his company participated in the development of the first amphibious planes produced in the United States. Later, the company would shuttle wealthy passengers from Manhattan to Long Island and back.

At the time, Richard E. Byrd, Charles Lindbergh, Wilmer Stultz, and Amelia Earhart stored their planes at Curtiss Field. Dick and Smith both became acquainted with them all. On one occasion, Dick and Wilmer Stultz were in Pennsylvania together picking up a new plane when they met Lou Gordon, an expert Fokker mechanic. Dick and Wilmer invited Lou to Curtiss Field to work on manufacturing planes, and that was how Gordon got the job as Amelia Earhart's mechanic, for which he would become famous.

Meanwhile, Dick needed more cash. He had dreams of building his own commercial airline, and his several-thousand-dollar allowance wasn't sufficient. He formally petitioned to have the trust company increase his allowance to $50,000. Uncle Will didn't share Dick's airline vision and thought the boy had lost his mind. But Will also knew that Mary's and Nancy's spending habits on clothes and food had spiraled out of control—he told himself that at least Dick was trying to be industrious.

Dick won the petition and increased his allowance to $50,000.

~ · ~

At age twenty-one, Dick watched as Charles Lindbergh rolled his airplane out from Curtiss Field in May of 1927. At eight in the morning, Lindbergh taxied the *Spirit of St. Louis* to the adjoining Roosevelt Field and departed for Paris, leaving cheering crowds behind. Dick and many other distinguished guests were there to see him off. After Lindbergh's flight, Dick was so inspired by the event that he decided then and there to work on his new airline.

His little brother, Smith, was even more inspired. By 1927, Smith was spending less time in high school and more time flying planes with Dick. He had become a seasoned pilot already, and participated in daring air races and stunt flying in New York and Winston-Salem, which was Smith's specialty. Smith also took flying lessons under Orville Wright and acquired an official license bearing his signature, just like his big brother. Eventually sixteen-year-old Smith dropped out of school for good to become a full-time pioneer in the new industry.

Both boys joined the Quiet Birdmen of America association, a secret aviation fraternity started by World War I pilots, officers, and Curtiss Field aviators in 1919. It was an aviation version of the Masons, and Dick and Smith were joined in the fraternity by Charles Lindbergh, among others. It was a fitting tribute to Dick's and Smith's growing obsession with aviation. Dick continued to be a charter member for most of his life.

After Lindbergh's historic flight, it seemed unthinkable that the owners of Curtiss Field were planning to sell the airfield to real estate developers. Dick intervened. In August of

1927, he bought the facility, upgraded the twenty hangars, and refurbished the entire field. In addition he bought thirteen passenger planes, and officially started his own airline—Reynolds Airways. It was one of the first domestic commercial airlines in the United States. The airline's office was headquartered in Midtown Manhattan in the newly constructed Graybar office building behind Grand Central Station. In addition, Dick took a five-year lease on Hadley Field in New Jersey as a second base for the airline, which would provide domestic service from New York to smaller towns in upstate New York, New Jersey, and Connecticut, and eventually to Winston-Salem. Dick served as president of his new airline and appointed a former Navy pilot, Tiffany Carter, as his vice president. To manage the books, Dick hired a young lawyer from Winston-Salem, Stratton Coyner. Dick was later quoted saying, "Things that facilitate transportation do the greatest good for civilization." It was clear that Dick meant, and acted on, what he said.

Curtiss and Roosevelt fields were still very popular after Lindbergh's flight, and Dick exploited the economic opportunity. Under Dick's ownership, Curtiss Field offered organized tours of Lindbergh's transatlantic takeoff site. Dick also offered flying lessons, many of which Dick and Smith taught themselves, and worked with the Plane Speaker Company—a maker of aerial speaker equipment—so advertisers could blast announcements from the air. It was also the era of Prohibition and, for a spell, his airline unwittingly assisted in illegal rum-running for mob boss Frank Costello until one of his planes crashed on a run.

Dick used the Garden City Hotel as his base and went into Manhattan regularly on the weekends. Both he and Smith were familiar faces in New York's fashionable cafés and speakeasies, and Dick even financed a couple of Broadway musicals just for fun. He spent piles of his new cash on expensive cars and gifts for his girlfriends.

Smith continued to dabble in stunt flying and often practiced flying over the Reynolda golf course and Winston-Salem's Miller Field, where Dick had just expanded his operations. When he was in New York, Smith became so attached to his brother's airfields that he slept in the hangar at Hadley Field when he was working. He brought two of his friends, Ab Walker and John Graham, to work for Dick, and to keep him company. Smith was thrilled when he personally met Charles Lindbergh, who wanted to try out one of Dick's planes at Curtiss Field and decided he would make Winston-Salem one of his stops on his national tour. Lindbergh's interest in Winston-Salem set Dick and Smith into a flurry of activity to upgrade the city's small Miller Airport in time. Dick donated money to build steel hangars, install electricity, and renovate the landing strips. On opening day ceremonies, there was an entertaining amateur air race, and Smith won.

A Taste for Alcohol

Along with developing companies, properties, and airplanes, Dick developed his drinking habit in New York as well. While the almost nightly rowdy parties in New York's speakeasies and cafés had been fun, they also fostered Dick's alcoholism. When Dick was under the influence, his behavior was often erratic, bizarre, and wildly unpredictable.

While Dick was working on his new airline, he rented a cottage in Long Beach, Long Island, which he shared with Smith's friend John Graham and a few servants that he'd brought up from Winston-Salem. But that fall—on September 11, 1927—Dick attended a play he had financed but had never seen before, called *Half a Widow*, at the Waldorf Theatre. A few days later, he got rid of his Long Island cottage and told his Winston-Salem servants they were no longer needed and that he would be sending them back home to Reynolda. Dick, John Graham, and another colleague, Manuel H. Davis of the Plane Speaker Company, moved into the Hotel White on Lexington Avenue.

On September 15, Dick cashed a check for $5,000, and told his chauffeur, John de Carlos, to buy $130 worth of train tickets for the servants to return to Winston-Salem, and asked him to see them off at Penn Station. Then he told the chauffeur to take his Rolls-Royce to the Mineola rail station, where Dick would pick it up at 11:00 P.M. after he visited the Nassau County Fair.

Dick picked up John Graham and the two went to the fair briefly but soon made their way to Rothman's Roadhouse in Oyster Bay, where they drank until eleven. Then they made their way into Manhattan to the Charm Club at 137 West Fifty-first Street, where they stayed until the early morning hours.

After a long night, Dick and John Graham left with a Broadway showgirl, Marie Houston, and Dick asked John to see Marie off at Grand Central Station at 6:00 A.M. That was the last anyone saw of Dick.

Meanwhile, at 12:30 A.M. the same night, late-shift workmen at Orchard Beach heard a loud splash in Long Island Sound. They found the noise peculiar but went on working anyway. A few days later, Dick's abandoned Rolls-Royce was found overturned in the water in Port Washington. The car had gone over a six-foot concrete pier at Chicken Point at the end of a mile-long rough dirt road. The car had apparently been driven to the pier with the headlights off. The workmen fished the car out of the water and it sat on the beach for several days, unclaimed, until John de Carlos retrieved it. He didn't say a word about what had happened and seemed unsurprised to see the car there.

Meanwhile, almost two weeks passed and no one had seen or heard from Dick. Uncle Will, Ed Johnston (who was still a guardian at the time), and Dick's officers at Reynolds Airways began to worry that something had happened to him. When they determined that the upturned Rolls-Royce was Dick's, they began to panic. They figured that the car went into the water about the same time that Dick would have been going from Long Island to Manhattan, but a thorough search around Chicken Point turned up nothing. Ed went to New York, enlisted the help of private detectives at the Val O'Farrell Agency, and initiated a nationwide manhunt. Uncle Will offered a large reward if anyone found Dick. The producers of *Half a Widow* were frantically looking for Dick, too, because they were relying on him to pay salaries and rentals or their show would close.

The case of the missing tobacco heir was all over the news. As the days passed, all kinds of tips came in. One couple thought they spotted him at a sporting event in Florida; others reported seeing him in Chicago. But most tips were coming from St. Louis.

As the days went on, some family members were decidedly unworried. One of Dick's relatives, H. W. Reynolds, said, "We think Dick is somewhere hiding, it's a habit of his to go away without telling anyone."

Eventually Dick's chauffeur came forward and said Dick told them he was leaving New York, and once he left his car in Port Washington for him, he was off duty indefinitely. Then, Marie Houston turned up in New York and told authorities she had gone to St. Louis to see a sick relative and Dick had paid her way, but she hadn't seen him since. John Graham was repeatedly grilled about Dick's whereabouts, but he refused to talk, saying he hadn't seen Dick since the morning of the 16th and he didn't wish to fuel speculation. Meanwhile, *Half a Widow* closed.

Finally, the investigators got a tip from a man named Charles Cruinshaw in St. Louis, who said he knew where Dick was but he wanted to secure his reward before he would reveal his whereabouts. Once investigators assured him that he would be paid, he said Dick could be found "in the fifth booth on the left side of the room at the Grand Inn of 910 North Grand Boulevard."

Sure enough, the detectives descended on a chop suey joint at that address and found a man fitting the description of Dick, sitting in a booth with a man and woman. The man's shirt was soiled, his tie crooked, and he carried an unmarked suitcase. When detectives first approached him, the man denied he was Dick Reynolds and said he was from Maine. Then he produced a driver's license with the name John Graham. Detectives said that Dick Reynolds was associated with a John Graham, and the man said he had heard of Reynolds and Graham of Winston-Salem but it wasn't him.

The detectives knew he was lying. Finally, Dick said, "This is getting on my nerves. Yes, I'm Reynolds."

While Dick talked, the man and woman he was with slipped out of the restaurant, never to be seen again. It had become a habit of Dick's to pick up "temporary friends" on such excursions, whom he kept around as drinking companions for days on end. The unidentified man and woman, as well as Mr. Cruinshaw, were likely more of his typical human collectibles.

Dick was further identified by an engraved green fountain pen that he carried with him everywhere. But Dick's explanation for his long absence only got weirder.

He said he left unannounced because he "did not wish to be bothered," and he first went to the heavyweight rematch between Gene Tunney and Jack Dempsey. Then he registered at the Claridge Hotel under the name Joy K. Fleet (named for a character in a film), where the bellboys reportedly enjoyed generous tips, and he attended the local horse and dog races in both Chicago and St. Louis. He said he'd only found out about the manhunt the day before and had confided in Mr. Cruinshaw that he was the man they were looking for. Dick offered no explanation for the Rolls-Royce, except to say that it must have been stolen, and claimed to have told both John Graham and Manuel Davis where he was going.

The newspapers were unsatisfied with Dick's nonexplanation. He continued to be questioned and he finally said he just got "fed up" with New York where "money talks." "No matter what I do, where I go, they've always got something to sell me. It's buy this stock or buy that. I just got fed up on society and the night life along Broadway and decided to take a sort of vacation," said an exasperated Dick.

∾ · ∾

While he was "on vacation," a tragic Reynolds Airways plane accident occurred on September 17. One of the sightseeing planes had crashed near New Jersey's Hadley Field, killing seven people onboard. Dick was so disillusioned by the accident that he left his officers to handle the day-to-day operations of the airline. Dick's fabulous aviation adventures in Long Island were dampened by this tragedy. All of the intensity, money, and interest he had poured into the industry abruptly dropped off. Dick always felt personally responsible for the crash, and carried the guilt of it for the rest of his life.

In October of 1927, Charles Lindbergh landed in Winston-Salem's Miller Field. Of the two brothers, only Smith was there to meet him. Two years later, Dick sold Curtiss Field for a large profit. Over the course of the next four years, Reynolds Airways moved its headquarters to Winston-Salem and would expand to Detroit, Philadelphia, Baltimore, and Myrtle Beach, but Dick was rarely around to see it. The airline was almost entirely run by Dick's employees.

After the St. Louis incident, Dick faltered for his next move. Looking back on it, he concluded that if he could go to such extremes to get away from the press, his family, and his obligations, it was time for a dramatic change. He vowed not to return to Winston-

Salem for seven years until he would get his full inheritance, which was growing by $1 million in stock dividends each year.

Dick moved back to Europe straightaway.

Dick in Paris and London

Dick returned to his apartment in St. John's Wood and took up another apartment in Paris. He spent time drinking and playing dominoes in Paris's most fashionable cafés and was a regular at Chez Fred Payne's on Pigalle's rue Blanche and Harry's New York Bar on rue Daunou. Fred Payne used to joke that he always knew Dick was coming by the noise of his Bugatti and his bellowing laugh, which could be heard halfway up the street. Although he tried to escape, the news agencies followed him there, too. He was still cursing Broadway and the fuss over his disappearance, saying he was "fed up" with the failures of the Broadway shows he financed and complaining about the manhunt. When asked if he was interested in getting married and settling down, he said, "Nothing doing."

Although Dick renounced Broadway, around this time he met a German dancer named Johanna Rischke and promised her a career in the theater in New York. Rischke, probably one of Dick's girlfriends, took Dick seriously and at his urging quit her job and prepared to move. She obtained a visa and later moved to America, along with a shaky contract that Dick set up with a dance company in New York.

Meanwhile, Dick loved life in Europe and spent more time cruising the Riviera in his boat. In spite of himself, Dick continued to be an accidental supporting character in the middle of major historical events. He returned to England when Amelia Earhart landed the *Friendship* in Southampton, and he greeted both Earhart and his good friends Wilmer Stultz and Lou Gordon upon their arrival. Dick was lucky enough to be a guest of honor at the Royal Aero Club in London when Wilmer Stultz spoke of the amazing experience of flying with Earhart. Earhart later sold the plane in England and gave Dick the aluminum pontoons for safekeeping. She couldn't have known that Dick was not the best guardian of precious artifacts. He stored them in a warehouse by the Southampton shipyard, but they disappeared before he could donate them to a museum as he'd intended. The pontoons were not the first and certainly would not be the last items of value lost to Dick's carelessness.

Dick continued to shuttle between London and Paris and sailed whenever he had the chance. As he developed his drinking habit, he also engaged in more peculiar behavior. He was seen hanging out in London's impoverished Limehouse neighborhood for weeks, dressed up as a beggar himself and calling himself "Jack Ashore" as he drank and cavorted with the locals. Sometimes he even rescued poor prostitutes who worked the Thames Embankment. He would give them money for a tryst, but instead of taking advantage of them he let them go. But Dick would soon learn that drinking and alcohol were not without their consequences—not even for a privileged young heir like himself.

Drunken Night in London, 1929

On the warm morning of May 14, 1929, Dick went out on a golfing trip with a man from Kew Gardens, Ron Bargate—another of his "pick-ups"—in the London suburb of Hurley. The golf got rained out, so the men went to the Old Bell Hotel to shoot darts and have drinks at around two in the afternoon. The two men spent several hours drinking Pimm's No. 1—a popular gin-based mixed drink—and both were slobbering drunk by the time they called it a night at 9:30. Bargate had passed out, so Dick carried him out to his rented car, a large green, six-cylinder Buick saloon with black wings, to take him home. It was still raining at 9:45 as Dick weaved down Bath Road toward London. Both Bargate and Dick threw up all over themselves repeatedly. Twice, Bargate leaned out of the back window to vomit, while Dick asked someone on the side of the road for directions to London. The back seat, the steering wheel, and the windows were covered in vomit. Dick swerved all over the road and drove at about 25 miles per hour, oblivious to the danger of his condition. His view was further obstructed because the windshield wipers weren't working. At one point the car veered to the side of the road and Dick felt a bump, but he didn't stop because he thought he'd just run up on a curb. He recentered the car and kept going.

Several witnesses reported seeing Dick swerving on the road and other drivers near him feared for their safety. One man driving behind him reported him to an officer on patrol. An officer from Chiswick police station spotted Dick's car as well and immediately followed him and pulled him over. As he walked to the car, he smelled the vomit right away, which was all over Dick's hands and clothing. The officer also saw Bargate passed out in the back.

"Sir, please step out of the car," the officer said.

"I don't know that I shall. Why should I?" Dick retorted.

The policeman motioned to him to do as he instructed.

When Dick tried to open the door, he slipped and fell down into the seat. He pulled himself back up and then stumbled and tripped as he got out of the car. The policeman caught hold of his hand to support him so he wouldn't fall. Dick's eyes were blood-shot and his hands were trembling. He couldn't speak clearly, but he was very happy as he chatted with the officer. The officer asked him what had happened to his car—the headlamp was smashed, its glass missing, and the front bumper was bent and broken off. Dick said, "I know all about that, that was done just after four o'clock."

The policeman administered a drunk driving test, which

Dick failed miserably. He was arrested on the spot. Dick said, "If you think I am drunk, Officer, you have made a big mistake."

Finally hearing the commotion, Bargate slowly came to. He saw the policeman talking to Dick and slithered out of the car, asking, "What's the matter?" Bargate couldn't even remember getting into the car in the first place, and he had no idea where he was. Another officer who arrived on the scene stayed with Bargate as they hauled Dick off.

On the walk to the station, Dick asked, "How much further is it? This walk is doing me good." When Dick arrived at the station he was questioned some more, and a surgeon confirmed his drunkenness. Dick was thrown into a cell and informed that he was charged with drunk driving, to which Dick, still very drunk, replied, "Impossible."

While Dick slumped obliviously, half asleep in his cell, the Chiswick station received information at two in the morning about a man who was badly injured in a hit-and-run accident at 9:45 the previous evening while trying to fix a light on his motorcycle. It was the same road on which Dick had been driving, and the officers recalled the damage on Dick's car. Witnesses of the hit-and-run said they had seen a dark-colored saloon car leave the scene.

Dick was further questioned but he had no clue what the officers were talking about. His car was examined the next day and the damage matched the damage to the motorcycle exactly. Apparently that bump in the road was twenty-one-year-old Arthur Graham, a Slough man who was found unconscious forty-two feet away with a broken thigh and six broken ribs, his arm chewed up in the rear wheel of the motorcycle.

The victim was now being treated at Windsor Hospital with grave internal injuries and he wasn't expected to live. He died three days later.

Dick was charged with manslaughter.

Prison Time in Wormwood Scrubs

Dick was in shock. He was just starting out in his life and he was indicted for a crime that could put him in prison for years. He couldn't belicve it was happening. Dick's Uncle Will got involved immediately and posted bail on May 22, and then set about preparing for trial, which was scheduled for June 18. Will hired the best lawyers possible for Dick's defense — he called Sir Hugo Cunliffe-Owen, head of the British American Tobacco Company, for help. He brought them Norman Birkett and Albert Edward Johnson, London's finest, to represent Dick. However, Dick would also be prosecuted by London's finest — Sir Henry Maddocks.

Dick lay low in his apartment, leaving it to the high-priced lawyers to miraculously make it all come out right. Before Arthur Graham passed away in the hospital, his family said they did not wish to press charges. Dick sent Graham's widow enough money to provide for her for life, hoping it would earn him a little sympathy in court.

But the British courts and the public were not impressed with the millionaire's gestures or his sense of entitlement, and there was great public outrage over the incident. For several weeks, American newspapers incorrectly reported that "Leslie Joshua Reynolds" was on trial for hitting a man in London, but by the time the trial began, the American press had caught on. The trial and the details of the accident were all over the news.

In London, the entourage around Dick seemed to work against him, and the court made a point of discouraging anyone from being persuaded by Dick's social status or generosity toward Graham's widow or with London's poor population. As the trial ensued at London's famous Old Bailey court on July 22, 1929, Dick was humiliated and scared, but he was clearly more concerned with his future than with the damage he had done.

He pled not guilty, and his legal team asked the court to consider his youth and tried to disprove the charges that Dick was drunk, bringing in experts who testified that the drunk driving tests were flawed. The bartender from the Old Bell testified that Pimm's No. 1 was diluted with lemonade, and that it was equivalent to only three whiskeys. The judge responded by reprimanding the Old Bell for letting two men drive home with even that much liquor in them. Witnesses at the Old Bell claimed that Dick didn't "look" drunk, and Ron Bargate claimed that Dick's hand was "steady" when he played darts, so he must have simply gotten sick from the food. Medical experts testified that Dick had a natural "lurch" in his step and normally dilated eyes, even when he was sober. Dick took the stand in his own defense, stating that he had only a few drinks and was swerving because he was blinded by the light of an oncoming car. But his defense team's far-reaching excuses were no match for the many witnesses who came forward attesting to Dick's drunkenness in Hurley and on the road. More credible witnesses said that the number of Pimm's No. 1s that Dick drank were the equivalent of seven whiskeys.

Dick was sure to be found guilty, but he received a surprising reprieve — on July 25 the constable reported that the jury foreman had spoken to one of the witnesses about the case — enough of a violation to declare a mistrial. A new trial was ordered immediately the next day.

In the new trial, Dick was much more nervous the second time he was sworn in, as the reality sank in that his money and family name would not save him in court. The evidence was repeated, and some of Dick's associates, like George Wells Orr, an attorney for the Reynolda estate, and other American businessmen flew in and testified to Dick's good character. The judge again went out of his way to make sure the jury did not take into consideration Dick's generosity with Graham's widow.

After only thirty minutes, the jury returned a verdict on July 31, 1929: guilty of manslaughter. Dick seemed unsurprised. In spite of the verdict, the judge took his age into account and gave Dick the lightest possible sentencing: jail for five months, with the potential for time off for good behavior. He was also responsible for paying the prosecution's legal fees. He was handcuffed and held in a cell at the Old Bailey and given the standard khaki-colored prison suit with broad black arrows before being hauled off alone in the Black Maria. First Dick went to Brixton Prison in South London and then to Wormwood Scrubs Prison in West London on August 1 to begin his term. Part of Dick was almost relieved to go to prison, just to have the ordeal over with. But he kept enough of his wits during the trial proceedings to attend to business beforehand: He sold large portions of his stock, reinvested it in foreign stocks, and moved his assets into foreign bank accounts for added protection.

At Wormwood Scrubs, Dick met a lot of colorful characters, but none of them were difficult or violent. Scrubs was considered a low-security prison, and Dick was assigned light chores—washing cells, making beds, and minor housecleaning. He was permitted to have newspapers, letters, and books as well, unlike other prisoners. Although neither Dick nor the warden ever confirmed it, there were widespread rumors that as a mon-eyed man of privilege and status, Dick was being furloughed on weekends and permitted to have conjugal visits with his girl-friends. Less far-fetched rumors included whispers that Dick was suffering from wicked alcohol withdrawal as well.

Dick's lawyers were trying to appeal the case to get him an early release, but Dick was too humiliated to appear on the dock in the black-striped prison garb. He told his lawyers he was depressed and dreaded contact with the outside world.

Dick would be forced to face that moment on November 11, 1929, when he was finally released. Dick informed authorities that he would be leaving London and going to Germany via Harwich on November 29—perhaps to reunite with his German girlfriend. The experience marked a turning point for young Dick. He felt shame and remorse over the loss of Graham's life and was tormented by the accident for the rest of his life. However, not even a profound lesson like a fatal drunk driving accident could force Dick to give up the bottle.

Once eager for the social life of an American expat in Europe, Dick was now desperate for a new kind of escape.

Release and Escape

Dick's fortunes were mixed when he regained his freedom. During his prison term, the stock market crashed on October 24, 1929. His finances and assets were virtually unscathed because of the transfers he had made to gilt-edged securities just months earlier.

While he was still in jail, Dick was also slapped with a $1.5 million lawsuit for the Reynolds Airways crash in 1927.

Hungry for normalcy, Dick returned to Winston-Salem after his stopover in Germany for the weddings of his sisters— Mary to Charles Babcock, a businessman who once worked with Ed Johnston in New York, and Nancy to Henry Walker Bagley. Both were married at Reynolda and Dick escorted both of them down the aisle. He learned that his brother, Smith, married Anne Cannon—a cousin to Dick's former girlfriend Ella Cannon—just a month earlier. Anne's father had discovered her and Smith in bed and drove them to a courthouse in York, South Carolina, the same night. They were married at midnight. Now Dick, the oldest of the four siblings, was the only one who wasn't married.

The weddings gave Dick a chance to reconnect with his sisters and brother, and they spent many late nights at Reynolda drinking, laughing, and playing practical jokes on each other. Dick was comforted by the company of his family, although he had a terrible feeling of regret hanging over his head. No one mentioned his jail time. He worried that he'd disgraced his family.

Before he let those thoughts linger, Dick made another quick change of scene. He reinvested in several American businesses since stocks were available at bargain prices. Then he moved Reynolds Airways permanently to Winston-Salem, and bought up large chunks of RJR Tobacco stock at a cheap price. He informed his Uncle Will that he would haul cargo in his freighter, the *Harpoon*, so he could take advantage of the entrepreneurship clause that R.J. had put in his will, which gave the heirs two dollars for every dollar they earned on their own. It also gave him an excuse to get away again. Dick's interests would soon take a new and lasting direction.

CHAPTER 5

Tragedy at Reynolda

1932

For two years, Dick had been sailing a new freighter, the forty-four-foot *Harpoon*, in Europe, Central and South America, and Africa with a German crew. Dick transported an occasional haul of tobacco and other freight in the *Harpoon* to make the case that his nautical cavorting was a proper "job," but also to justify tax write-offs and give himself an excuse to sail. He carried cargo all over the world but didn't get to traverse all the oceans as he intended. He later said, "I was always trying to get to the Pacific, but I was never able to get a cargo there."

Dick continued to argue with his Uncle Will about how his inheritance would be administered. Even after his embarrassing disappearing acts and jail time, Dick was intent on squeezing as much money out of his uncle as he could. He knew what he wanted and had learned early on how to take legal action to get it. Dick had even filed a lawsuit against Will and the trust in 1930 to fight for every last dollar he thought he was owed on the two-for-one matching funds clause. He lost.

Undeterred, Dick dressed up his freighter and transformed it into something of a luxury yacht. The boat had accommodations for eight guests and was fully serviced by a crew of World War I veterans, who originated in Bremen. Germany was suffering from a serious depression, and cheap German labor was easy to come by. Dick paid each crewmember about a dollar a day and covered their room and board. His first mate was a former U-boat captain from the North German Lloyd line. The man claimed to have been the one who fired the torpedo that sank the *Lusitania* during World War I, and he was later decorated with a medal and citation for it. Dick saw the medal and took his word for it.

Dick continued to pick up some of Germany's best sailors and craftsmen for a pittance. He hired a steward named Cornelius and an excellent chef, Karl Weiss, who had once been a skilled carpenter and cabinetmaker and had lost many family members in the war. Weiss would go on to become Dick's personal chef for the rest of his life. They came into Dick's life when he was docked in Bremen and Cornelius and Karl rushed up the gangplank, begging to join Dick just as he was set to sail.

Slain Brother

In the summer of 1932, Dick sailed on his fancy freighter, bound for Dakar and Capetown with a German girlfriend (who may or may not have been Johanna Rischke), his crew, and two other friends from England.

The freighter was docked in the Canary Islands when Dick received terrible news from his Winston-Salem lawyer and trusted confidant, Stratton Coyner, who had gone to great lengths to track him down: Smith had committed suicide by shooting himself. At the time, Dick was recovering from jit-terbugs—severe symptoms that can be caused by either alcohol withdrawal or an infection in individuals who have been drink-ing heavily for long periods of time—and was suffering hal-lucinations, panic attacks, and fits of paranoia. Dick never said whether he had stopped drinking or had been drinking through an infection, but it was likely the latter.

Alarmed and frightened by his hallucinations and uncontrol-lable trembling, he had himself chained to a tree in a desperate effort to stop the shakes. Dick never told anyone who did the chaining, although it was probably a member of his crew or the friends he had onboard—all of whom were apparently appalled by Dick's condition. Dick never mentioned experiencing delir-ium tremens like this before or after.

When Dick received the cable that Smith had shot himself, he responded to the crisis the way he always did—he drank even more. This time, the peace of the ocean next to him couldn't keep him from drowning his sadness in alcohol.

Dick's girlfriend and guests didn't know what to do except con-sole him the best they could. But he wanted nothing to do with them and drank until he passed out. When he came to the next day, his guests had left and caught a different ship back to Europe.

Dick sobered up. He had to get back home. Although he was emotionally drained and booze-fogged, he managed to put together a wild itinerary in 1932 that would make today's most sophisticated traveler swoon. Dick sailed to Dakar and anchored his boat, leaving his crew to sail the *Harpoon* back to Germany. He then took the first transatlantic passenger ship he could find—a French Aéropostale mail boat that was going from Dakar to the tiny port city of Natal, Brazil. They embarked on a rough, stormy journey across the ocean that took several gruel-ing days. Dick wondered if he would make it across alive. He was horrified by the condition of the ship, and when they docked in

Brazil, he advised the crew to get another ship for the return trip because this one wasn't fit for sailing. They didn't listen to Dick, and on the way back to Dakar the ship sank in the middle of the Atlantic, killing all onboard.

Dick picked his way homeward. He wanted to get to Rio de Janeiro, where he might find a main airliner that would take him directly to the United States. But the only flights from Natal terminated in the city of Manaus, a former boomtown but now a remnant of the rubber trade located in the middle of the Amazon jungle. Dick would have to stay in Manaus for a day and night and then charter a plane to Rio. He bided his time visiting the Teatro Amazones and wandering through Tenreiro Aranha Square, all the while consumed with thoughts about Smith.

Were his uncle and sisters handling the investigation properly? He had received word that Smith's death was ruled a suicide, but Dick felt strongly that his brother was not the type to take his own life. When he arrived in North Carolina, many people were going to have to answer to him.

Maddening Journey Home

Dick finally caught a plane to Rio de Janeiro, where he could surely make another air connection straight to the United States. But his journey to the scene of his brother's death stalled yet again. He had arrived at the start of a three-month civil war — the Paulist Revolt of 1932. When soldiers marching through town handed him a machine gun to protect himself, he wondered how he would get out. Dick holed up with American airmen in a hotel and dodged bullets that blasted through the windows in the night. By dawn, the local authorities managed to subdue the rebellion temporarily, but all flights out of town were booked. Much to Dick's annoyance, reporters found him in Rio, and he was quoted saying that he was "profoundly shocked" by Smith's death but he would form no opinion until he talked to investigators. Dick finally found a steamboat, the *American Legion*, which was set to sail to New York via Trinidad.

When the ship docked in Port of Spain, Dick caught a plane to Cuba. He landed in a small airfield in Cienfuegos to avoid the publicity that was already swarming around the United States about his brother's death. Reporters were eager to talk to Dick. While Dick's sisters grieved and tended to the funeral arrangements in Winston-Salem, Strat Coyner met him in Cuba, with the three-hundred-page coroner's report in his hands. If Dick's sisters or anyone else in the family had heard from Dick up to that point, no one knew it—they were likely protecting him as he attempted to make his way home undetected. Dick and Strat drove from Cienfuegos to Havana and then flew to Miami on a Pan Am Airways flight. An official on the flight had radioed Miami and reported Dick's arrival and told the press that he had traveled under an assumed name. In Florida, they rented a dark sedan and drove up to Winston-Salem, where Dick read the testimony from an inquest held weeks earlier as well as a coroner's report several times in the car. Dick finally arrived in Winston-Salem, incognito. His gritty, primitive, ten-thousand-mile journey home had come to an end, a month and a half after Smith died.

When Dick arrived, Reynolda had been closed for some time, so he stayed with Strat and contacted his sisters to get their version of the tragedy. Dick had read the coroner's ruling and had concluded, contrary to publicized reports, that Smith's death was a murder, not a suicide. Dick wanted Smith's already buried body to be exhumed for an autopsy. There was a lot to sort out.

Smith's Tumultuous Life

After Dick left to sail on his freighter in 1930, Smith continued to hone his skills as a pilot, and he won several races up and down the coast. In 1931, he took on his most ambitious quest yet—he embarked on one of the first around-the-world flights with a small Savoia-Marchetti amphibian plane with an 85 horsepower engine. He first took the *Berengaria* to London with his amphibian as his "luggage." Dick met him to help him get through customs in Southampton, and then Smith departed for the 128-day trip from London to Hong Kong. The flight took him to exotic locations including Tunis, Cairo, Gaza, Baghdad, Karachi, Bangkok, and Hanoi. The flight set the unofficial record for the fastest flight from London to Hong Kong, but Smith was unable to complete the journey home because he had mechanical failure in Zhanjiang. Smith kept a journal of the brave, hair-raising, and often life-threatening flight, which would be one of his greatest accomplishments.

❧ ⦂ ☙

However, Smith's personal life wasn't as successful as his aviation adventures. Two years before his death, young Smith and his then wife, Anne Cannon, were having marital problems soon after their hasty wedding in late 1929. They'd only been married a month when Anne got pregnant, and by the time she was due to have the baby in August, she and Smith were already on the brink of divorce. Anne gave birth to a girl, also named Anne, on August 23, 1930. By then they were effectively separated.

Smith left and spent much of his time in New York with his sisters, patronizing speakeasies, having affairs, and living the wild life, just as Dick had done before him. Because Smith had pursued his aviation interests with Dick instead of going to college, he was unanchored by any responsibility outside of his own young family, whom he had now effectively deserted.

In the spring of 1930, while Smith was still very married to pregnant Anne, he met the famous Broadway torch singer Libby Holman at one of her plays in Baltimore. Libby was as famous for her throaty, soulful voice as she was for her bisexuality, having been linked to Louisa Carpenter of the DuPont family for years. When Smith first met Libby, who was a decade older than he, he was instantly infatuated. He made no secret of his attraction for Libby and he clung to her with the unabashed abandon of a schoolboy. After Smith's long and dogged pursuit of her, in which she refused his advances numerous times, Libby finally gave in to the wealthy heir.

Smith wasted no time moving to divorce Anne so he could marry Libby. Anne didn't protest a divorce, having long since fallen out of love with Smith. They obtained a divorce in Reno, Nevada, just as quickly and easily as they had gotten married. Smith's grounds for divorce were that "she likes big parties and I like small parties." Anne added that Smith used foul language that left her upset. This was all the Reno court needed to hear. Although he had not yet come into his inheritance, Smith agreed to give Anne a healthy settlement of $1 million, which she was satisfied with, as well as a trust for baby Anne. Beyond that, Anne waived all further rights to Smith's estate. The two of them parted amicably, and Anne went on to take care of Smith's daughter on her own.

The same day the Reno divorce went through, Smith took out a license to marry Libby. In one short year, Smith had been married, made a father, and divorced, and now he was about to get married again. He was nineteen years old.

A Party and a Gun

Without a word to the family, Smith eloped with Libby in Monroe, Michigan, on November 23, 1931, just a week after his divorce from Anne. Dick was still out of the country in his boat at the time, and Mary and Nancy had no idea that Smith's teenage passion had reached such a pitch.

Many of Libby's friends also wondered what she was doing— marrying a teenager when she could have had any man she wanted. While it was evident that Smith was crazy about Libby, her affection for him seemed reserved; although she was earning $150,000 a year on her own as an actress, most assumed she married him for money. Some of Libby's friends countered that her dear "Smitty" was already possessed by a jealous love for her and had threatened suicide a number of times if she wouldn't marry him. On at least one occasion Smith flew into a rage after a fight with Libby and nearly crashed when he took off on a plane that was low on fuel.

No one could agree on the true nature of their relationship, nor would they have cared if Libby hadn't played such an important role in what happened next.

Right after Smith and Libby got married, Smith left for his incredible global flight. He said he wanted his excursion to bring him fame, but he would end up being more famous for the events that soon followed. Libby met him in China for a honeymoon when he suspended the flight in April 1932. By May, they finally made their secret marriage public in an announcement in Manhattan, and Smith made plans to study aeronautical engineering at New York University in the fall. By June, they decided to move to Reynolda for a few months. They spent the summer entertaining Libby's friends from New York and Smith's friends and family in Winston. That summer, Smith continued to make provocative threats that he would kill himself when he and Libby fought, even alluding to his own imminent death in the family Bible one night. He taunted Libby with a story about the time a fortune-teller in New York told him that 1932 would be a "dangerous period" in his life. Libby interpreted it as emotional blackmail, rooted in his possessive jealousy.

Smith threw a big weekend-long party at Reynolda with a group of Libby's theater friends from New York and some local

Winston-Salem friends. The weekend got off to a miserable start. Smith and Libby were fighting. He repeatedly accused her of flirting with his friends, and, to spite her, sent a telegram to Dick, who was off the coast of West Africa, saying he was going to join him there soon. Then Smith left the party with his secretary, Ab Walker, that night to pick up some girls, who were believed to be prostitutes.

Dick received the telegram the next day. That night, Smith and Libby argued again while their friends celebrated the twenty-first birthday of Smith's friend Charles Gideon Hill, over a barbecue and gallons of illegal corn whiskey at the boathouse overlooking Lake Katharine. It was late on the night of July 5, 1932, and most of the partygoers had either left or passed out in various spots throughout the house. Smith and Libby retreated to the master bedroom and continued to fight. Smith accused Libby of flirting with Ab.

In the early morning hours of July 6, a gunshot went off on the sleeping porch. Ab heard the shot down below in the reception hall. Libby ran out to the balcony and screamed, "Smith's shot himself!"

Ab ran upstairs and found Smith lying unconscious on the bed, a bullet wound in his right temple. An automatic .32 caliber Mauser pistol, belonging to Smith, was on the floor.

The Questions Begin

According to Libby, the possessive and jealous Smith had an inferiority complex and had repeatedly threatened to kill himself. He had also repeatedly accused Libby of cheating on him without evidence. The night of the party was no different. When they had argued in the bedroom that night, Smith again accused her of being unfaithful and again threatened suicide. He had begun packing his bags, saying he was going to run off and join his brother on his freighter. Meanwhile, Ab was downstairs closing up the house.

When Libby called Ab for help, the two of them rushed Smith to Baptist Hospital. Libby's negligee was soaked in blood, and Libby and Ab convened in a nearby hospital room. There was nothing the doctors could do for Smith and he was pronounced dead four hours later. The death was deemed a suicide.

While there were many questions, Mary and Nancy presumed it to be the correct conclusion. Robert E. Lassiter, still Smith's guardian at the time, issued a statement saying they believed it was a suicide, although they were perplexed as to why he would kill himself. Uncle Will was at a horse race in Cleveland, Ohio, when he heard the news, and he rushed back to Winston-Salem to make funeral arrangements for his nephew.

Meanwhile, investigators had found the gun and the bullet on the floor of the bedroom, along with blood on the bed, bedroom floor, and bathroom, and a blood-stained towel. Fingerprints of the guests were taken, and guards patrolled Reynolda.

An inquest was held on July 8 at Reynolda. In front of a jury, Libby, Ab, and several other of the partygoers were questioned about the events the night of Smith's death. Dressed in a negligee and perched provocatively on a bed in Reynolda, Libby claimed she couldn't remember anything because she had been drinking. Ab and the other guests backed the story that Smith had shot himself, but their testimony was often vague and inconclusive. Every inch of Reynolda was examined in front of several witnesses.

On July 9, at 11:00 A.M., Smith was buried next to his parents in Salem cemetery, and all the Reynoldses, excepting Dick, joined both Libby and Ab in mourning his tragic death.

After the funeral, investigators found flaws in the coroner's report. That changed everything.

On July 11, Smith's death was ruled not a suicide, but death at the hands of "a party or parties unknown." At the time, neither Libby nor the Reynoldses were sure what to make of the ruling. Needless to say, the investigation would likely go on much longer. By July 13, they were all mentally and emotionally exhausted. Everyone left Reynolda—Mary and Nancy to New York—and Libby was picked up by her parents.

Two weeks later, the grand jury had reached a conclusion as a result of what they found to be damning testimony during the inquest. Libby and Ab were indicted on first-degree murder charges. The accusations sent shock waves through Winston-Salem and New York. The charges were later reduced to manslaughter after both Libby and Ab posted $25,000 bail. Libby's bail was paid by none other than her rumored lover, Louisa Carpenter. In addition to the conflicting testimony, the jury found that Ab had appeared to have manipulated the crime scene after Smith was rushed to the hospital that night. In particular, they suspected that he had at first hid the gun and later moved it to the bedroom where Smith was shot for investigators to find.

Meanwhile, reporters complained that Dick Reynolds had "thwarted all efforts to ascertain his whereabouts," as local officials repeatedly said that they expected Dick to add pressure to the case once he arrived. Tensions were running high between the Reynolds and Holman families. Libby's father, attorney Alfred Holman, called the indictment a "dastardly frame-up." Libby had fled her father's home and gone into hiding, while reporters scattered throughout the country trying to find her.

By the time Dick's tedious, piecemeal trip from the Canary Islands had delivered him to Winston-Salem, the publicity and hysteria had already traumatized Mary and Nancy. Then rumors spread that Libby and Ab were having an affair, and that Libby was pregnant with a child that may or may not have been Smith's, which further complicated the mess. The siblings were now suspicious that Libby had killed Smith, with Ab as a

potential accomplice. The press was inclined toward the Reynoldses and speculated that Libby and Ab were having an affair
and had been confronted by Smith before the shooting.

When reporters finally found Dick, who was holed up at
Stratton Coyner's apartment and wearing a mourning band on
his left sleeve, he said, "Smith was a very level-headed boy. I
knew him better, perhaps, than anyone else. When I received
the brief cable telling of his death, I felt sure he had not taken
his own life. I thought probably it had been an accident." He
also said that Smith "did not have an inferiority complex" as
Libby claimed, and that he "was not of suicidal temperament."
He added that he "wanted to see justice done."

As promised, Dick conducted a secret exhumation and
autopsy of Smith's body—at midnight—to determine where
the bullet had entered and exited. The grisly task was conducted
by four surgeons, one of whom included longtime family friend
Dr. Henry Valk. The results of the autopsy suggested he was
shot at close range—a distance of three to five feet—rather
than point-blank—a distance less than three feet and much
more common during a suicide, as the original coroner's report
stated.

Afterward, Dick met reporters at the tobacco offices and said,
"I believe my brother's death was murder." Dick's statements
only exacerbated the local hostility toward Libby and caused the
Holmans to take a hard line. They prepared for trial by making sure the court would hear everything about Smith's behavior prior to the shooting. Everyone eagerly awaited the October
trial.

Then, a shocking change of course: Three months after the
indictments, the charges against Libby and Ab were dropped
due to lack of evidence and Uncle Will's sudden recommendation that the trial not go forward. Will had talked to Ab personally about the case and discovered more information than he

wanted to know about Smith and Libby's relationship. It was presumed that Will was afraid of the information that might come out about his nephew if the trial went on. The details of Smith's love life and infidelities might prove embarrassing for the family. Libby had already publicly discussed Smith's sexual insecurities, which she believed contributed to his suicidal behavior, and indicated that she would not hesitate to reveal any and all details about her and Smith's personal life in order to clear her name. Dick initiated a publicity campaign of his own that highlighted Smith's accomplishments in order to counter Libby, but his efforts were no match for Libby's scandalous revelations. Will famously hated publicity and scandal, so rather than fuel these stories, he wanted the charges dropped. He wrote to the officer handling the case, Carlisle Higgins, that they would be "quite happy" if the case was dropped. The more Dick learned in Winston-Salem, the more he, too, became embarrassed.

Dick issued a statement: "I have stated that I did not believe that my brother committed suicide and I'm still of the same opinion. His death might have been accidental. I believe a lengthy trial with the evidence now available would accomplish nothing toward clearing up the mystery and would only result in undue hardship for the accused and heartaches for all concerned. The whole truth of what happened that night at Reynolda will probably never be known." Dick further suggested that there might have been a "scuffle" during which the gun discharged accidentally.

While Will also did not believe Smith committed suicide, he hinted that he, too, considered the shooting an accident after carefully reviewing the circumstances. Libby was infuriated when the case was dropped. She wanted full "exoneration" at the trial, which now would never happen.

No evidence of an affair between Libby and Ab was uncovered. Libby also confirmed that she was pregnant and unflinchingly claimed the child was Smith's.

~ · ~

To this day, Smith's death is a mystery. The most likely story is that Smith did threaten to commit suicide and held the gun to his head. Libby probably rushed across the room to stop him, and in the ensuing "scuffle," as Dick said, the revolver accidentally went off. Perhaps Smith's suicide threat was supposed to be a dramatic maneuver intended to manipulate Libby—but instead ended in tragedy. With his daring excursions and risky lifestyle, Smith had tempted death numerous times during his short life. But it was his emotional insecurities, not a stunt flight or mechanical failure over the Sahara, that ultimately led to his demise.

No matter what happened, Libby refused to speak about the incident for the rest of her life. No one but Libby, and perhaps Ab, would ever know what really happened.

Emotional Aftermath

Smith's death permanently tainted Libby's life. Not only was she implicated in the death, she bore a child in Philadelphia on January 11, 1933, that the Reynoldses refused to acknowledge. The boy was named Christopher "Topper" Reynolds. Libby never forgave the Reynoldses and referred to Winston-Salem as the "hick town that tried to lynch me." Long after the fact, officials in Winston-Salem revealed that the grand jury had only indicted Libby and Ab because they knew they were lying during the inquest and wanted it forced into open court. Those claims were little consolation to Libby.

The inevitable battle over Smith's estate shortly followed in the spring of 1933. Before he had married Libby, Smith had named Dick, Mary, and Nancy, his daughter, Anne, and even murder suspect Ab Walker the heirs and beneficiaries of his estate, but since Libby and now her child were involved, the matter became complicated. Smith had made the will before he was twenty-one, which was potentially invalid, and Libby argued that he died intestate. Ironically, Smith's will stated that no one could contest it.

Although the Reynoldses had money of their own, they still suspected Libby was partly responsible for Smith's death and were sickened by the thought that she would receive Smith's fortune. Libby was pitted against the Reynolds siblings, and then Anne Cannon jumped in to lay claim to more of the estate for her daughter as well. Although she had previously waived her rights to Smith's estate in the divorce settlement, Anne tried to claim that she had been in poor health during her Reno divorce from Smith and that she had not been in her right mind. Therefore, she was Smith's lawful widow, not Libby. Dick responded by saying if Anne took this route, he would countersue so she wouldn't get anything at all. They all battled over the details for three years, with twenty-two lawyers involved and fees mounting to millions of dollars and the case traveling to the Supreme Court of North Carolina before it was settled. The parties finally agreed to split Smith's inherited fortune, which he never had the chance to spend himself, between Christopher and Libby, who would receive 25 percent of Smith's estate, or $7 million; baby Anne and Anne Cannon, who would receive 37 percent, or $9 million; and the Reynolds siblings, who received the rest. Libby received an additional $750,000 from Dick so she would cease litigation, and she would have access to her son's inheritance for her lifetime.

Years later, ex-wife Anne developed a much more amicable relationship with the Reynolds siblings, but she was unhappily married a few more times and became an on-again, off-again alcoholic. Baby Anne grew up to be a sweet and responsible young woman who made the Reynoldses proud.

Libby and Christopher didn't have a happy ending. Libby married an actor, Ralph Holmes, who died of a drug overdose in 1945. Christopher, who grew up to look just like Smith and who was the center of his mother's life, died on August 11, 1949, at the age of seventeen, in a tragic hiking accident on Mount Whitney. Libby inherited all that Christopher would have received from Smith's estate. Some members of the Reynolds family still doubted Christopher's paternity and found it embittering that this woman, who may or may not have been responsible for Smith's death and who was married to him for only a year, would receive Smith's money.

With the money Dick received, he founded the Z. Smith Reynolds Foundation in 1936, which he also served as president. Some said he and his sisters did it just to ensure that Libby wouldn't get access to any more of Smith's money, but the foundation did fund many good works for the city of Winston-Salem. Today, it funds the Z. Smith Reynolds Airport, Wake Forest University, local hospitals, parks, schools, and other projects. Through the years, Dick, Mary, Nancy, and their Uncle Will poured money into the foundation, and the coffers still show no signs of running dry. It turned out to be one of Dick's proudest accomplishments.

Young Dick was despondent after Smith's death. He decided to anchor himself in Winston-Salem and spend time with his family as they all recovered from the shock of their loss. Dick's aunt and uncle, and many cousins and relatives, were a great source of comfort to him. They had all been deeply affected by Smith's death—although they lived separate, often wild lives, the orphans and their extended family were bonded in the common burden of living up to the Reynolds name. Dick, Mary, Nancy, and Smith had cemented their relationship and their devotion to each other the day Katharine passed away. No matter where their adventures led them, they knew and understood each other the way no one else did. Dick and Smith shared their love of flying together in New York, and Smith and Nancy spent weeks at a time together in the speakeasies and theaters of New York. The loss of Smith was another blow to the orphans, once a family of six and now down to three before they reached the age of thirty.

CHAPTER 6

Love, Yachts, and Politics

1933–1941

While Dick was recovering among his North Carolina connections, he met the woman who would become his first wife. Elizabeth "Blitz" McCaw Dillard was in her mid-twenties and unmarried, and she had taken a liking to Dick after she was invited to a few barbecues at Reynolda. Blitz was from an upper-middle-class family and was the granddaughter of a tobacco farmer as well. She had known the Reynolds girls since they were kids and went on to Sweet Briar College in Virginia after high school. All her girlfriends were married off and Blitz was on the hunt for a good husband. She quickly grew on Dick—he found her to be bold, fun, and outgoing. Dick thought she was the prettiest woman in Winston-Salem and they began dating. But Blitz wasn't his first North Carolina love.

As a teenager, Dick's local sweetheart had been Ella Cannon—a cousin of Smith's ex-wife. They had dated throughout their

71

teens, and Ella wanted to get married. Dick told her they should wait—they were young, and he wanted to be sure they were ready. Ella was crushed by Dick's hesitation and broke up with him. But Dick never stopped loving Ella, even after he met Blitz, and Ella married his good friend Emory Flinn years later. In the summer of 1934, Ella had just given birth to a son with Emory, when she tragically and mysteriously fell off her penthouse balcony while Emory looked on.

Dick was so disturbed by her death that he had recurring dreams about Ella for the rest of his life.

Wedding Bells

Blitz and Dick had been dating for two months and their relationship had quickly grown intense. According to Dick, he had been drinking one weekend in late December of 1932 and had halfheartedly proposed to Blitz. The next morning, a group of Dick's friends called him in fits of laughter, congratulating him on his engagement. Dick was stunned to learn that Blitz's father had announced in church that morning that Blitz would soon be wed to Richard Reynolds. Dick claimed he couldn't even remember what he said. Yet another milestone in his life had been fogged by alcohol.

All day long Dick received good wishes from friends and relatives. They all liked Blitz and couldn't have been happier that Dick would likely settle in Winston-Salem with her. It looked like Dick would have to see this "engagement" through.

Dick soon found himself at the St. Paul's Episcopal Church's altar on January 1, 1933. After a modest ceremony, he did what he always did best: He threw a big party at his father's old Fifth Street house and invited all the neighbors. It was one of the last parties the old house would ever see.

The Era of Blitz

As Dick and Blitz settled into their marriage, Dick eventually showered her with attention and affection, and enjoyed treating his new bride like a queen. Both of them were the life of the party everywhere they went. There was no hint of unhappiness—in fact, their love was deepening.

Amazingly, they first moved into Reynolda, even though it had just been stained by tragedy. But they wouldn't stay there long. On April 14, 1934, Dick and Blitz traveled to Baltimore where Dick would finally receive his full inheritance. At the age of twenty-eight, he inherited over $25 million, which made him even richer than his Uncle Will. The news made headlines. One of the first things Dick did with the money was build a hundred-square-mile estate named Devotion in Surry County, not far from his mother's Mount Airy birthplace. The estate was located sixty miles north of Winston-Salem, and included eleven thousand acres of untouched wilderness and wildlife. Waterfalls, trout ponds, and lakes were scattered throughout the acreage, and Dick went to work building the twenty-room main house—Long Creek Lodge. The house was built over a dam by one of the lakes and was surrounded by a variety of multipurpose buildings—a movie theater, cheese-making shed, barns, servants' quarters, and power supply house. It dwarfed Reynolda and every other place he'd lived.

In support of the Depression-era recovery effort, Dick turned the building of Devotion into his own WPA project— the relief measure created under President Franklin Roosevelt to put unemployed men back to work. Dick paid workers double the standard wage for construction and prolonged the building process so the men could stay employed for as long as possible.

Dick looked for more things to do in Winston-Salem. He

asked his Uncle Will for a position on the board of RJR but he was voted down by the board, who thought he didn't have sufficient business experience. Dick was disappointed, but he didn't fight it. Instead, he invested heavily in local business and real estate and began buying solid gold bricks, which he felt were necessary to back up currency. As his business ventures grew more complicated, he hired an accountant, Grey Staples, to manage them but soon fired him when he and Coyner discovered that Staples had embezzled $150,000. When Dick fired him, Staples committed suicide. Dick felt responsible for his death, and to make amends to his family, he hired Ledyard Staples, his brother, to work in his stead, whom he kept in his employ for the rest of his life.

Dick also took advantage of his time in the community to give back to the city that helped make his father a rich man. He donated land and financed the 186-acre Reynolds Park— the first public park in Winston-Salem and the first accessible to the black community. Dick doubled this effort as another WPA program and put dozens of unemployed men to work. When it was finished, it included an eighteen-hole golf course, tennis courts, the city's first municipal pool, an amphitheater, and picnic areas. Dick appeared at the opening ceremonies.

At home, Dick and Blitz threw grand parties, sometimes numbering in the hundreds of attendees, which sometimes lasted for days. They went skeet shooting together at Roaring Gap and attended the Kentucky Derby with their friends. They soon became interested in horse racing and joined the Hambletonian Society, a horse racing club that hosted the country's most famous horse race. Dick's Uncle Will was one of the original founders of the society, and Will's fastest racehorses were named Dick Reynolds and Mary Reynolds. On July 7, 1933, Dick Reynolds won a pacing stake in Cleveland, and on August 17, 1933, Mary Reynolds won the Hambletonian at Goshen,

New York, as Dick, Blitz, Mary, and her husband, Charlie Babcock, watched.

By 1934, Dick and Blitz started training their own horses at Seminole Park in Orlando, Florida, which Uncle Will partly owned. Dick's best horses—Red Dewey, Joshua, Erla, Mack Abbey, and Taffy Volo, went on to win numerous races up and down the East Coast throughout the 1930s. And in 1937, Dick became vice president of the Mineola Driving Club in Garden City, Long Island.

It wasn't long before Dick's past came back to haunt him, though. At a horse race in Goshen, Dick was served with a $140,000 lawsuit by the German dancer Johanna Rischke. She alleged that Dick persuaded her to abandon her dancing career in Europe several years earlier on the promise of a theater contract in New York that never happened. At first, Dick didn't take the suit seriously and tried to claim that she had no grounds to file the suit because she was in the country illegally. But the courts forced Dick to respond. Eventually, Dick settled the case with Rischke, whose role in Dick's life was never clarified, but not before he had a lot of explaining to do with Blitz.

Although the Johanna Rischke situation was thus put to rest, it was not the last Dick would see of such cases. He had a pattern of neglecting "unfinished business," and he often failed to keep the many reckless promises he made to the people he picked up. There always seemed to be something—or someone—that would get in the way of his new loves.

Around the same time as the Rischke case, the old lawsuit over the Reynolds Airways crash was finally resolved. Dick was ordered to pay the victims' families $20,000 in damages after several years of litigation. At that time, Dick dissolved Reynolds Airways and renamed the Winston-Salem operation Camel Flying Service.

In a relatively short time, Blitz and Dick's union produced

a big, growing family. They had four beautiful boys in seven years: Richard Joshua Reynolds III (1933), John Dillard Reynolds (1936), Zachary Taylor Reynolds (1938), and William Neal Reynolds (1940). They were Dick's pride and joy. Along with Devotion, Dick built a huge, yacht-shaped townhouse for his family in Winston-Salem called Merry Acres. But he and Blitz raised the boys at Devotion, where Dick took them outdoors for a variety of activities. He built a skeet shooting range, tennis courts, and a jungle gym, and took the boys horseback riding and canoeing on the estate, much to their delight.

After a while, Dick was anxious to travel the world again as he had often fantasized, but he hadn't bargained for the burden of a family. First, he ordered a customized private plane—a trimotor Stinson monoplane made in Detroit—to be flown to Winston-Salem, should they ever need to take off on a whim. They still hadn't made one trip on Dick's precious freighter, the *Harpoon,* which Blitz urged him to sell. She thought a freighter wasn't a good place for bringing up a family. Blitz increasingly spent her time with Winston-Salem society people, which bored Dick. But Dick would come up with plenty of activities to keep him busy.

In 1934, auto pioneer Howard Coffin invited Dick on a hunting vacation on the Georgian island he owned called Sapelo, with the intention of asking him to invest in his neighboring Sea Island Hotel. But Dick was interested in Sapelo, not Sea Island. Georgia's coastal islands were already occupied by some of the country's wealthiest men. J. P. Morgan and the Carnegies owned the neighboring islands, and the Vanderbilts and Rockefellers vacationed on Jekyll Island. Sea Island was increasingly developed by millionaires like Coffin. But Sapelo Island, with its thousands of acres of untouched landscape, natural beauty, salt marshes, oaks, and wildflowers, was a sight to behold. It had recently been featured in *National Geographic,* and the island had been visited by two presidents, Charles Lindbergh, Henry Ford, and other prominent men who had appreciated its beauty. Eventually, Coffin gave in because he needed the capital. Dick bought the land and Coffin's mansion, the South End House, for less than $1 million. The sale included the entire island, except the settlements by the island's indigenous residents.

Dick took such an interest in the conservation of the island that shortly after he bought it he joined the American Wildlife Institute, which aided the government in protecting the nation's wildlife. For decades, Sapelo would continue to be Dick's head-quarters for conservation and preservation efforts.

When Dick bought the island, he added the 124-foot *Zapala* to his fleet. Coffin accepted the deal, although it pained him to give up the majestic yacht. At the time, Coffin had lost nearly everything in the crash of 1929 and would take whatever he could get. The price—$50,000—for the *Zapala* was a fraction of its worth and Dick knew he'd nearly stolen it. The elegant yacht, which was originally built by Luders Marine Construc-tion, was already famous for its luxury. It included a walnut din-ing room, social hall, three mahogany double staterooms, two single staterooms, four bathrooms, and large deck space. It had two eight-cylinder Winton engines of 500 horsepower each and a cruising speed of 17 knots. After Dick acquired this yacht, his interest in boating grew even more.

He thought if he built a bigger yacht, he could change Blitz's mind about cruising with the family. He soon began work on building his next boat, the *Lizzie McCaw*. The work gave him an excuse to be off on his own with his true favorite lady, the open sea. He hired a group of yacht builders, Sparkmen & Stephens, who built the *Lizzie McCaw* with surprising speed and success. While spending time with the builders, Dick became acquainted with the yacht racing circuit and took an interest in the possibility of racing himself.

In 1937, Dick began to fulfill his dream of yacht racing, participating in numerous races up and down the Atlantic Coast and Europe and almost always placing well. Dick first took the *Lizzie McCaw* to compete in the six-hundred-mile Fastnet Race at the Royal Ocean Yacht Club off the southern coast of Ireland. At first, his entry was disqualified when his skipper didn't see the signal to start the race. But the officials decided to forgive the error and Dick won fifth place.

Dick eventually threw himself into yacht racing with the same abandon he'd once shown to aviation. In December of 1937, construction began on his new yacht at Nevins Shipyard in City Island. Sparkman & Stephens were constructing the fabulous single-mast, fifty-five-foot cutter, called the *Blitzen,* and many other smaller speedboats for Dick. Dick's ploy to entice Blitz to the open water worked when he gave the yacht her nickname.

In 1938, Dick launched the *Blitzen* and entered the yacht in the world-class thrash from Newport, Rhode Island, to Bermuda. A great sailor named Robert Garland, who would become a life-long friend, joined him on the race. Dick was triumphant when he won the Class B division. Next, Dick raced the 225-mile Block Island race at Bayside Yacht Club in Queens, where Dick took the lead with the help of a generous southwest breeze.

But the 1939 Honolulu Fastnet Race was the big win he was most proud of.

Dreams Chased

The son of tobacco lord R. J. Reynolds was the big draw at the 1939 international Fastnet Yacht Race in Honolulu. Dick, who was about to cause an upset in the yachting circuit, had created a media frenzy.

Since the sloops had launched from the Golden Gate Bridge

in San Francsico for the brutal 2,085-mile race, reporters already wondered if the *Blitzen* might be the surprise winner. On July 6, the *Blitzen* reported in at 130 miles southwest toward Honolulu and was in second place. By July 16, the *Blitzen* was 605 miles from Honolulu, but the *Fandango* was still ahead at 585 miles to the finish. On July 17, Dick's yacht lost its headsail and they had to press on using only the lower sails. Dick slipped to third place.

As the race neared its end, Dick and his crew had gone for days without sleep, and they were wet and worn from the salt spray. Some crewmembers were seasick. But Dick's expression was intent—his eyes steely and focused on Diamond Head in the distance as the sun disappeared on the horizon. The beautiful *Blitzen* had inched back to second place in the race, which was proving to be one of the most competitive in history. Dick was coming down the home stretch with the 106-foot *Contender* ahead and the *Fandango* behind him, while the glistening blue Pacific pushed them along.

At thirty-three, Dick had acquired his impressive fleet of yachts and sailboats, like he always wanted since he was a little boy playing on Lake Katharine. He joined the Sea Island Yacht Club and the exclusive New York Yacht Club in 1937, with its sloping, yacht-shaped windows and nautical architectural design, the same year he built the *Blitzen*. After he first raced her in Bermuda, where he obtained a handicap allowance based on *Blitzen*'s weight, he then took her to the British Fastnet and made a third place showing. Next was second prize in the Miami–Nassau run, and first prize in a Nassau course, which Blitz watched from the air on a chartered plane. Then he earned two more firsts from St. Petersburg, Florida, to Havana, and Havana to Key West, barely beating his friend Harkness Edwards both times. Dick was a bona fide expert yachtsman, reearning his title, "Kid Carolina."

Kid Carolina Strikes Again

As Dick sailed, he thought about Blitz. The marriage was starting to falter and their petty arguments intensified. Each time they fought, Dick showered her with gifts, but they would fight soon again anyway. He rarely saw his young boys anymore. It seemed only yesterday that Blitz had become pregnant with their first child in 1933, and shortly after the news hit the press, trouble began. On October 28 of that year, a note arrived at Reynolda threatening to kidnap Blitz unless a ransom of $10,000 was paid. Without even telling Blitz about it, Dick immediately called J. Edgar Hoover, the director of the Bureau of Investigation— the predecessor to the soon-to-be-formed FBI—who advised him to make a decoy package, while federal authorities kept a night vigil at the drop-off site. When a former Reynolds security guard and unemployed textile worker, John Lanier, showed up to retrieve it, he was arrested on the spot. Dick had compassion for Lanier and asked the court to treat him fairly. When he was sentenced to five years in prison, Dick lobbied for his parole. But it was an ordeal that reminded Dick that he had to protect his family from the curse of wealth.

Dick sold his sister Mary his share of Reynolda in 1934, and she moved into their childhood home permanently. Mary refurbished the property and added an indoor swimming pool, shooting range, bowling alley, billiard room, squash courts, and a complete bar. To honor her brother's love of yachting, Mary had a large mural painted in Reynolda's basement art deco bar featuring Dick and Blitz at the bridge of the *Blitzen*.

Lately Dick had felt disconnected from his sisters. Mary had devoted herself to her marriage and Nancy had moved to Connecticut. And Dick still missed his brother, Smith, whom he felt had really understood him.

It had been only seven years since Smith was shot in their

family home. The young man had been poised on the brink of glory, almost circling the world by plane and breaking aviation records. Dick recalled their excitement over receiving their pilot's licenses from Orville Wright. Smith loved boats, too. They spent wonderful years together during Smith's short life.

Professionally, Dick had everything to be happy about. He had just invested heavily in Chrysler, General Motors, and Cannon Mills, all of which were bringing in healthy returns. He had made significant strides with Autolite and the Fortune 500 company Atlas Powder. At home, he was in the process of successfully memorializing Smith with the development of the Z. Smith Reynolds Airport, another WPA effort, in Winston-Salem. The Z. Smith Reynolds Foundation, which was headquartered in his office at Sapelo, was already making huge advances in eradicating syphilis through its $7 million donation to research. It was so successful that the federal government had been using the foundation's approach with their own national health campaigns.

Dick had many projects that he wanted to undertake for the community. After Smith's death, he had softened toward his hometown and had been inspired to do good things with Smith's money. Although Dick had always sought to help the poor since his days in London, he was now driven to do even more for those less fortunate. It gave him a sense of purpose that he otherwise found hard to come by. He had already built Reynolds Park for the poor, donated RJR stock (which yielded dividends of $5,000 per year) to North Carolina State University and become one of that institution's most prominent benefactors and trustees, and worked to rebuild Winston-Salem's hospitals—but he wanted to do more.

Meanwhile, back at the yacht race, night fell and Dick was rounding the bend at Diamond Head. The *Contender* was ahead of him and Dick knew he wasn't going to catch up under the weight of the *Blitzen*. The *Fandango* was inching closer and closer behind. They pressed on hard and crossed the finish line. The *Contender* was already resting in front of them. They beat the *Fandango* by fifty-two seconds.

As the winners were announced for the toughest and most revered yacht race of the year, Dick's *Blitzen* was declared the winner due to the handicaps it faced in the last three days of the race. It was the most prized American yacht trophy, and Dick was crowned one of the world's leading yacht racing captains.

The Honolulu race was a stunning example of what Dick was capable of achieving when he committed himself to a goal and stuck with it long enough to see it through. Whether he could repeat such challenging exploits, in life and in love, was uncertain. While the *Blitzen* had won, the real Blitz was herself in need of some of the same attention.

After the race, Blitz flew to Pearl Harbor clipper base to meet Dick and celebrate with him. They stayed in Honolulu for several weeks and attended parties and took cruises. By this time, Dick was spending about $1 million per year, and $20,000 sailing with Blitz to Europe whenever he could convince her. In addition to the sailing, they went to the Caribbean regularly and flew hundreds of guests and musicians to meet them at Sapelo for parties and hunting trips. But it remained to be seen if the good times between them would last.

Political Ventures

Soon, the dimpled, sandy-haired prince who had already worn so many hats in his professional life would take a new direction. Dick had proven to be charismatic, jovial, and welcoming on the home front, and had a genuine compassion for people of every background and social status. In public life Dick was respected and admired, even in the face of brewing controversy over the danger of the cigarettes that made him and his family so wealthy. That led him to the inevitable transition to politics.

In 1940 and 1941, Dick traded in yacht racing, temporarily, for the national political stage. He jumped into politics headfirst and full bore, as he did all his endeavors. On January 4, 1941, he was appointed treasurer and chair of the finance committee of the Democratic National Committee by chairman Ed Flynn. This honor came after he had successfully helped Franklin Delano Roosevelt win his third term as president. In late 1940, the DNC had looked to Dick for help when FDR was losing in key states and the election was in jeopardy. They had run out of money to continue the expensive radio ads they needed to swing the election back in his favor. In September of 1940, Dick, having already given FDR a $10,000 donation in his first election and another $20,000 for this one, jumped in and loaned the Democratic Party a total of $300,000 in cash through the New York, New Jersey, and Illinois organizations. The campaign turned out to be the country's most expensive in history to that time. Financially, he gave the Democrats unprecedented power and leverage against the wealthy Republicans, who had long been subsidized by the Rockefellers and DuPonts. At a time when his entire hometown, including his own family, had come out in support of Wendell Willkie, Dick favored FDR, whom he had loved since he first ran in 1932. At the time, Dick was so swept up in the spirit of reform that he got involved with the North Carolina Democratic Party. Dick was quoted saying he backed Roosevelt because "I liked his program." Dick fully credited FDR with inspiring him to become politically active.

Dick became very good friends with FDR, and Dick's funding was considered the turning point in FDR's third-term win. Even before he became treasurer, Dick had already proven to be a talented political fund-raiser, and FDR had commissioned Dick's assistance for his campaign. Dick campaigned hard for

FDR, making calls and raising money wherever he could. This was scandalous to the Reynoldses, especially Uncle Will and his wife. They and almost all of his family opposed a third-term election for FDR because FDR had overseen the filing of a price-fixing antitrust suit against several tobacco companies, including RJR. As Dick moved to Raleigh to campaign exclusively for FDR, Will stopped speaking to him. Blitz even said publicly that her marriage might be in trouble if FDR was reelected. None of Dick's friends and peers would donate, and Dick even got into a fistfight with one of them over it.

Following the election, Blitz set aside the political differences when she and Dick were invited to FDR's inauguration. At the same time, Dick was subpoenaed by a federal grand jury over the funds he had loaned the party, which had not been repaid and far exceeded the cap on the amount of money an individual could donate. Dick was forced to demand repayment on the loans so they wouldn't get in trouble, which left the party in debt. Dick went to work and announced that they would hold a five-week fund-raising drive, saying the party "must rely upon relatively small donations to carry on its work, and this is more true now than it ever was before." Dick held fund-raisers and $100-a-plate Andrew Jackson dinners, held by North Carolina's Young Democrats club, to help refill the party's coffers. Dick said, "These dinners are the chief source of revenue for the national committee, and we hope that sufficient funds will be raised to pay the deficit." The first time Dick attempted to host the famous dinners, the event was abruptly canceled when FDR announced that he wouldn't be able to attend. The following year, Dick's hosting duties were much more successful.

When he wasn't busy with the Democratic Party, Dick took an interest in his airlines again. Dick allowed his much neglected airline, Camel Flying Service, to fold and sold the planes to Thomas H. Davis, who renamed the company Piedmont Airlines. Then Dick invested heavily in Eastern Airlines and became its largest stockholder, under the condition that the airline move its North Carolina hub to the Z. Smith Reynolds Airport, which Dick was in the process of building. Dick also went back to his Uncle Will and again asked for a seat on the board of RJR. Since Dick decided to name his fourth son — William Neal, born in 1940 — after his uncle, the tensions between them over politics had healed. Since Dick seemed to be settling down in Winston-Salem for good and had exhibited more responsible behavior, Will would consider the request more seriously this time.

In April of 1941, Dick decided to run for mayor of Winston-Salem. Former mayor Marshall Kurfees had urged Dick to run, and withdrew his own candidacy to support him. Some thought Dick's mayoral ambitions were another one of his adventures or stunts, intended to capture the imagination of an easily bored playboy, but those who knew him well said he was serious. He was called a neophyte by the newspapers, and when asked why he was getting involved in politics now, Dick said, "I've always had a deep interest in social legislation." Three weeks before voting, Dick had already won. The last Democrat opposing him for the nomination withdrew, and Dick had no Republican challenger.

At the same time, Dick ran for a recently vacated North Carolina congressional seat, which would be filled via a special election among Democratic state delegates. But he faced heavy opposition from another candidate named Clyde Hoey, who had the support of former governor O. Max Gardner. Although many of the state's delegates liked Dick, Hoey and Gardner had much more political clout and threatened some of the delegates with their political jobs if they voted for Dick. Just before he took office as mayor of Winston-Salem, Dick was defeated by Hoey in a landslide.

At home, Dick would be the city's youngest mayor at the age of thirty-five when he took office on May 12, 1941. He pledged to work with the Board of Aldermen to make Winston-Salem one of the greatest industrial cities of the South, and he became tremendously popular for clearing out slums and building housing for the poor and expanding tax burdens to residents outside the city limits who worked inside the city. His efforts again faced major opposition from the city's wealthy, including his family, who had large estates outside the city limits and had managed to escape paying property taxes for the city until then. Dick wasn't intimidated and, with the help of a supportive City Council, passed the tax laws.

When Dick had first approached the Board of Aldermen about clearing the slums, they responded that Winston-Salem had no slums and rocked their chairs in silence. Dick exhibited his unpolished diplomatic skills when he replied angrily, "You mean you're going to sit there and rock like a bunch of dictators and not even consider the question?" Dick had photos taken and put together a report that directly countered the board's claims and angered slumlord owners. The photos showed overflowing sewage in some of the city's neighborhoods and notices of condemnation on homes that were owned by city officials and politicians. In one area, thirty-two families had a single cold water pump. After a contentious town hall meeting, the City Council voted to approve Dick's plan to receive federal Housing Authority grants. This gave him the chance to apply for funds he needed to tear down the slums and build new housing units. Dick raced to Washington to obtain a special hearing with the Federal Housing Authority and was granted $1.4 million to build 338 housing units for the poor. He named Strat Coyner the head of the local Housing Authority. Dick also irked the Board of Aldermen when he required that the city's movie theater open every Sunday for visiting soldiers. Needless to say, Dick was very popular among the common people of Winston-Salem.

Breakdown Ahead

President Roosevelt became close to Dick, especially after the election. He and Eleanor often extended White House invitations to Dick and Blitz. Blitz put aside the political disagreements when these invitations came along, and she became a familiar face in Washington's social scene. She even chaired and hosted some political dinners and activities on Dick's behalf during the first part of FDR's third term. But her interest didn't last long.

After about ten years of marriage, the tension between Dick and Blitz was running high. Since 1937, Dick had been traveling to Washington and Raleigh often, first to work on his boats, and later to attend to his DNC business on a near weekly basis. He traveled to state conventions all over the country giving speeches and fund-raising, and even when he was in Winston-Salem, he was tending to his mayoral duties. The more involved he got in politics, the more he was gone. Dick's political endeavors continued to be a point of contention between Dick and Blitz. She mocked his Democratic principles and told him that he had "no sense, no education, and stayed drunk all the time."

In December of 1941, Roosevelt wrote Dick a letter, saying he would make it to this year's Jackson Day Dinner, barring any "wars" or "catastrophes," and invited Dick to meet with him on December 7 to discuss DNC affairs. That very day, the bombing of Pearl Harbor put an end to the FDR visit, while Mayor Dick Reynolds called on Winston-Salem residents to remain alert.

At the time, Dick was also considered a prime candidate for the Senate but gave up those plans when the war started. Dick was a patriot at heart and he would do everything in his power to serve his country. That meant dropping whatever he was doing to support the war full-time. Dick purchased the bankrupt Seattle-based American Mail Line, which he rehabilitated to aid the war effort. He renovated the company's existing ships and built new freighters to service the war. In May of 1941, Blitz served as hostess for the launch of the first completed ship — a new, 450-foot C-2 called *China Mail,* which was built in Chester, Pennsylvania. Shortly after, Dick loaned the *Zapala* to the military and turned his attention to the U.S. Navy.

CHAPTER 7

Love and War

1942–1950

In 1942, much to everyone's dismay, Dick abandoned his mayoral post in order to join the war effort. It would make his mayoral career the briefest in Winston-Salem's history, and the city was sorry to lose him. He'd just finished improving and paving city streets in addition to all of his prior accomplishments. The many hats Dick wore served him well with the people of Winston-Salem. When the city was threatened with a taxi strike, Dick sided with the drivers and told them, "I understand your position, fellows. I used to be a taxi cab driver myself." It was true—Dick had driven a cab in Norfolk, Virginia, during one of his excursions running away from Ed Johnston. His willingness to associate with ordinary citizens and find common ground helped them reach a deal much more quickly.

In the spring of 1942, Dick's ailing Uncle Will finally gave him a seat on the board of RJR, which he had long sought. Will resigned as chairman of the board of directors and Dick was appointed in his place. But by that time, Dick had made up his mind to volunteer for the Navy. It was the last time he would ever take an interest in working for RJR.

President Roosevelt assured Dick he could be excused from active combat, especially as a politician, a young man with four children, the owner of AML, and as the treasurer for the DNC, but Dick insisted. He would give it all up for the chance to serve. Neither the president nor Blitz, nor Mary and Nancy, were pleased with his decision. Dick formally resigned from the DNC on June 4, 1942. After only two years, he had eliminated the party's debt, except the money that had to be repaid to Dick for his radio loans. Dick offered to donate the note in honor of FDR's Warm Springs Foundation in Georgia, but Roosevelt said it wouldn't be necessary. The president expressed gratitude for all that Dick had done for the Democratic Party.

Blitz was very unsupportive of Dick's decision and Dick's sons would soon learn what life would be like with a full-time absentee father. Dick spoiled them but found them annoying and too needy. He was often visibly relieved when he could get away from his family. While Dick spent time in recreational activities with the boys, he left it entirely up to Blitz to meet their every-day needs. Dick was never around anymore to take them out-doors, and Blitz wasn't always the best caretaker herself. Once, Dick and Blitz threw a huge party at Devotion, with hundreds of people from Winston-Salem streaming into the mountain estate. The adults got terribly drunk and the children were run-ning around, completely unsupervised, underfoot. The boys even rowed around in a canoe and helped fish drunken partygo-ers out of the estate's large lake. The activities at Devotion were very often inappropriate for growing boys. Dick was oblivious.

Before Dick left for war service, he attended the dedication of the newly refurbished Z. Smith Reynolds Airport, which was the last event over which he presided as mayor. Dick announced that Z. Smith Reynolds Airport would soon be Eastern Airlines's North Carolina hub—a symbol of Winston-Salem's economic future. Dick, his sons, and his nephews pulled the cover off of a large marble bust of Z. Smith, erected on the second floor balcony of the terminal. The caption below the bust described Smith's global flight in 1932. Thus the late teenager, high-school dropout, aviation stuntman, twice-married father of two, and possible murder victim was forever memorialized at Winston-Salem's airport and at the city's most generous foundation.

Dick had already taken a leave of absence from both the mayoral and DNC posts on June 17, 1942, and announced his plans to join the Navy as a lieutenant on August 9, 1942, after he completed his training. He issued a statement saying that he wished to keep his commission quiet "until he had completed preliminary training" and that he "had no desire to claim anything that he had not earned." Dick was eventually selected for the naval air intelligence corps. He requested active combat and served as chief navigator of the USS *Makin Island* in the Pacific until 1945. Winston-Salem would need a new mayor.

Marriage Abandoned

When Dick arrived in California for training during the summer of 1942, he'd already begun several extramarital affairs with a variety of women he'd picked up around the country. He was back to collecting people for his entertainment. He had mistresses from San Francisco and Philadelphia, whom he lavished with expensive gifts, and whom he brought to meet him periodically during the training. He felt only a little guilty because he had Blitz and the boys visit him in California during this time, with all his girlfriends waiting on the sidelines.

While Dick was away, Blitz spent her time volunteering at hospitals and gathering donations to aid the war effort. She did her best to entertain the boys at Devotion, now completely on her own. None of them heard from Dick much during his time in the service.

Meanwhile, Dick's most prized love interest in California would step into his life right before he deployed. Marianne O'Brien was a sultry film and stage actress whose real name was Marian Byrne, and she was arguably the most glamorous of Dick's lovers. She was under contract with Warner Brothers and had been working in bit parts in various films when she met Dick. She was used to the attentions of rich and famous men, having been chased by Frank Sinatra, Prince Aly Khan, Aristotle Onassis, and Cornelius Vanderbilt. But only one would capture her heart.

San Diego, California, 1944

Dick was in San Diego docked on an escort carrier, the USS *Sangamon*, preparing to leave for combat duty in the South Pacific. At the time he was serving as an intelligence officer and shipped servicemen from San Diego to Hawaii and back. On one break, back in San Diego, a drunken Dick partied at the Hotel del Coronado with his fellow servicemen.

He bought round after round for his comrades and surprised them with an extra treat that evening. Dick had called Warner Brothers Studios in Los Angeles and asked them to send down a few showgirls to entertain them before they deployed. Marianne O'Brien was one of them. She had been a chorus girl on Broadway for many years, and had even performed with the embattled Libby Holman years before, but she had so far landed only a few small parts in Hollywood. She was under contract but was far from carrying a major motion picture, and could use the extra work.

The lovely twenty-nine-year-old New Yorker was the daugh-

ter of a nightclub performer, Mae Byrne, and the stepdaughter
of Abe Attell, a former featherweight boxing champion and
nightclub host. Marianne grew up in the theater district and
had only recently moved to Los Angeles. But California wasn't
home, and the older she grew, the more she was being passed
over for leading lady roles. Still, the Warner Brothers girls were
in high demand for servicemen either going to or returning
from the war. She would be one of three beautiful women sent
down to San Diego's luxurious Coronado Island to entertain
Dick Reynolds and his military boys.

This particular job would prove to be a lucky one. Dick
was smitten by Marianne. After the performance, Dick offered
Marianne and the other girls a ride back to Los Angeles and
sent them generous thank-you gifts. The exchange eventually
sparked a romance that would last through the war.

Dick was looking for someone who would be proud of his
choices and who would represent a return to the playboy lifestyle
he had long missed. He sought to renew his sense of youth at a
time when he was feeling suffocated by his family and rejected
by Blitz. Marianne seemed to be the woman that could give him
a fresh start, and her breathtaking beauty didn't hurt.

Marianne was looking for a wealthy man to give her the status and comfort she sought as a struggling actress. Nearly all of
her friends and peers were married, and her acting contract was
about to expire. Dick seemed to embody her ticket out of the
tumultuousness and unpredictability of Hollywood.

By the time Dick's unit shipped out, he was already considering divorce from Blitz. As he wrote to Marianne from abroad,
he knew his relationship with Blitz was over. The hard part
would be finding an efficient way of getting out of marriage.

Dick and Marianne both had a passion for New York and
made plans to rendezvous at the latest theater show once Dick
returned from the service. As his year in the Pacific wore on, he

wrote to Marianne regularly while he was lonely at sea, and her fanciful letters in response gave him just the boost he needed to get through some of the toughest moments in the war. By the summer of 1945, Dick relinquished his other women and proposed to Marianne via letter.

Active Service

When Dick shipped out to the Leyte Gulf in the Philippines in 1944, his duty in the Pacific would be strenuous and long. For seventeen months at a stretch he was in combat as a chief navigator without leave. He'd served with the Navy's Seventh Fleet under Admiral Calvin Durgin, who led a fleet of baby flat-top aircraft carriers. Even under the great physical and mental strain, Dick was an excellent navigator. But the absence of liquor onboard made the strain of war much worse. Dick's chef, Karl Weiss, used to send Dick whiskey and bourbon in tins marked "Berry Juice" and milk bottles marked "Sapelo Island Milk," which he stashed away in his cabin. Every now and then the ships docked, letting the sailors go ashore, and Dick would open his tins of "berry juice" and "milk" and pass them around to his fellow sailors. After the war Dick proudly displayed one of the "milk" bottles, complete with white paint and a silver foil cap, in his library at Sapelo.

Dick's fellow officers included Price Gilbert, who went on to become the head of Coca-Cola, and Thomas Gates, who eventually became defense secretary under Eisenhower. Together, Dick and his shipmates fought the battles of Okinawa, Iwo Jima, and Leyte Gulf. They also fought in the Battle of the Philippines in January 1945, in support of General Douglas MacArthur.

During the Battle of the Philippines, Dick had to navigate the *Makin Island* under constant enemy fire. Other American ships all around the *Makin Island* were being hit by kamikaze pilots, and Dick carried out a series of sixteen emergency turns in less than an hour to avoid the Japanese planes. This was Dick's first close encounter with the extreme danger of the war.

Then, in the battle of Iwo Jima, Dick watched as 25,000 of his comrades lost their lives. Again, Dick's expert navigating helped the *Makin Island* avoid kamikaze attacks. Ships all around the *Makin Island* did not have the same luck. Dick's escort carrier helped land some planes from the sunken carriers, but not all. As Dick watched ships and planes all around him burn, he, Gates, and his fellow sailors knew they were changed men.

Dick's ship emerged unscathed by kamikaze planes in both the Philippines and at Iwo Jima. The *Makin Island* went on to support the battle of Okinawa, and Dick's tour of duty ended after the atom bombs were dropped on Japan. After the war, Dick received two Bronze Stars and a Navy Citation from the president for meritorious service as a lieutenant commander and for his exceptional navigation skills. His comrades had nothing but praise for him and he felt the same about them.

When the war ended, he funded and published a book, a catalogue of his time as a navigating officer on the USS *Makin Island*, for his fellow sailors and their families, to the tune of $60,000—chump change to Dick. He produced thirty thousand copies of *Escort Carriers in Action in the Pacific* for the military personnel involved in the conflict and sent copies to Carnegie libraries throughout the country.

Postwar Activities

For the past several years, Blitz had made no secret of her resentment over Dick's activities, which not only kept him away from home but persisted despite the continuing opposition of their peers and his own family, who still disapproved of his high-tax, New Deal politics and ambitions. Blitz also opposed many of

Dick's decisions as mayor, which led to more taxes on the rich to support the poor—and stood in support of his angry, wealthy Winston-Salem constituents. Her constant resistance to Dick's choices concerning his military service and political policies left some wondering if Blitz's opposition had more to do with intimate troubles at home. People speculated that Blitz had paid allegiance to the Republican Party purely out of spite. Although Blitz knew nothing about Dick's extramarital affairs, they fought often. It also didn't help that Dick, although still quite young, had become a full-fledged alcoholic before he even left for the war. All the sophistication and responsibility of politics and White House dinners couldn't stop his habit. Those who knew Dick intimately noted that he was never quite the genius he could have been because of his increasing dependence on the bottle.

When Dick left for the war, he was succeeded as mayor by J. Wilbur Crews and had no more obligations to the city. Dick was honorably discharged from duty in September of 1945 when his unit returned from the Pacific. When he finally arrived on American shores after the war was over, he didn't go directly to Winston-Salem. In fact, he had lied to Blitz and told her he wouldn't be home until Thanksgiving. He immediately got in contact with Marianne, who met him in California, where they resumed their love affair. Dick was stateside for two weeks before he even called Blitz.

Dick's plans for divorce were already in motion. No one knows where he learned such sophisticated tactics to get out of his relationships, but he would implement a doorstopping technique that would become his trademark. The first step was to hide his intentions behind a smokescreen of affection, nonchalance, and unpredictability. Then he would activate his lawyers: This usually meant preparing some kind of advanced maneuvering to protect Dick's finances and make the coming legal action as efficient as possible. One of these maneuvers was the famous "residency trick," which Blitz would soon get to know. Then, when he was ready, he would deliver the final blow, the coup de grâce, to knock his unsuspecting opponent off balance.

On September 21, 1945, at 6:30 A.M., Dick finally called Blitz and said he was in New York, stopping for a visit. What Dick was really doing was seeking the advice of lawyers in New York and courting Marianne. When Blitz asked him what he was doing there and when he would be back home, he hung up. Blitz was baffled by the call, and she didn't hear from him for another five days.

When Dick finally did call again, he informed her that he wanted a prompt divorce so he could marry a new lover he'd acquired in New York. Blitz was shocked. Dick had just written her a sweet letter telling her how much he missed her and the boys and that he couldn't wait to see her. It was the smoke-screen ploy to catch her off guard as he initiated divorce proceedings—a diversionary tactic that Dick would use repeatedly in the future. Dick had also purchased a house in Sunset Island, Florida, for Marianne, and he sought to establish residency in the state, which had more relaxed divorce laws—this was the "residency trick."

Blitz begged and pleaded with him to return to his family. How could he do this to her? To the boys? Dick coldly said there was nothing she could do about it, and if she fought it, he'd report it to Walter Winchell, leaving Blitz embarrassed and ashamed. Just to make sure she understood, he called back a few minutes later and repeated himself. This was the final coup de grâce.

It turned out that Winchell had already been informed, and the news that Dick Reynolds was getting a divorce hit Winchell's radio show. Gossip columnists also reported that Dick had already given Marianne $100,000 in gifts.

Everyone in Winston-Salem and even Sapelo Island was up

in arms. Dick's family and his own employees loved Blitz and couldn't understand his actions. Blitz's father, John Dillard, hurried to New York to try to talk Dick out of it, but Dick wouldn't budge.

Faced with the humiliation of divorce and the prospect of becoming a single mother of four, Blitz still fought to keep the marriage intact. On October 19, 1945, she heard rumors that Dick was ill in a hotel in New York. She rushed up to see him and found him suffering from a bad cold and alcohol poisoning. In spite of her kindness, Dick belittled her from his sickbed and again reiterated his desire for a divorce with much hostility. Blitz left in tears, again, humiliated.

A week later, Dick told Blitz he was going down to Winston-Salem and asked her to meet him at the rail station in Greensboro. She thought he intended to reconcile, but when he arrived, it became clear that he had no intention of patching things up. He was only there to greet his boys and, more important, retrieve his things. On arrival in Winston-Salem, Blitz refused to let him in to Merry Acres or to see his sons.

In retaliation, Dick phoned all the stores where he kept credit accounts for her and the kids and had them closed. Dick then left town to tend to business at American Mail Line in Seattle. In November, he called Blitz at five o'clock one morning and simply said, "You will never know how much I hate you."

Blitz had had enough. When Dick filed for divorce (after he had safely established residency in Florida) from Dade County, he argued that he had told his wife he had no intention of living with her upon his discharge from the Navy and accused her of "mental cruelty" and an "ungovernable temper"—another trademark legal tactic. Blitz immediately countersued. After fourteen years of marriage, Blitz formally filed for divorce in Forsyth County. She accused Dick of "extreme" cruelty and said he publicly embarrassed her, verbally abused her, and deserted her and their sons. She said it would be detrimental to the children to be around their father and that she should be awarded full custody. She fought for at least half of the estate. With four kids to care for, Blitz had a lot of sympathy from the courts and Dick didn't stand a chance in limiting the amount of money she would get out of him. With little fanfare, the divorce was finalized in 1946, and Blitz was awarded $9 million in cash and assets for their sons, along with the fabulous townhouse, Merry Acres, and the country estate of Devotion, outright. Dick kept his yachts, private plane, and Sapelo Island. It was considered the most lucrative divorce settlement in U.S. history.

Although they were well provided for, the boys would never feel close to Dick. They would not see him for two years after the divorce. Dick wasn't the slightest bit heartbroken over his split from Blitz, except for the breathtaking amount of money he had to part with. He quickly recovered and made plans to marry Marianne as soon as he could.

Mary and Nancy were furious with Dick for leaving Blitz and abandoning his sons. They were even more incensed that he had run off with a woman who, in their minds, was a gold digger. More than anything, Mary and Nancy were embarrassed by Dick. Nancy, especially, would later seek to bury in obscurity Dick's mistakes, including the products of those mistakes—his children.

Dick was relieved to be out of the marriage. He had moved on to a new life in New York, Florida, and Sapelo with Marianne. But this break from Winston-Salem and the solidarity of his family would be the beginning of the end for him. His alcoholism would engulf him, and despite wild successes, his businesses would fail to satisfy him. All of the things money could buy would not bring him the happiness he sought. Only his boats would bring him hints of joy.

Enter Wife No. 2

As soon as the divorce was final, Dick was married to Marianne in New York on August 7, 1946, in her parents' apartment by a city magistrate, Raphael P. Koenig. Marianne's mother, stepfather, sister, and a few other friends and family witnessed the nuptials. None of the Reynolds family attended. Dick was happy to be back in one of his favorite cities, and Marianne saw her childhood dreams fulfilled when Dick bought her a huge twenty-two-room duplex at One Beekman Place. The Beekman Place apartment included a sixty-foot living room with one entirely glassed-in side that overlooked the East River. It was just blocks from where Marianne grew up as a child in a much more modest apartment.

Dick maintained his extravagant lifestyle with Marianne, and the pair used Beekman Place as their launchpad for many wild nights in New York. As he had done with Blitz, Dick threw Marianne huge parties in New York, Sapelo Island, Miami, and on Dick's yachts, parties that sometimes lasted for days on end.

Dick's divorce from Blitz and marriage to Marianne effectively estranged him from his sisters, who refused to meet her. Although Mary and Blitz didn't always get along, Blitz was family and the mother of their nephews, and they found Dick's abandonment of her unforgivable. Dick didn't let this worry him, though. As his mother, Katharine, had done before him, he wanted a fresh beginning with his new spouse. He knew they would get over it eventually. And Marianne was pregnant with his fifth child.

Dick set about spoiling his new bride. He spent tens of thousands of dollars renovating Beekman Place to fulfill Marianne's every want and need. As a wedding gift, he deeded the entire island of Sapelo to her on a napkin. It was another of Dick's reckless promises that he had no intention of keeping.

At Dick's insistence, Marianne gave birth to little Michael Reynolds in July of 1947 on remote Sapelo Island, without adequate medical services available. The birth was difficult for Marianne, who nearly died when she lost too much blood. She was saved by Dick's personal pilot, who flew off the island to retrieve pints of blood from a local blood bank. In spite of the ordeal, Marianne was excited to have a baby in her life, and Michael's birth healed tensions between Dick and his sisters as well, just as Dick predicted. Mary and Nancy made up their minds to accept and embrace Marianne, although behind her back they continued to poke fun at what they considered to be her unrefined behavior and flamboyance.

Dick's joy at his newborn son didn't last long. According to him, Marianne drank heavily during her pregnancy and after Michael's birth. In September, Marianne left Sapelo with the baby and went to New York on her own after a falling-out with Dick. Dick begged her to return to the island, but Marianne refused and told Dick that if he came to New York, she would "take care of him." Dick went to New York anyway, and when he arrived at One Beekman Place, he found Marianne drinking most of the time, with Michael in the care of nurses. She often went out all night on her own, and on one occasion the servants found her passed out in the baby's nursery with a cigarette burning on the floor. The baby was still sleeping in the crib. Luckily, nothing had caught fire, but cigarette smoke twirled up next to the baby. The servants fought with Marianne to get her out of the room. Marianne grabbed Michael and lurched back and forth over an open window with the baby in her arms. Eventually the servants wrestled the baby from her and carried Marianne to bed.

Dick was alarmed by the incident. He confided to his sisters that he felt he had made a mistake in marrying Marianne, but Nancy, by now the family leader, urged him to make the marriage work for the sake of the baby. Nancy was tired of defending Dick's womanizing, and she was adamant that he commit himself to his wife and children. Dick didn't know it, but Marianne had also confided in Mary that she felt increasingly ignored by Dick.

Dick took Nancy's advice and tried to put the incident behind him. In December of 1947, Dick threw Marianne a surprise birthday party at New York's Carnival Café. Dick's guests took over the entire balcony, which looked down on a horseshoe-shaped dinner table. Marianne walked in and asked "What's this?" Dick said, "Honey, it's a surprise party for you." Dick spent an exorbitant amount of money on roses that decorated the place and guests were served filet mignon and champagne, while the waiters enjoyed high-dollar tips.

Back at Devotion, Blitz had become something of a drinker since the divorce, and continued her policy of refusing Dick access to his sons as a way to punish him, even though Dick only halfheartedly tried to see them since he returned from the war. In the years to come, Dick would spend more time searching for fresh projects, new things to build, and new boats to sail than he would seeking out his boys.

Meanwhile, Blitz aimed to raise them so they would be the opposite of their father in every way. They were made to do chores and work in the house and on the estate, and in the process they became full-fledged outdoorsmen. In Dick's absence, the boys' other male relatives, like Uncle Will and Mary's and Nancy's husbands, tried to spend more time with them and act as makeshift father figures for the attention-hungry youngsters.

~ · ~

Michael wasn't yet one year old when Marianne became pregnant again. Dick became enraged and accused her of deliberately getting pregnant so she could get more money out of him. Dick drank more and Marianne grew deeply depressed, even picking up a smoking habit in spite of the fact that she was pregnant.

Marianne spent more nights out on her own. Dick began having mild health problems at the time and was often resting or recovering from hangovers. Marianne, who was growing more bitter by the day, used to mock Dick's illness and sometimes kicked him out of the bedroom. When he wasn't around, Marianne would ask the servants, "What happened to the dope?" or "Where is the body?"

When he wasn't fighting with Marianne, Dick got involved in politics again. He was asked to bail out Harry Truman, who was in need of emergency campaign cash in order to beat Thomas Dewey in the election of 1948. Dick grudgingly donated tens of thousands of dollars to his campaign but told Truman he was still upset for not being paid back the hundreds of thousands of dollars he loaned the DNC during and since FDR's election, which now amounted to about $270,000. On inauguration day, Truman called Dick into his office and told him, "I owe my election to you." After Truman won, he arranged a secret deal with the IRS so Dick could write off all the campaign donations to FDR and Truman as "bad debt" on his tax returns. Again, Dick and his wife soon accepted White House invitations from another sitting president. Dick was later praised as one of the few wealthy men of the era who stuck by President Truman.

In business, Dick was elected vice president of Consolidated Caribou silver mines, one of the leading producers of silver ore, and joined other former presidential aides in investing in the company. Dick also made one of his smartest aviation moves at this time. In 1949, he invested in a small crop-dusting airline that was run out of Atlanta, called Delta. Dick bought the majority of the airline's shares and poured money into it over the next two years. By 1953, Delta had expanded to international passenger service and became a world class airline.

For a moment, Marianne and Dick would know joy again. Marianne gave birth to another boy, Dick's sixth son, Patrick, in December of 1948. Marianne and Dick decided to commemorate the birth of their second son by making a vow to sober up and start a new business together. They opened up the Sapelo house and turned it into the Sapelo Plantation Inn, in part to help cover the soaring maintenance costs for the house. The chatty brochure read, "Expert and thoughtful attention given to every detail to make your stay comfortable and enjoyable... careful selection of guests assures you of congenial companions during your visit."

Dick also added a subsidized boys camp to another part of the island for underprivileged families in McIntosh County, but closed it just a few years later when he discovered that the "underprivileged" boys from Darien were being dropped off in expensive cars.

With the two baby boys in the care of nurses and governesses most of the time, Dick and Marianne gave up their vow of sobriety and resumed partying throughout their sons' infancies. They sailed to Miami Beach, Sapelo, New York, and the French Riviera on a regular basis.

The more they drank, the more verbally and physically abusive both Dick and Marianne became. Dick often became furious when Marianne wore revealing clothing in the presence of other men, which was the primary source of their arguments. Once Dick tackled Marianne to the ground in a choke hold and she pushed him back against a fireplace mantel, knocking him unconscious. When the fights were really bad, she hurled furniture and dishes at him and mocked him for being a coward when he didn't fight back. On one occasion, Marianne backed Dick up against the wall of their garage, cursed at him, and said, "You're a sissy, why don't you stand up and fight?" Then she picked up objects in the garage and threw them at him. Most of them broke on the floor, but one hit him and cut his forehead. In New York, their fights and screaming matches sometimes got so bad that Dick would call the police to scare Marianne into submission. Marianne also called the police to have Dick arrested, but when they arrived, they couldn't find any reason to. The police never arrested either of them for domestic disturbances, but they spent plenty of time acting as marriage counselors. In record time, the romance and the marriage had spiraled into violence and loathing.

It had been only a few short years and two kids, and Dick was increasingly abandoning Marianne, just as he'd done with Blitz. Even when they were on vacation together, Dick spent more time eating and drinking with his yacht crew than with Marianne. Marianne was bored with the isolation of the yacht and Dick's drunkenness, and she usually bolted ashore, alone, whenever they docked in a major port in France or the Mediterranean. Marianne's many lonely nights and Dick's drinking eventually drove her into the arms of other men. By 1950, Marianne had attracted the attention of some of the world's most famous playboys. But Dick wouldn't be lonely.

The Knickerbocker Ball

The striking, raven-haired, former British correspondent for the *New York Times* named Muriel Marston Greenough had attitude, passion, and a major temper. The Canada-based socialite, born December 28, 1918, to Thom Marston and Eleanor Heselton, looked like a 1940s version of Meryl Streep and was once a familiar face at the Garden of Allah in Los Angeles with Dorothy Parker and Robert Benchley, founders of the famous Algonquin Roundtable. She was also friends with Maurice Chevalier, Gloria Swanson, and Charlie Chaplin. As a young woman, Muriel even appeared in several foreign films with her famous friends.

She attended school at Havergal College in Toronto, the Château de Broussailles in Cannes, and Le Lierre in Paris before she married Colonel Harold Laurence, a Bengal Lancer, at the tender age of sixteen and traveled around the world with him. The couple spent three years in India, where Muriel studied Sanskrit and Hindu practices under the guidance of a maharajah. But Muriel was much too young when they married and the relationship didn't last—they were divorced in 1939. Upon her return to England, Muriel reported on the Blitz in Britain and was offered a job with the *New York Times* to write about the blackouts, wartime fashion, and female wartime workers. But she did not emerge from the war unscathed. Muriel narrowly escaped Nazi bombs on numerous occasions and watched as friends were killed right before her eyes. She was an extreme claustrophobic, and no matter how traumatized she was by the bombings, she wouldn't go down into the bomb shelters or the Tube to escape. But on one occasion she was forced into a cellar, where she was trapped with a fellow war correspondent, Richard Greenough. When they emerged three days later, they were in love.

At the time of their marriage in 1946, Greenough became a director for the United Nations Relief and Rehabilitation Administration and was stationed in Prague. Their marriage put an end to her career at the *New York Times* and Muriel devoted herself to a life of social dinners and events. But when Greenough cheated on her in 1950, Muriel started divorce proceedings. She continued to live off Richard Greenough as well as money she had obtained in her divorce from Laurence, and her own family's money. Muriel was already well off, but she wasn't filthy rich, and her mother, who had grown up poor, wanted to see her daughter become a Vanderbilt or a DuPont. During the fall of that year she attended the Knickerbocker Ball at the Waldorf-

Astoria, looking for love. There she introduced herself to Dick Reynolds—a move that would forever alter her fate.

❧ ⸱ ❧

It was getting late—a cold November weeknight in Manhattan when only the independently wealthy considered going out. The Waldorf-Astoria was hosting a big charity ball and everyone would be there. Muriel lay half asleep in her Upper East Side apartment when a friend from her interior designing days, John, called. "Did you forget that the Knickerbocker Ball is tonight? Where are you?"

"I can't be bothered. I'm exhausted and I have a splitting headache."

"Another hangover?"

"Very funny."

Muriel hung up and returned to bed.

John called back. "I trust that you're getting dressed."

"I told you, I'm not going."

"Meet me on the corner of Park in an hour."

"Fine. There better be some rich eligible bachelors there."

Muriel rolled out of bed and dressed. She left her Seventy-ninth Street apartment at ten and met John on the corner of Fiftieth Street.

"You look gorgeous, as always," said John.

They kissed each other's cheeks and walked to the hotel. Doormen ushered them to the main ballroom where music was playing. The doors opened to a large crowd of well-heeled New Yorkers dancing, drinking, and smoking inside the massive, balconied room.

"Let the party begin," John said with a wink.

An hour later, Muriel was dancing with John when she felt a tap on her shoulder. She turned around to see a dashing blond man who clearly had had one too many. He smiled from ear to ear.

"May I have this dance?"

John motioned for her to go on and Muriel joined Blondie in a two-step. Muriel looked into his eyes and felt as though she'd met him before.

"My name is Dick. And you are?"

"Muriel."

"It is *very* nice to meet you."

Dick looked at Muriel so intently that she had to look down at her feet to conceal her blush. They danced and talked for the better part of an hour.

"How about a drink, Muriel?" They walked to the bar and sat down. Dick asked Muriel lots of questions about herself, which she loved. As they talked, Muriel kept up with Dick, drink for drink, which he loved. Dick was impressed by this very attractive woman who could match him in both booze and brains.

Finally Muriel said, "I really should get back to my table. My friends will wonder what happened to me. Won't you join us?"

Dick happily followed Muriel to her table and sat down with her friends. His star power at the party was evident—all eyes followed the blueblood heir, and Muriel found that their table was suddenly the center of attention. Dick mingled easily with New York's millionaires, who in turn adored Dick's relaxed Southern charm and his soft North Carolina drawl. His popularity was enhanced by his excessive smoking and drinking, giving those around him permission to party with abandon. He was the life of the ball, and Muriel couldn't take her eyes off him.

Later that evening, Dick invited Muriel, along with the better part of the crowd at the Knickerbocker Ball, to join him for a nightcap at One Beekman Place. Muriel walked outside into the still energized New York night to meet Dick and his instant entourage, who were in a limousine waiting outside. The smell of sewage, manhole steam, alcohol, and perfume filled Midtown's post-party early morning air. It was a classic mid-century New York City night and, as usual, Dick Reynolds was at the center of it all.

They pulled up to One Beekman Place. The small, hidden, riverfront street on Manhattan's East Side ran from Forty-ninth Street to Fifty-first Street and was the place where millionaires congregated. Dick's enormous twenty-two-room duplex was a sight to behold. In addition to its sweeping views of the East River, it included a bar custom-made for Dick, which, Muriel observed, was as large as the bar in Club "21." The apartment was already heaving with guests by the time Dick and Muriel arrived. A beautiful, buxom redhead was making the rounds. Muriel settled down with a martini and observed the scene. As the night groaned on and the crowd grew more and more intoxicated, Dick invited Muriel to his study. He was fascinated by Muriel's history as a writer and thought she might be interested in his own publishing endeavors. He pulled out his self-published book, *Escort Carriers in Action in the Pacific,* and spoke about his wartime experiences.

As Dick rambled on to Muriel about the war, pointing to different pictures of aircraft carriers, Muriel, smitten, was less interested in the carriers than she was in Dick's handsome face. She started to feel guilty that she was keeping the guest of honor distracted for so long.

Muriel was flattered to have Dick's full attention, but she would soon have to go home. The more she drank, the more her headache came creeping back. She eventually excused herself from Dick, regretting having to do so, and retrieved John. On her way out, the lovely redhead bid her goodbye. With barely a glance over her shoulder, Muriel walked back out into the pre-dawn city with John.

On the way home, the twosome gossiped about the party and Muriel gushed about Dick. John informed her that Dick was *the* Dick Reynolds, of the Reynolds tobacco fortune. The name still didn't ring a bell. John asked Muriel if she had heard of Camel, and she said, "Of course."

"They're the Camel people. One of the richest tobacco families in the country." Muriel nearly swooned as dollar signs flashed in her head.

John also told her that the redhead was his wife—a B-movie and Broadway actress.

Muriel was appalled. "What? That bimbo was his wife?"

"I'm afraid so. Sorry to dash your hopes."

"Someone needs to rescue that man."

John went on to tell Muriel that Dick was once married to a nice woman, Elizabeth "Blitz" Dillard, who came from another respected tobacco-farming family in Winston-Salem. Dick was married to her for years and they had four children. But when he returned from the war, he left her, and then, seemingly out of nowhere, showed up in New York with Marianne O'Brien, aka Redhead.

Muriel quietly processed this information.

"All right, honey, this is your stop," said John as he kissed Muriel goodbye.

As Muriel waited for the elevator in her building, she pondered Dick Reynolds. Why would he leave his aristocratic first wife for a theater girl? He seemed awfully drunk all night—maybe he was just another alcoholic who tired of wives after a while and went in search of something younger.

Muriel also contemplated Dick's clear interest in her. The attraction she felt was definitely mutual. She wasn't the beauty that Marianne was, but maybe Dick was starting to tire of Redhead. Maybe it was time to coerce Dick Reynolds to move on to brighter, and more refined, pastures.

CHAPTER 8

Destiny Calls

1950–1951

A couple of weeks later, Muriel and her mother were planning a long trip to Europe, and she decided to throw a goodbye party in New York before their departure. Muriel invited both Dick and Marianne via telegram, in order to get a little more face time with Dick. The same day, Dick called her.

"Thank you for the generous invitation."

"You're quite welcome. Will you and your lovely wife make it?"

"I think so, yes. But we must go to the theater afterward. Would it be possible for us to come early?"

The night of Muriel's cocktail party, Dick and Marianne showed up, both sober and crisp. This time around, Marianne looked really beautiful to Muriel. She could understand why Dick fell for her. In the course of their conversation, Marianne revealed that she and Dick had two small children. Muriel suddenly felt embarrassed by her barely concealed attraction to Dick. Marianne invited Muriel to a Christmas party later that month, but she declined the invitation since she would be traveling. Dick, becoming more drunk by the minute, didn't want to leave Muriel's place. Marianne finally dragged him out the door a couple of hours later.

After he left, Muriel considered their family, and she felt further shame for coveting Dick. Although her own marriage had failed, she wasn't interested in becoming a home wrecker. Her ex-husband Richard Greenough had cheated on her and she was very lonely again, but that didn't give her license to steal another's husband.

Muriel and Eleanor

Muriel and her mother left for their cruise in December 1950 and sailed the Mediterranean. Onboard they met a group of RJR Tobacco employees who were traveling with their wives and children from Macedonia, where they worked in the tobacco fields. Turkish tobacco for Camel cigarettes had been grown and harvested there for over forty years. The tobacco they grew had to be aged for several years before it could be shipped out and manufactured into cigarettes. The employees informed Muriel that they had a handsome benefits package from the company— they were granted long leaves of absence and took all-expenses-paid holidays to Greece and other destinations of their choice. It was obvious that thirty years after their deaths, R.J. and Katharine's legacy at the tobacco company lived on.

In the course of their conversation with Muriel, she told the employees that she had recently met R. J. Reynolds Jr. in person. Muriel said they looked at her, dumbfounded, as though she said she had met "God." Muriel began to absorb the weight of the kind of man Dick Reynolds was. And she still couldn't contain her growing feelings for him.

Muriel had originally planned to take the cruise alone, but her mother, Eleanor, wanted to go along. Eleanor was a constant thorn in Muriel's side — she relied heavily on her young daughter, financially and emotionally, while also criticizing every move she made. Eleanor always found a way to squeeze herself into Muriel's life, which strained every relationship she ever had. She also had an obsessive love of money that drove her incessant demand that Muriel be constantly attached to a rich man, first marrying her off when she was only sixteen. Sometimes Muriel wondered if her mother would doom her to a life of loneliness.

On this trip, Muriel was reminded why she wanted to travel without her mother in the first place. Every plan she had made for herself—a relaxing sail through the Mediterranean and the North Africa coast, and an extended stay in Cairo—was derailed for weeks on end because of Eleanor's demands. They got only as far as Gibraltar and Tangiers, Morocco, before Eleanor coerced Muriel to go straight back to Spain and the French Riviera, and all the while they suffered many misadventures. They missed boats and planes, and their car broke down in Spain. By the time a truck full of orange farmers picked them up in Valencia, all Muriel could do was cry on the side of the road. After their car was repaired, they finally made it to the Riviera, where Muriel had given up entirely on her North Africa vacation.

Muriel and Eleanor had many friends scattered around Cannes and they were happy to be in a place that felt like home after their wild trip. They checked into the Carlton Hotel and settled in for several weeks.

As Eleanor hobnobbed with elderly folks she knew, Muriel took long walks in the hills along the border with the Italian Riviera by herself. She would pack a picnic lunch and sit alone, looking out at the breathtaking panoramic views of the Mediterranean. She thought a lot about Richard, and how she was twice divorced before she was even forty years old. She hoped to find someone new, and she thought a lot about Dick. She still felt horrible, pining for a married man, but she couldn't help it. He had money, he was handsome, and he was a warmhearted and bubbly American. What a catch he was—too bad he was caught up with a Broadway floozy like Marianne O'Brien. Muriel felt the jealousy rising up in her. *No, don't go there. Don't ruin your vacation with these thoughts.*

Muriel spent her nights gambling. The first time, she became enraged when she lost $200 right off the bat. Determined to win it back, she kept gambling, winning some, then losing, and then losing more. Muriel was hooked. She spent the next month in Cannes and Monte Carlo with her mother, gambling. She managed to lose $5,000 of the $7,000 she had left for the rest of their holiday.

After two months in the Riviera, Muriel had lost too much money to take her mother anywhere else. The only thing left to do was cut their vacation short and go back to London and hibernate for the rest of the year. And hopefully find a new husband somewhere.

The Ritz

Muriel moved into the small vacant home at 73 Lyall Mews West near Belgrave Square that she once shared with Richard Greenough. It was May 1951 and Muriel was bored, since she was broke and had no plans for the rest of the summer.

A few weeks later, her old friend and neighbor, Thea, called and invited her to lunch at the Ritz, and Muriel accepted. As always, Eleanor wanted to tag along.

At 1:00 P.M. that Friday, they met at the Ritz. The dining room was nearly empty as Muriel sat down with Thea and her mother to eat. Much to Muriel's surprise, three tables away sat Dick Reynolds, who was just finishing his dessert. He looked up and smiled at Muriel. She said, "Aren't you Dick Reynolds?"

"Yes, I am," Dick said, as he got up and went over to their table.

"Do you remember me?" asked Muriel. "I was at the Knickerbocker Ball?"

"Of course. How could I forget?" Dick said, as he reached for Muriel's hand.

"Won't you join us for coffee?" asked Muriel.

And so he did.

Muriel couldn't have been more happy or excited to be in Dick's company, and Eleanor couldn't have been more pleased that her daughter had gotten the attention of a Reynolds. Dick left a searing impression in the minds of the women at the table. He was jovial, handsome, fun-loving, and, especially to Eleanor, he was *rich*. After a lingering talk over lunch and coffee, Dick stayed on with Muriel after Thea and her mother excused themselves. Muriel's luck seemed to be unending—Dick later confessed to Muriel that he had not been getting along too well with his wife while they were traveling through Europe the year before.

Dick told Muriel that a few months after the Knickerbocker Ball, he had had a big fight with Marianne. One evening, after Dick got very drunk on their yacht, the *Zapala*, which was docked in France, Marianne disappeared for a week. When she returned, she claimed that she had been out with girlfriends, but Dick found out she had really been with Porfirio Rubirosa, which was later reported in Walter Winchell's gossip column. Muriel gasped. She knew exactly who Rubirosa was, of course. Not only was he Doris Duke's ex-husband, he was probably the most notorious playboy in the world. If a woman was seen with Rubirosa, there was no question she was sleeping with him. Several society people had seen Marianne and Rubirosa together and Dick was sure that he'd caught her in a lie. On another night in New York, Dick was out with friends at the El Morocco club when he caught Marianne and Rubirosa in an embrace. *How stupid of Marianne, to sabotage a marriage with a man like Dick,* Muriel thought.

Dick said that the marriage had been in trouble for some time anyway. He had long since grown weary of Marianne's insatiable love of the theater, café society, and fancy hotels, while he preferred his yacht, the ocean, and the open wilderness. He also disclosed that she was cruel to him—she verbally and physically abused him, threatened him, pushed him around, and threw things at him, once cutting his forehead. She called him a "sissy" and mocked his recurring illness, calling him "the body" when he wasn't around. Dick even wanted custody of his two children if he pursued a divorce—he told Muriel that Marianne drank during both of her pregnancies, and told the story of when Marianne was once found in Michael's nursery asleep with a burning cigarette.

Then Marianne's relationship with Rubirosa began. Dick said he had heard rumors that Marianne was seeing Rubirosa for months before it was verified, and that she was also dating Prince Aly Khan. Dick suspected that her affair with Rubirosa had begun as early as the summer of 1950 when they were in Capri and Paris. Rubirosa was following Marianne all over Europe and even tried to call her at their house on several occasions. One night at the Hotel George V, Dick got very drunk and fought heavily with Marianne. He left her to go to a bar, and she retaliated by disappearing for the night. When he sobered up the next day, he went on the hunt for her, questioning her friends all over town. Some lied and claimed she had been with them, others simply wouldn't disclose her location. Dick hired investigators to find out where she went, and they learned she was with Rubirosa. Dick didn't say anything to her at the time.

As always, Dick was an expert at protecting his own interests and assets when he was ready to dispose of a wife, and he soon deployed the "smoke screen." In late 1950, he made a conscious decision to stay with Marianne through the holidays and kept his suspicions of her affairs a secret for a while. He lavished her with expensive gifts and jewelry so she wouldn't suspect anything. Before he had heard of the affair, Dick had renovated his yacht so that he, Marianne, and their two boys could live and travel on it in the Pacific for at least a year or two. Now, Dick planned on making that journey alone. But he wasn't even sure if he would divorce Marianne just yet — it might be too much trouble.

It wasn't until the affair with Rubirosa became public that Dick knew the marriage was over. He finally dealt Marianne the coup de grâce and threatened divorce for the first time. But Marianne wouldn't be swayed so easily. She angrily defended herself, saying that while she had spent time with Rubirosa, she had not slept with him and that the gossip columnists were lying. Dick wasn't sure what to think.

To clear his head, Dick sailed to the Virgin Islands for a few weeks. From there, he activated his lawyers, got his financial affairs in order, and organized his income taxes to prepare for a possible divorce. Marianne called daily, trying everything she could to win him back. When he returned to their Miami home, Marianne convinced Dick to give it another try. They threw a party and invited Marianne's family down for a reunion. Marianne, on her best behavior, implored Dick to take her and the family on a vacation in the Caribbean after the party. They needed to spend some family time together, she said, and focus on mending their recent disagreements. Dick apprehensively went along with the idea.

They sailed the Caribbean and eventually checked into a hotel in Puerto Rico, where Dick took Marianne and the family out to dinner. As the night wore on, she became drunk again and openly flirted with male guests at the restaurant. Dick and Marianne exchanged insults and jabs. Dick already felt his compromise was a huge mistake.

Before the night was over, Dick tiptoed out of the hotel and walked to the docked yacht to begin his solitary journey right then and there. By then it was January 1951. He would make arrangements for Marianne and her family to fly home on their own.

Marianne woke the next morning to find that Dick was nowhere to be seen. She was furious. In the meantime, Dick was en route to Sapelo Island.

On Sapelo, Dick closed down the severely neglected Sapelo Plantation Inn. When he wasn't there to supervise everything, his manager, Frank Durant, often ran it for himself as a country house, and sometimes even refused guests so he wouldn't have to work. On one occasion, friends of Dick's tried to make a reservation, and Dick knew from the logs that there was plenty of availability, but Durant pretended it was booked so he could have a two-week vacation. Dick never confronted Durant and kept him in charge in spite of these warning signs, but he soon realized it would be impossible to continue the business unless he gave it his personal attention. Dick entertained the idea of building an eighteen-hole golf course, but his financial advisers convinced him he'd never make a profit for the same reasons.

Dick then set sail for Panama, carrying seaman's work permit papers he'd acquired when he carried freight there on the *Harpoon*. Dick's plan was to cross the isthmus over to the Pacific, but he was restless and irritable for most of the journey, thinking about what to do with Marianne. After sailing for several weeks, he received word from Camper Nicholsons shipyard in England that he had an offer to buy his current yacht. Dick planned to use the proceeds of the sale to start work on a new sixty-five-foot teakwood yacht. Dick immediately ordered the yacht be turned around and set sail for England, where he would sell the boat and start work on his new one. It was a dramatic move that symbolized his new intentions.

As always, Dick had a drink in hand almost continuously as the ship churned through the Atlantic. With hardly a moment sober from Central America to England, he contemplated the direction his life was going yet again. He had been here before. He just never thought it would fall apart so soon. He never thought Marianne would cheat on him either. How he missed those passionate first days with gorgeous, carefree Marianne. In 1946, not long after they married, Dick threw her a large birthday party at Sapelo, which made headlines. It was a good year in many ways. Dick had sold his Eastern Airlines stock when the company reneged on its agreement to make Winston-Salem the hub of its North Carolina operations. He used the profits to buy up more stock in Delta, keeping it in competition with Eastern and raising the stock value. Dick always knew how to make his money and investments work in his favor.

Dick wanted to impress Marianne, so he chartered five airlines to bring guests in from Winston-Salem, New York, and Miami. He loved spoiling his new wife. He had even scribbled out the note that deeded her all of Sapelo just to prove his devotion to her. It was hard to believe those heady days and nights had soured so quickly. He now regretted ever marrying Marianne and even lamented his bad judgment in leaving Blitz for her. While the marriage brought him two more beautiful boys, he felt they were the only good things to come out of it. By April 1951, he told Marianne that it was over and he was never coming home.

He finally missed all his boys. Before he arrived in England, he contacted Blitz and invited his two oldest boys, whom he had hardly seen since he left her, on a cruise for the first time. She agreed that they could join him once he docked in Europe.

Dick drank so much that he was seriously ill by the time the yacht docked in Gosport, England, and he had to see a local doctor. He was advised that he had to stop drinking and get plenty of rest. It would be the first warning of many to Dick to stay off the bottle. When Dick finally recovered, he finished the arrangements for his yacht at Gosport, and traveled to Ireland where he ordered a small, twenty-seven-foot day sailor, called the *San Dera*. About a month later, he headed to London to visit for the day. It had been a while since he had been there. The place brought back bittersweet memories.

While he had a terrific love for the city and the countryside, he had also spent time in jail in England as a youngster. A chill went down his spine at the thought.

On his arrival in London, Dick was starving and headed for the Ritz for lunch. He sat down for a quiet meal alone and that's when Muriel caught his eye.

Looking back, Muriel said it was nothing less than destiny that they should be there at the same time.

❧ · ❧

After Dick charmed Muriel over lunch, he decided he would spend the night in London.

"Would you like to go to the theater with me tonight?" he asked. Muriel had another date that night, but canceled in order to accept Dick's offer.

"Are you sure you're comfortable with that? Would your wife mind?"

"I'll pick you up at seven."

After going out with Muriel, Dick ignored the doctor's orders to stop drinking and he set about working on two projects: building his yacht, and winning Muriel's heart.

CHAPTER 9

Dick and Muriel's Secret Affair

1951

Dick picked up Muriel for their first real date in front of her home in the quaint, cobblestoned street of Lyall Mews. They walked the short distance to the West End to see a play and have dinner at fashionable Quaglino's.

In the restaurant's inviting sunken dining room, Dick had an amazing time with Muriel, who challenged his wit and stimulated his intellect. He'd already told himself that he wasn't going back to Gosport the next day. After a romantic evening, Dick asked her out for a second date the next night.

Dick ambled back to Lyall Mews the night after, already enjoying the familiarity of Muriel's street. He asked if they could stay in and talk instead of going out.

While Muriel cooked, Dick talked and drank. As his body warmed with the spread of alcohol, he disclosed to Muriel again just how miserable he was with Marianne. After the birth of their first child, Michael, Dick had wanted to leave Marianne.

But his sister Nancy convinced him not to. Soon they conceived their second child. Dick said that he missed his sons terribly, but he just couldn't cope with Marianne. Especially not now, after this affair.

As the liquor poured, Dick went on and on, rehashing his relationship troubles with Marianne. Muriel listened intently, wincing at the right moments and sympathizing at others. On the inside, she couldn't have been more delighted.

Dick was slightly ashamed of himself. Even he couldn't believe he was sitting in another woman's living room, tired of Marianne after only a few years of marriage. Dick could be fickle, and while Marianne had cheated on him, he was also relieved to have a good excuse to end the marriage. He complained to Muriel that he wasn't crazy about Marianne's family and he suspected she had ties to the Mafia because of her stepfather Abe Attell's boxing associations, and because Marianne admitted that she had dated men who were secretly in the Mafia. She was a city girl, and he, a country boy, and eventually their ideologies clashed. It never occurred to Dick that his behavior might have pushed her away.

Muriel's little house was cozy and Dick felt safe there. Muriel took pity on him. He seemed sad and conscious of having made many mistakes in his life. He felt guilty about leaving his first wife and his four boys for Marianne in the first place. Blitz didn't forgive Dick for a long time—only now was Dick allowed to see them again. Dick had missed out on so much. And now he would leave two more boys behind with Marianne if he went forward with his plans.

Rain was pouring in London and Dick and Muriel stayed up all night talking, drinking, and smoking. It was 3:00 A.M. before Dick finally left.

Shortly after, Dick sent Muriel a beautiful bouquet of red roses accompanied by a note that said he was going down to

Gosport to tend to his yacht, and he'd like Muriel to join him. She was welcome to bring her mother, too.

The following weekend, Muriel and her mother drove down to Gosport to see Dick's yacht. He had dinner waiting for them on the boat, and let them stay overnight. He was charming and sweet as ever, and Eleanor was as impressed as she had been at the Ritz. The next morning, Muriel sat with Dick on the deck, watching the boats come in and out of Gosport harbor. Dick was having such a nice time, he didn't want Muriel to leave.

~ · ~

Dick's sons would soon join him for their highly anticipated around-the-world trip. Dick said it was his goal to be back in four to six weeks, and he wanted Muriel to have dinner with him the very night he returned. Muriel couldn't imagine he would make good on that date. She was sure he would end up back in America with his wife instead. She nonetheless promised to be available when he returned.

The weeks passed, slowly but surely. The evening Dick was to return, Muriel got ready and waited for him at Lyall Mews. The night dragged on, seemingly endlessly. Muriel had all but given up when her doorbell rang at nine. Her heart jumped to her throat as she rushed to answer the door. There stood Dick with a fez on his head and two bottles of champagne.

"I told you I'd be here. Sorry it's so late." He kissed her on the cheek and let himself in. "The champagne is still cold so let's open it now."

After a few drinks, Dick and Muriel walked to a sensuous private club, the Belfry, on West Halkin Street. As they sat in circular booths, surrounded by heavy velvet curtains and dark, mahogany-paneled walls, Dick chatted about his trip with his teenage boys and his assistant and yacht captain, Peter Barber, who had come along to chaperone the boys. Barber had been a captain during the war and had known Dick since his early yacht racing days. Dick trusted him completely with his most valuable yachts and sailing expeditions.

The boys were in for the trip of their lives during their reunion with their father. They first sailed across the Pacific and down to Australia, where Dick had hired a private plane to take them over the Great Barrier Reef. From Australia they sailed to Singapore, where Dick took the boys out to dance clubs and hired Chinese call girls to entertain them. From Singapore, they sailed across the Indian Ocean to Egypt, where, again, Dick ordered a troupe of Arab dancers for his boys, and then took them camping out in the desert for five days. Muriel was riveted by Dick's sense of adventure.

Candles flickered against the dark wooden walls as Dick leaned over the table and talked about his travels. He loved sharing stories with Muriel, who seemed cool and laid-back, but also sophisticated and well traveled. It was a relief to talk with a woman who could relate to him intellectually and with maturity and understanding. When Dick was feeling euphoric, he kept up the drinks to make sure the good feeling didn't go away. He ordered several more rounds for himself and Muriel and they drank at the club and later at her house until four in the morning.

It was nearly dawn when Dick, who was by then extremely drunk, tripped up the stairs to Muriel's bathroom while she waited for him in the parlor. After some time passed and he still hadn't returned, Muriel went upstairs to see what happened.

"Dick, are you all right?" she called.

He was passed out on her bed. Dick had ended the long-awaited date night with this worldly, intelligent woman, who had listened to his stories all night, by falling asleep on her. He was lucky that Muriel was so good-natured about it.

Muriel was still trying to behave like a lady, although she wrestled with the both humorous and enticing image of Dick in her bed. She took a deep breath and reluctantly shuffled to her guest bedroom.

The next morning, Muriel slipped out of her apartment early for an appointment and when she returned in the afternoon, Dick was gone.

He finally called a few nights later and apologized for passing out at her house. He invited her to join him and his sons for a night out at Ciro's on Bond Street. Muriel wondered what Dick's sons would think of her showing up, but she accepted the invitation anyway.

Muriel met Dick and the boys, Josh and John, at the club and found the young men sweet and polite. They did appear to be a little perplexed by Muriel's presence. Nevertheless, they all went out and enjoyed themselves immensely. The boys were ecstatic to be spending so much time with their father. The trip had marked a return of Dick to their lives; he had been almost completely absent since 1942.

Their vacation with their father wouldn't last much longer. Dick soon sent the boys back to America so they could return to school in the fall. They would also go back to playing second fiddle to Dick's boat building and marital troubles for a while. Dick told Muriel that Marianne had turned up in Paris looking for him. She didn't know he was in London, and Dick wanted to keep it that way. Apparently she'd phoned Gosport repeatedly trying to find him, but they hadn't told her where he was. Dick felt he must go to Paris to talk to her about the divorce.

"Are you sure you want to do this, Dick? Especially with your youngest sons, who are still just babies?"

"I'm sure. I've been miserable in this marriage for some time. The boys will be all right. I'll make sure they're provided for, just like I did with my oldest sons."

They said goodbye as Dick prepared to catch an early morning plane for Paris.

∾ · ∾

He'll most certainly reconcile with Marianne, thought Muriel. *I'll never see him again.* Surely, once he saw Marianne's gorgeous face again, he would fall in love all over.

Nevertheless, Muriel sat around her house again that night, hoping Dick would show up. She prepared a small meal and waited.

That night, Dick knocked on her door. Muriel couldn't believe it.

"You're here!"

Dick let himself in.

"I told you . . ."

"Tell me what happened."

Dick poured himself a glass of gin and told Muriel that Marianne wasn't giving up on the marriage without a fight. Dick was sure she was still carrying on an affair with Porfirio Rubirosa, but he made Marianne a generous settlement offer and told her it was in her best interest to divorce him as soon as possible. She refused. Dick told her that he would go back to America right away to pursue the divorce if she didn't accept his offer.

"I need to get away. I'd like to make you an offer, too. Come to Italy with me."

"What?" Muriel stared at Dick incredulously.

"Let's go away together. See if we like one another and then discuss things more seriously later."

"What are you trying to say?" asked Muriel.

"I want to spend some time with you. But I need to tell you something."

Dick told Muriel he had been having an on-again, off-again affair with a girl in Ireland since he had arrived in Europe in the spring: more of Dick's unfinished business.

"I haven't told anyone. When I first went there and ordered

the *San Dera,* that's when I met her. I promised her that I'd take her on a trip. That was before I got to know you."

Dick felt he should go see the girl in Ireland and formally break things off. At least this time he would deal with another broken promise in person. Muriel thought it was an excuse to carry on his affair, but she accepted that he should go and talk to her. Not to be outdone, Muriel told Dick that her ex-husband Richard Greenough was still trying to win her back and they were due to meet the following week.

"Like you, I'll just meet him to tell him there's no chance of reconciliation."

Muriel went on to say that she thought her husband had emotional problems—always leading a double life—and she wanted to be a friend to him. The irony wasn't lost on Dick, who was essentially doing the same thing.

"Well, I better go." Dick kissed Muriel goodbye and told her he'd call when he got back.

Muriel did meet up with Greenough while Dick was away and told him that she and Dick were seeing each other. Although Greenough was upset, he eventually understood and was grateful to at least have Muriel's friendship.

Dick again shocked Muriel when he returned from Ireland and went straight to her doorstep. He said he had broken things off with the Irish girl. Muriel reported the story of Richard to him as well. Now the only thing in the way of their romance was Marianne, but Dick was undeterred. He knew how to play this game. The next day they flew to Italy.

Milan was breathtaking this time of year. Dick and Muriel arrived at the majestic Villa D'Este and checked in under assumed names. "As I am sure you can understand, we need to be discreet. Marianne is hot on my heels," Dick explained.

Muriel was taken aback by the elegance and enormity of the suite, which took up an entire floor. A wide, sumptuous living room connected the two bedrooms on either side and had sweeping views of Lake Como.

"It's magnificent!" Muriel exclaimed.

Dick and Muriel sneaked around the villa like a pair of fugitives. They never left the suite or went down to the lobby at the same time. The first night they had a romantic dinner in their room alone.

With their bellies full, Dick and Muriel sat on the illuminated terrace sipping brandy and smoking Winstons. Cellists and violinists played soft music in the garden. Dick's handsome, kind face looked even softer in the moonlight. She was having a wonderful time and wondered what Dick was thinking. He caught her stare and turned to her. It had been a relatively innocent courtship thus far, and Dick meant to change that.

"I thought of you a great deal while I was away on my trip, and I like you very much, Muriel." Dick smiled.

"I feel the same way."

"I've become very attached to you," said Dick. "I want someone to stay with for the rest of my life. I need a woman in my life, and I want you to be my sweetheart on this trip."

"What did you mean, then? Are you trying to tell me you love me?"

"If everything works out with my divorce, I'd like to marry you one day," said Dick.

The Italian Idyll

A heated love affair ensued at Lake Como.

In between numerous trips to their bedrooms, Dick and Muriel took boats around the lake, wandered off for awe-inspiring drives in the mountains, and shared many intimate lunches and dinners around the clock. Romance seeped into every corner of their excursion.

From Lake Como, Dick and Muriel traveled to Florence, stopping for lunch in Siena. They ate in the thirteenth-century town square, which hosts the famous horse race, the Palio, each year. In this delightful medieval town, Muriel would witness one of Dick's more serious drinking binges for the first time. Up until that point, Dick had been drinking moderately, at least by his standards. Muriel noticed that Dick could be excessively high-strung and often needed a drink to calm his nerves. Not that Muriel minded, normally. She was endlessly fascinated by Dick and found him to be incredibly entertaining when he drank, even if his ramblings made her a bit nervous.

But this particular episode in Siena was alarming. Dick gulped hard liquor hour after hour. At four in the afternoon, Muriel was still trying to get him to leave the restaurant so they could go on to Florence. She tried to hide her impatience. After all, they were having such a good time; she didn't want to ruin it. But as Muriel gently nudged Dick to get him moving, he growled, "I don't feel like it!" It was the first indication of trouble for Muriel, and their vacation had just begun.

Eventually, the pair grumpily moved on to Florence. Dick continued to drink heavily all night. Muriel didn't want to talk and they read in their own corners of their hotel room. Dick finally approached Muriel and rubbed her back.

"If I'm ever unpleasant while I'm drinking, just ignore it because I can't help it. I don't mean it. I know I can be mean sometimes when I drink. But I always make things right as soon as I'm myself again. And I want you to know I meant every word I said at Lake Como."

Muriel took his word for it. But a little voice in the back of her mind told her to be wary of this other side of Dick.

The next morning, Dick was visibly hungover, sick, and acting erratic. Muriel had the urge to take care of him and nurture him. This man could be an unpredictable train wreck at times,

but he could also be incredibly sweet. He clung to Muriel—
he was needy, tender, and impossible at moments like this.
Muriel peeled him off herself and went out to a local pharmacy
to retrieve medicine for him. She also called room service to
have clean robes brought up and the bedsheets changed—Dick
was running a high fever and had sweated through the material.
When she returned, she ordered him to the shower and fed him
orange juice and broth. It had been a mess of a day, as Dick's
health went from bad to horrible. After a full day of Muriel's
nursing, Dick's fever finally went down, and they had a quiet
dinner on the terrace, overlooking the Arno River.

After two more days of rest, Dick finally regained his health
and swore he would stop drinking for the rest of the trip. "Why
don't we go sightseeing tomorrow?" asked Muriel. She was eager
to get on with their holiday.

When Muriel woke up early the next morning, she caught
Dick lacing his coffee with brandy. Muriel was stunned that he
had caved in to the bottle so soon but didn't say a word.

They went to the city's premier museums, including the
magnificent fifteenth-century Medici Riccardi Palace. They
admired the Baroque architecture and arched windows and took
in all the exhibits. In the Renaissance-style courtyard, sculp-
tures and other works of art were on display.

The next day, Dick and Muriel packed up and traveled to
Rome. When they arrived, they checked into the Excelsior in
the heart of the Piazza di Spagna. As always, they checked in
under assumed names and arranged for two sets of suites with
separate entrances. The celebrity-rich hotel towered over Via
Vittorio Veneto. Their double suite rooms were decorated in
rich mahogany and blood-red velvet. The rooms were again
connected by a living room area.

Muriel wanted to take Dick clothes shopping. She chose
beautiful Italian suits for him and requested that the best tailor

in town meet them at their hotel room to have Dick measured. Dick thought the suits Muriel picked out for him were fabulous and he ordered ten more. Emboldened, Muriel added a dinner jacket, four silk suits, and four wool suits. Muriel smiled at Dick as he got measured, looking like a boy on the first day of school.

When the tailor left, Dick went back to bed, saying he didn't feel well again, which he blamed on an old sinus and lung problem from his youth. Muriel followed him and held his hand while he lay down. He clung to her, a sadness washing over his face. Muriel was stunned by his sudden depression.

"I can't believe you would order me all these things. No one has ever bought me clothes before. At least not since my mother. I'm always the one getting things for everyone else." Dick smiled wearily at her.

He seemed so touched and melancholy, Muriel wasn't sure how to respond. This big, important man looked so small and childlike before her now. She couldn't imagine that she was really the first person in his adult life to buy him clothes.

"Why don't you get something for yourself?" he suggested.

"I've done enough shopping in Rome for a lifetime. Don't worry."

"Please. Sorelle Fontana's is down the street. Get the best dresses you can find."

Muriel left Dick to sleep and strolled down Via Veneto. She was greeted by dressmakers at Fontana's and given the royal treatment as she picked out three dresses.

Dick felt better the next day, so they checked out of the Excelsior and drove to Naples for ten days. Dick phoned ahead to make reservations for them at the Caruso Belvedere at Ravello and managed to snag the last rooms.

As usual, the hotel was spectacular. Muriel was getting used to this lifestyle, fast. *It's no wonder Marianne's having such a hard time letting go,* she thought.

They had a stunning view from their patio, which was perched in a limestone cliff a thousand feet above the Mediterranean. In the distance, they could see fishermen in their tiny boats, seemingly oblivious to the day's end. It was breathtaking. Perfect. Dick and Muriel couldn't imagine a time when they'd ever been as happy as they were then, sitting on the terrace that night. With Dick's illness behind him, their romance was quickly rekindled.

After watching those fishermen every night, Dick was in the mood to drink and sail. One night they were feeling mischievous and left their suite to go down to the fishing village. Dick had managed to convince some of the hotel staff to join them for a little boat party, and a collection of bellboys, waiters, and bartenders followed them. Dick boldly sauntered out to the dock.

The local fishermen looked surprised to see the tipsy, well-heeled couple and their entourage, carrying a case of wine and headed in their direction. Dick made a deal with one of the fishermen to let them go sailing in his open boat. The man agreed, for a fee. Dick looked around at all of the boats and decided on one that could fit them all. The catch of fish from that day was emptied, and everyone snickered with amusement while Dick and Muriel helped their guests into the boat. Dick assured his passengers that he was a sailing pro as they floated out into the black Mediterranean night.

A good hour passed and they had completely lost sight of land when the staff became nervous. But Dick sailed on, merry as ever. As the winds picked up, water splashed into the vessel and it listed heavily to starboard. Some of the passengers started shouting and begging Dick to turn the boat around. Broken from his blissful, nautical stupor, Dick whipped the boat around and quickly sailed back toward land. One man lay prone at the bottom of the boat and the rest looked pale and panicked, clearly wishing they had never come out into the sea, in the middle of the night, with a couple of drunken foreigners. Dick and Muriel, however, couldn't stop laughing.

It had been close to two hours since they'd left when the faintest line of the spiky mountain range began to emerge. Muriel smiled—she couldn't believe Dick had managed to navigate them straight back to the village in the murky waters, with no compass, rough weather, and a weak little fishing boat. He was a pro, just as he said.

Dick had been sailing along the coast for twenty minutes when he abruptly turned right. He'd found the precise harbor at the base of the mountains from which they came.

Relief washed over the faces of the hotel staff. As Dick pulled the boat ashore, his guests kissed the ground as they disembarked. Dick and Muriel cracked open the wine and passed around the drinks to their now very happy passengers. The group became festive in their relief and partied with Dick and Muriel on the shore until three in the morning.

After their rousing Naples adventure, Dick and Muriel decided to visit Pompeii. They filled up on Italian wine and fine food before hitting the streets.

"Did you know that we once lived together in Pompeii? In another life?" asked Dick.

Muriel gasped. "I have felt the same way! Doesn't it seem as though we've been here before?"

Perhaps it was reincarnation, déjà vu, or just whirlwind lust, but Dick and Muriel never felt more connected to each other than they did in that moment.

❧ · ☙

By the time they arrived in Rome, Dick had fallen ill yet again. He said it was just his old lung problems from childhood. He told Muriel about the operation he'd had that removed all of his defenses, and dust would get into his throat and lungs, making it difficult to breathe. Perhaps it was the dust in the Italian summer countryside?

Dick and Muriel checked into the Villa d'Este La Fontana dell'Organo in Tivoli outside Rome. Dick marveled at the dragon fountains that burst up from the organ terrace in the front of the hotel and pondered the engineering that was required to create them.

"These were built hundreds of years ago. Amazing," whispered Dick.

He went on to explain in detail how they used hydraulic engineering to calculate the water pressure needed to create the fountain. Not only did Dick have a soft side—he loved poetry and riding horses—he was enthralled with design. With every engineering feat they came across, Dick could talk about the nuts, bolts, and mechanics of how something worked, whether it was a yacht, an airplane, a train, or a fountain like this. He stood there in front of the Villa d'Este and analyzed the construction of the garden—how it had been originally built, the planning that was required. When he was done, Muriel appreciated their surroundings in ways she never would have before.

Over a lunch of fresh trout from the hotel's pond, Dick told Muriel of his love for boats and airplanes in particular, and talked about his ventures with Delta Airlines back in the States. They wandered around Rome and strolled by all the breezy outdoor cafés, stopping for a glass of wine or a cappuccino. At the end of the day, they landed at the Casino Borghese Gardens, where there was a spectacular flower show. Dick and Muriel had dinner there, among hundreds of plants in full bloom. They drank and smoked cigarettes after their meal against the backdrop of live piano music and fragrant flowers while Dick told Muriel more stories about ancient Rome.

At the villa in the Casino Borghese Gardens, Dick professed his love to Muriel again. He got down on one knee.

"I feel like I'm already married to you, Muriel. In fact, let this be our first day of marriage." Dick declared Muriel his first and only wife and told her they would be together forever.

Their brief Italian idyll had officially put a halt to Dick's post-Marianne dream of a lasting, solitary escape at sea.

CHAPTER 10

On the Run

1951

D ick abruptly decided they must go back to England at
once so he could continue work on his yacht before the
summer's end.

He checked into the Dorchester Hotel and offered to buy
Muriel a new apartment in her neighborhood. While Dick went
to Gosport to inspect the *Aries,* which Muriel named after Dick's
zodiac sign, Muriel looked for a new place. She settled on 15
Grosvenor Square, which had once belonged to the Duchess of
Westminster.

When Dick got back from Gosport, he went straight to
Muriel's apartment with another bad cold and fever. Muriel put
him to bed, and Dick asked her to retrieve his belongings from
the Dorchester and check him out of his room.

"But what will we say if people see you here?" asked
Muriel.

"I don't know—say I'm your husband."

"We can't say that."

"Okay, say I am Richard Greenough," joked Dick.

"All right, fine. But if the gossip columnists hunt you down here, don't blame me."

Return to America

Dick had to return to Winston-Salem for his niece's wedding, and he wanted to get back to New York and find a way to shake Marianne into an agreement as quickly as possible. Now Marianne had become the woman who was in the way of his future with a new love. But, as always, Dick underestimated his opponent. Dick was well aware that if Marianne found out about his affair with Muriel, he'd lose his infidelity grievance in the divorce. The pair again went on the run, catching a train from England to Naples, where they caught up with the *Saturnia,* which was bound for Halifax. Their antics aboard the ship were reminiscent of an *I Love Lucy* episode. They had adjoining cabins, but they weren't connected, so each cabin had its own separate balcony. Dick was still paranoid that they were being watched, even on the boat—he had Marianne under constant surveillance and assumed Marianne had hired private investigators as well.

Each night, no matter how rough the mid-Atlantic waters were, Dick climbed out the window of his cabin onto the balcony, and then stumbled over to Muriel's balcony where she reeled him in through the window as his legs kicked in the air. Every time, Muriel worried that Dick would fall into the sea. One morning, when Dick was climbing back out of her window to return to his room, Muriel caught the eye of an elderly couple staying in the cabins above them, who were glaring down at them in horror.

Upon the *Saturnia's* arrival in Canada, they headed straight for Montreal, where Stratton Coyner was waiting for them at the Ritz. Dick talked with Strat for hours about the divorce, and he convinced Dick to meet with Marianne personally to sort out the details.

First, Dick had to go to Winston-Salem to see his niece, Mary Katharine Babcock, marry Kenneth Mountcastle Jr. He reunited with his family and paid a visit to his ailing Uncle Will, who had slipped into a coma. Just five days after Mary's wedding, Uncle Will died at age eighty-eight. The entire city of Winston-Salem mourned Will's passing, and he was honored for the many gifts he left behind for the city—a hospital named for his wife, millions of dollars to the Z. Smith Reynolds Foundation, and the donation of his estate, Tanglewood, to the city to use as a public park.

Just a month after Uncle Will's death, one of his and Dick's wishes would soon be filled. With the help of the Z. Smith Reynolds Foundation, Wake Forest University would be moved to Winston-Salem, and President Truman was due to arrive for opening ceremonies. But Dick didn't stick around long enough to greet the president. He wanted to get back to New York and deal with his marital problems.

While Dick was away, Muriel was at her house in Oyster Bay, Long Island, preparing for an extended stay. Dick had ordered a new green Buick for her and she stocked up the place with groceries and supplies. Dick soon joined her and worked on a divorce strategy.

For weeks, Dick had meetings on and off with Marianne, who, according to him, was uncooperative. Dick at least took advantage of the meetings to see his two baby boys, whom he hadn't seen in months. One night, Marianne begged Dick to go out with her for a few drinks and promised him she would come to some sort of agreement.

They agreed to meet at a bar on Third Avenue. Before he left for the night, Dick asked Muriel to call the police if he didn't return by midnight. He feared that Marianne was trying to kill him using her Mafia connections. This paranoia would become yet another hallmark of Dick's.

Trouble at One Beekman Place

Police burst into an apartment at One Beekman Place at three in the morning. They had received a frantic call from a Long Island woman who begged them to check on Dick Reynolds. The police officer from the Fifty-fifth Precinct was familiar with Dick. He'd answered so many domestic calls for Dick and Marianne Reynolds that Dick had given him a key to the apartment and told him to help himself to the bar or food at any time. He got calls from both Dick and Marianne, but mostly Marianne when she was drinking. There was always some fight, which required nothing less than a police presence to end. Still, the officers never arrested either of them but took on recurring roles as referees.

Tonight the officer was worried by the Long Island woman's urgency. She said she was a friend of Dick's and that he had asked her to call the police if she didn't hear from him.

The officer knocked on the door a few times, but there was no answer. Using his key, he opened the door and went inside, searching the beautiful twenty-two-room duplex on Manhattan's Upper East Side. All the lights were on. He cracked the door to the bedroom and discovered Dick passed out on the bed. A notorious drunk, Dick likely had had one too many, as usual. The officer repeatedly tried to wake him up, as he'd done so many times before. But he wouldn't budge. He was out cold.

The officer walked out of the apartment and gently closed

the door behind him. When he reached the station, he called the woman back. Muriel Greenough was her name.

"Ma'am?"

"Yes! Is he all right?" gasped Muriel.

"Yes, he's just fine, Mrs. Greenough. He just had too much to drink, and he's sleeping."

"Did you wake him?" asked Muriel.

"Well, I certainly tried, but I couldn't shake him. I'm sure he'll be fine, Mrs. Greenough." The officer hung up the phone.

As Muriel placed the phone on the hook, she felt a sense of panic. Dick could always be woken up, at least when he'd been with her. *What if Marianne tried to do something to him? What if she poisoned him, for God's sake!* Dick swore to Muriel he wasn't planning on drinking, but they both knew that was a promise he would find hard to keep. Maybe Marianne deliberately tried to get him so intoxicated that he blacked out. Maybe she was trying to lure him back to the apartment and commit some terrible act.

~ · ~

After Muriel had dropped Dick off earlier that evening, she went to a local bar to have a few drinks with friends for a couple of hours. On her way back out to Oyster Bay, she crashed her new emerald-green Buick in a frightening head-on collision on Route 25. Muriel had a bad cut on her forehead and the car was totaled. It was a miracle that Muriel wasn't seriously injured. Still in shock, she left the car on the highway and took a taxi the remaining distance to her home. When she got there, she lay down in the dark house, feeling shaken and unwell. Dick didn't know about the accident.

Now Muriel was so worried about him, she couldn't concentrate on her own injuries. Muriel waited until 3:00 A.M.—she knew that with the upcoming divorce from Marianne, anything could have held him up and she didn't want to interfere. Then

Muriel panicked over the thought that perhaps Dick had decided to get back together with Marianne. Maybe she would never hear from Dick again. With the pressure of his family and his kids, maybe he had changed his mind.

So she had called the police and gotten the unsurprising news that Dick had broken his promise not to drink. There was nothing she could do about him now but go to sleep and hope he would call her back first thing in the morning.

At five the next morning, the phone rang.

"Dick! Are you all right?"

"I've been up since four A.M. and I can't find my clothes. Looks like Marianne hid my wallet, too."

"Oh, my God."

"Well, it's quite all right, dear. I checked into the Vanderbilt Hotel and borrowed the butler's overcoat. I even got a pair of shoes and trousers from him."

"What on earth happened to your clothes?"

"Never mind that. Can you get me some clothes here at the hotel? I need to sleep at the moment. I'm taking a couple of sleeping pills—I feel awful."

"I'll come into the city this afternoon and bring you a suitcase. But I can't come in the Buick. I got into a terrible wreck last night and it's totaled."

"What!"

Dick was shocked and worried. He grilled Muriel about her injuries before he was satisfied that she was all right. He immediately sent for a new Buick to be delivered to Muriel's home within hours. Once it arrived, she drove into the city to retrieve Dick and drive him back to Oyster Bay.

❧ · ❧

When Muriel picked Dick up in the city the next evening and drove him back to Long Island, he relayed his ordeal. He said

Marianne had been friendly and cooperative over drinks, which she continued to order for him. Dick claimed that he couldn't remember anything after the first drink, except that he felt very sick. Dick wove a dramatic tale for Muriel, whether or not it was true. The next thing he knew, he said, he was back at the apartment with Marianne and he blacked out. "She probably put something in my drink. I really don't know how I got there."

Muriel gasped in disbelief. She told Dick that she had called the police to check on him. They simply informed her that he was drunk and passed out. Dick regained consciousness about an hour later and vomited blood.

Dick convinced himself that Marianne tried to lure him back to the apartment to have him "taken care of" as she used to enjoy telling him.

Dick said, "I don't want to go anywhere near her after this."

In addition to his clothes, Marianne had also stolen his passport and his wallet, which contained a bearer's check in the amount of $15,000. Apparently Marianne thought taking Dick's passport would force him to stay in the country, but he'd find a way around that.

"What were you doing with $15,000?" asked Muriel.

"I meant for it to be a gift to you. I'd been meaning to buy you a beautiful piece of jewelry for weeks, but I hadn't found anything that I liked for you yet. When you mentioned that bracelet you saw at Van Cleef & Arpels, I had the check made out that day so I could give it to you when I got home. As a matter of fact, I need to contact Van Cleef and tell them not to honor the check."

Dick made up for the lost check by buying Muriel a Golconda diamond and $100,000 worth of jewels.

The next week, Dick invited Muriel to meet his good friends Mr. and Mrs. Robert Garland of Dick's favorite yacht builders, Sparkman & Stephens. Dick had worked with Garland when he

The turreted Victorian home on Fifth Street in Winston-Salem, where Dick grew up. *(Courtesy Forsyth County Public Library Photograph Collection)*

R. J. Sr. with his four young children in front of their beloved Fifth Street house. From left to right: Nancy, Mary, Dick, baby Smith, and R. J. *(Courtesy Forsyth County Public Library Photograph Collection)*

Katharine and R. J. Sr. pose with their children in front of the Fifth Street house. Katharine holds Smith in the background, while Mary, Nancy, a cousin, James Dunn, R. J., and Dick are seated. *(Courtesy Forsyth County Public Library Photograph Collection)*

Twenty-two-year-old Dick at a cafe in Paris after he became "fed up" with Broadway and moved abroad. His love of alcohol would soon land him in serious trouble in Europe. (CORBIS)

Dick at the time of Smith's death in 1932. (CORBIS)

Dick and Blitz join Mary and her husband, Charlie Babcock, to watch Uncle Will's horse, Mary Reynolds, win the Hambletonian—and its top prize of $50,000. (CORBIS)

Blitz and Dick with their friends Katherine and Harkness Edwards, in a photo taken just a month after Dick had come into his $25 million inheritance. Dick was well known throughout the 1930s among the yachting and horse-racing sets, where Edwards was also a regular competitor. *(CORBIS)*

Dick's 55-foot cutter *Blitzen* sails into Havana harbor to win the St. Petersburg-Havana race of 1939. *(CORBIS)*

Dick and Blitz celebrate *Blitzen*'s Honolulu Fastnet win at Pearl Harbor Clipper Base. *(CORBIS)*

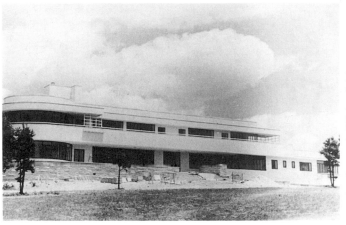

Dick and Blitz's Winston-Salem showplace, Merry Acres, built to resemble the deck of a ship, in 1940. *(Courtesy Forsyth County Public Library Photograph Collection)*

A rare image of Lieutenant Commander R. J. Reynolds Jr. and CQM A. K. Horton in the chart room of the USS *Makin Island* during World War II. *(Courtesy National Archives Still Picture Division)*

Dick and his second wife, Marianne O'Brien, at their wedding in New York in 1946. The ceremony took place in the bride's mother's apartment on East Fifty-second Street. None of the Reynolds family attended. *(Associated Press)*

Dick and Marianne holding their young sons, Michael and Patrick, in their Miami home, December 1948. A year later, they would be separated. *(CORBIS)*

Blitz with her and Dick's four sons, Josh, John, Zach, and Will, at their country estate, Devotion. Their father had been gone almost ten years at the time this photo was taken. *(Courtesy Forsyth County Public Library Photograph Collection)*

The vast Reynolda estate that Katharine Reynolds completed in 1917. The mansion can be seen at upper right, with Lake Katharine behind it. The farm buildings are to the left, and the greenhouse and gardens are at the bottom. *(Courtesy Forsyth County Public Library Photograph Collection)*

Dick and his third wife, Muriel Greenough, depart Miami for London to launch the *Aries* and begin their long honeymoon in the Pacific. *(CORBIS)*

Dick and Muriel on a tour of Dick's private island off the Georgia coast. *(Associated Press)*

Dick and Muriel in front of the famous South End House on Sapelo Island, three days after their wedding was held there. *(Associated Press)*

Dick and Muriel recovering at the Monte Carlo Hotel in Miami after they abandoned their burning yacht, the *Scarlett O'Hara*, and made it to shore in a dinghy. Such adventures were commonplace for Dick and Muriel by that time. *(CORBIS)*

Blitz with her and Dick's four sons, Zach, John, Will, and Josh, at Merry Acres, Christmas, 1957. Dick's boys grew up spending very little time with their father. Just a few years after this photo was taken, they would lose Blitz, the only parent they knew, to cancer. *(Courtesy Forsyth County Public Library Photograph Collection)*

Dick and his fourth wife, Annemarie Schmitt, on Sapelo Island, where Dick announced their recent marriage in the South China Sea. *(CORBIS)*

Dick and Annemarie after their March 15, 1961, wedding on the USS *Rotterdam* in the South China Sea. Dr. Hans Lindemann can be seen to the left of Dick, and his wife, Ilsa, is to the right of Annemarie. Previous wives Muriel and Marianne believed this photo was doctored as part of a conspiracy. *(Associated Press)*

Dick's sister Nancy dedicates a portrait of Z. Smith Reynolds at Wake Forest University. Nancy was said to be so traumatized by Smith's shooting and the subsequent publicity, it caused her to become obsessed with controlling the family image. *(Courtesy Forsyth County Public Library Photograph Collection)*

Katharine Reynolds's 64-room "bungalow" as it looks today. The home's two side wings are hidden by trees and foliage, making it look in this view a third of the size it really is. *(Author Collection)*

built the *Lizzie McCaw*. Garland told Muriel that he had been with Dick during some of his most dazzling races, and the Garlands greatly respected Dick's sailing skills.

The couple would hide out in Muriel's Oyster Bay home for weeks, cooking, leaving the curtains drawn at all hours, and sneaking in and out of the house at night so people wouldn't see them. But Dick was impatient for his precious boats, especially after reminiscing with the Garlands. He justified the purchase of another boat by telling himself it was the best way to hide from Marianne. Dick asked Garland to help find a local motor sailor. With the *Aries* in Gosport nowhere near completion, Dick decided to purchase the *White Heron,* a forty-five-foot sailor that Garland recommended, at a shipyard in Long Island, and Dick brought Peter Barber to New York to oversee the work. He gutted and remodeled the ship's galley and ordered new instruments. Muriel chipped in and ordered, at Dick's expense, all of the china, flatware, and covers for the interior. It was a project for Dick to sink his teeth into for the next couple of months. His goal was to have it finished by Christmas.

In November of 1951, Dick had fallen so ill again, Muriel checked him into a hospital in New York. Dick was advised again by doctors to quit drinking and smoking immediately. He had advanced liver damage, a weak heart, and weak lungs, which they traced to his childhood lung difficulties. It took Dick a week to recover in the hospital, but when he did, he ignored doctors' orders and went right back to abusing himself and spending money.

It was December, and Dick and Muriel were still on Long Island. One day, Dick went into the city and ordered a television set for Muriel from the Liberty Music Shop in Manhattan, as well as equipment from Hammacher Schlemmer. Everything arrived in good order in Oyster Bay, but the stores inadvertently sent the bills to Dick's Beekman Place address. Now Marianne had Muriel's address and their cover was blown. Luckily, Dick and Muriel had already planned to leave town that day and drive south in a Nash Rambler Dick had recently purchased. But it would be even more difficult now for Dick to obtain a divorce on the grounds of Marianne's infidelity with Rubirosa.

Journey to Mexico

They drove south toward Knoxville, Tennessee, where Strat Coyner was staying at the Andrew Johnson Hotel, which Dick owned. Dick wanted to see if he could make arrangements for a quick and easy Mexican divorce and Muriel would get her chance to meet Strat formally. On the way, they stopped for the night in Ocean City, Maryland.

Dick needed lightweight pants since he hadn't prepared for the Southern heat. Muriel went into the shoddy little town to shop, but the best she could find were a pair that was two sizes too big for him. They were good enough for Dick and he yanked them on before they rushed out the door. Dick was antsy to get his hands on some more liquor. He wasn't feeling great and it was his all-purpose cure.

They found a liquor store, where Muriel waited outside for Dick to pay for a few bottles. When he came out and turned around to walk toward her, his beltless trousers slid down to his knees... and he happened to be without underwear at the time. As traffic whizzed by, Dick stood there for a minute with the bottles in each hand, and then carefully knelt down, placed the bottles on the ground, and calmly pulled his pants back up. Muriel was doubled over with laughter. They immediately went back to the store to buy Dick a belt.

They finally got out of Ocean City and drove through the rolling Appalachians for two days to Tennessee. Dick pulled up to the Andrew Johnson Hotel in Knoxville, which was the tallest building in Tennessee at the time and the same hotel in which Hank Williams would spend his last night alive, not long after Dick and Muriel were there. Dick had purchased it on a whim in the early 1930s for almost nothing. When he had checked in, the clerk was rude to him. Dick figured if he owned the place he could have the clerk fired, so he did just that: bought the hotel and fired the clerk.

Dick introduced Muriel to Strat. But Strat, who was always on hand to clean up Dick's messes, was more concerned with the business at hand. He advised Dick that it was legal to get a Mexican divorce, but probably risky at best. Dick insisted on looking into it, so after just one day, they bid Strat farewell and headed for Mexico, via Texas.

Dick grew more remote and distant as their journey wore on. He didn't say much for the two days they were in Texas, and he stayed in his own room. Muriel wondered if he was second-guessing his decision to get a divorce. He insisted that he just didn't feel good—but Muriel found out later he was drinking alone. Dick was an expert at closeted drinking. Muriel learned that when he was remote like this, he'd started one of his secret binges. She didn't realize what she was up against—an average binge meant at least a bottle and a half of liquor per day.

Eventually, they drove across the border and trailed down to Mexico City. Dick continued to be angry, temperamental, and argumentative on the journey. Muriel was in for another disastrous trip with Dick. When they reached Mexico City, no rooms were available at the Great Hotel where they planned to stay, so they checked into a different one, but went straight back to the Great for drinks. Dick attempted to cash two traveler's checks at the front desk to pay for the drinks, but the clerk refused to cash them unless they were staying there. Dick replied, "But these checks are acceptable anywhere." But the receptionist still refused. Dick flew into a rage, ripped up the checks, and threw them in the receptionist's face. Drunk and red-faced, Dick stormed out of the hotel.

Muriel followed Dick out onto the street, begging him to let it go. She was desperate to turn the sour evening around. Predictably, Dick hurled himself into a drinking rampage that lasted until four in the morning. Muriel was quickly becoming familiar with, and exhausted by, these late night, outburst-induced excursions. She wondered if Blitz and Marianne went through the same thing.

Dick never did get around to consulting with anyone in Mexico City about a divorce. The next day, they drove to Acapulco so they could relax on the beach and at least try to make a vacation out of the trip. Dick fought with Muriel the entire way. For the first time, he slapped her across the face.

Muriel's jaw dropped. She jumped out of the car and leaned up against it, holding her head in tears. Unable to bear the thought that their relationship was taking this kind of turn, Muriel told herself that Dick was simply under too much stress with the divorce. He was on the verge of a nervous breakdown. This wouldn't last. The drinking wouldn't last after they were married.

The more Muriel invested in this fantasy, the more bitter she grew toward Marianne and any force that she blamed for Dick's unhappiness.

Dick was apologetic and conciliatory the next day. Muriel accepted his apologies. She refused to let his behavior ruin the rest of their trip.

They managed to enjoy roasting hot Acapulco eventually, especially after Dick sobered up. They spent their days sunbathing and their nights talking until the roosters crowed at dawn.

CHAPTER II

Return to Sapelo Island

1952

Since the wrangling in Mexico was in vain, Dick was eager to hit the water. Dick and Muriel ditched the Nash Rambler in Mexico and flew to South Carolina, joined Peter Barber and the *White Heron* in Charleston, and sailed for the holidays.

On Christmas Eve, they docked off the coast of Florida, and Dick's oldest son, Josh, joined them for Christmas dinner onboard. Josh seemed elated to be in the presence of his father, who had rarely made himself available to him. He didn't know exactly what he wanted to do after he finished his last term at Culver Military Academy in Indiana, which Dick had also attended. Josh only knew that he wanted to do something to make his father proud, and at least get his attention.

After the holidays, Dick told Muriel that he wanted to show her his prized possession, Sapelo Island. He said he wasn't sure what to do with it, and he wanted her opinion.

Dick's love for the island was evident. He had bought it in his twenties and repeatedly hid out there when he sought refuge. Muriel also realized that maybe the peace of the Georgia island was what Dick needed as he became ill more frequently. Perhaps it was time for Dick to slow down on the traveling and stay at the place he called home.

Sapelo Island, 1952

The minute they set foot on the island, Muriel felt as if she'd stepped back in time a hundred years.

The twelve-mile-long island was situated fifty miles south of Savannah, and contained 16,500 acres of usable land. Sapelo was the largest of Georgia's Golden Isles and the fourth largest island on the Atlantic Coast. A third of the salt marshes on the East Coast could be found in the Golden Isles, home to fiddler crabs, herons, and egrets that occupied miles of undeveloped beaches. Sapelo contained thousands of acres of wildlife as well: whitetail deer, wild turkeys, hogs, cattle, and the Guatemalan chachalaca bird. The isolated land appealed to Dick's desire to be surrounded by water—it was like one enormous yacht all its own, floating on the coastal sea—the ultimate captain's lair.

As they drove down the dirt roadways from the loading dock, the path to the house was flanked by six-hundred-year-old oak trees dripping with Spanish moss. The house gradually peeked out from behind the trees until it opened up in its entire splendor. Maybe it was the fact that it had been closed for many months, or maybe it was the swift breeze that picked up around them, but Muriel found the mansion haunting and mysterious. The grounds were eerily quiet—there wasn't a soul in sight. And the nineteenth-century, Spanish-style South End House stood before them like an old fortress—the only sign of life on an ancient land.

As they pulled up to the house, Italian-style gardens spread out before them. Five large columns guarded the hundred-foot patio, where Dick kept antique, Goya-tiled, wrought iron patio furniture that his sister Mary had imported from Spain. Two sets of steps led to a reflecting pool in the shape of a four-leaf clover, surrounded by oversized twelve-foot terra cotta jars scattered throughout the lawn. A long, symmetrical pathway cut through gardens, which were littered with azalea, gardenia, and wisteria. Beyond the garden, the path snaked into a small grove and emerged at a beachfront pool a mile away. Large nets hung between the pool and the ocean to protect swimmers from sharks.

When Dick and Muriel arrived that winter, the house had been closed down for months. Immediately upon his arrival, Dick looked happier than he had since Muriel met him. He exuded immense pride in his island treasure, and he talked about the many ideas he had for developing Sapelo over the years. He hoped Muriel would be the kind of partner to help him make a successful business happen there.

When Dick bought the island in the 1930s, he added his own personal touch, as the previous owners, Howard Coffin and Thomas Spalding, the island's first, nineteenth-century plantation owner, had done before him. He hired an interior designer from Atlanta, Phillip Shutze, to remodel the house from top to bottom, renovated and rebuilt the farm buildings, and added new plumbing and air-conditioning—in fact, the South End House was one of the first homes in the South to have this luxury. Dick offered Muriel a personal tour of the grounds.

The main section of the house resembled Dick's childhood home, Reynolda—a central hall flanked by two sets of wings. The main drawing room and entrance hall were marked with large central fireplaces. Pointing in each direction were hallways leading to the dining room, additional sitting rooms, two wood-paneled libraries, and Dick's office.

Behind the central hall was the solarium, which overlooked Dick's lovely heated indoor pool. Grecian pillars and statues surrounded the well, and floor-to-ceiling windows provided panoramic views of the back gardens. To the left and right of the pool room were two sets of bedrooms. Dick took one suite and designated the other, which had previously been occupied by Blitz and Marianne, for Muriel.

From the dining room, a hallway led to the all stainless steel kitchen, and a separate dining room, bedrooms, and bathrooms for the staff. From the main library a long, narrow hallway, also with floor-to-ceiling windows, led to another small living room, kitchenette, and nursery that Dick built for his children, with additional bedrooms and bathrooms for caretakers.

On the second level was a beautiful ballroom encircled by a rooftop terrace that opened to the back side of the house. The ballroom was painted to look like a circus tent, complete with painted circus animals and ceramic statuettes. The work was done by renowned Atlanta artist Athos Menaboni, whose murals of circus characters, birds, and images of Dick's friends posing with pirate characters covered the ballroom, four rooms on the main level, the pool room, and the basement. The pirate murals were inspired by neighboring Blackbeard Island, which was named after the famous pirate and rumored to contain buried treasure. Dick had commissioned Menaboni to paint the murals twenty years earlier, when the Italian artist was a relative unknown. He later became one of the world's most famous painters of birds. In addition to the Menaboni art, Dick kept one of Gilbert Stuart's famous George Washington paintings in the house.

Underneath the house, tiny winding cellar stairs led to an adult playroom. The basement comprised a cozy lounge and another fireplace that partygoers used for roasting marshmallows. Behind the sitting room were a bowling alley, pool tables, a Ping-Pong table, and a large bar in the shape of a yacht. Tucked into a corner by the lounge was a wine cellar with a maze of side rooms that ran underneath most of the house, and one side room included a gun room where Dick kept hunting weapons, ammunition, and fishing tackle.

Down the road from the South End House, Dick hired designer Augustus Constantine to help him build a new stable and barn for his livestock and an office block for farm personnel and visiting scientists from the University of Georgia, whom Dick invited to study the salt marsh ecology on the island. To accommodate the guests, Dick let them use the forty loft spaces above the barn as well as additional apartments in the complex. He also bought a fleet of jeeps for everyone to use. Dick took Muriel up to a 250-foot attic that housed a full-size, hundred-seat movie theater complete with a professional-grade projector and perfect acoustics. When Dick first built it, he was interested in film and photography and had already made a handful of films. These days the theater was used to show Dick's favorite movie, *Gone with the Wind*, which played once a week when Dick was in residence.

Near the barnyard were large carriage houses, stables, and fuel and oil tanks. A boathouse with a lift for Dick's boats stood near the marsh side of the waterfront, and a larger, corrugated iron building housed Dick's yachts.

A third of a mile down the beach path from South End House was a 250-foot greenhouse that Howard Coffin had built, which Dick had not maintained since the war. Some of the glass had been broken and Dick gave orders to a farmhand to have it redone for his new girlfriend. Muriel was an avid garden lover and promised to fill the greenhouse again.

A smaller, three-story, three-bedroom home named Azalea Cottage sat hidden in the woods near South End House. Dick said he often used the cottage when he needed to get away from everyone.

Dick had recently fortified the island with an electrical supply house and generator with enough electric units to supply power to the entire island. Dick named his small electric company Atlas Utilities and had three electricians on staff to maintain it. The utility line eventually included a radio microwave transmitter that connected to a tower at the marsh landing dock in Meridian and provided electricity to the island's indigenous residents for the first time.

Many of the island's residents were Dick's employees — they worked as gardeners, maintenance men, cattle farmers, and gamekeepers — and he was committed to improving Sapelo's conditions for them. He built a school for the local children and maintained a ferry, designed by Sparkman & Stephens, of course, to the mainland, which was the only means of transportation across Doboy Sound to Georgia. Dick kept a standing offer to send any of the island's residents to vocational schools and training at his expense. Many of the residents were also expert shrimpers, fisherman, and duck and turkey hunters.

Since Dick had purchased the island, he turned Sapelo's main industries to cattle farming and timber. The businesses provided employment for the residents of the island and helped to pay for operating and maintenance costs in keeping up the estate.

The rest of the island comprised an eclectic array of locations, old tabby (a building mixture of lime, sand, oyster shells, and water) ruins, lighthouses, cabanas and bathing beaches, a cemetery, additional cabins and swimming pools for the Sapelo Boys Camp, and Dick's private hangar and two-mile-long airstrip. When he built the airstrip in 1934, it was the largest in the country. He stored his D-3 airplane in the hangar.

❧ · ❧

As Dick and Muriel concluded their tour and stood in front of the empty South End House, they agreed to keep Sapelo as their base after they got married. Dick loved his Southern roots, but he said that he would never live in Winston-Salem again.

For a moment, Muriel considered that maybe she and Dick should start somewhere new together, but Dick's life and desires had been disrupted too many times by demanding wives and children, and she thought Dick should be in familiar surroundings. Muriel grew comfortable with the idea of leaving behind her own friends and interests and devoting herself to Dick in this strange place.

Muriel later acknowledged that agreeing to this might have been one of her gravest mistakes.

⁓ · ⁓

Dick wanted to sail again while the island was being reopened and prepared for their permanent return. He introduced Muriel to his manager, Frank Durant, and best farmhands: Fred Johnson, Martin Hall, and James Banks. Dick asked some of them to join him on their next sailing trip.

Fred Johnson was one of Dick's favorites. He was a kind young man who was one of Dick's most devoted employees, and he often worked for Dick personally. He was tall and handsome and was married to a lovely woman named Flora, who, Dick said, was one of his "best ladies maids." She took care of his boys when they were young and she was beloved by both Blitz and Marianne. Muriel was also impressed by Flora from the first time she met her and regretted that she wouldn't have the chance to work with her because she was starting her own family. Lately, Dick had dramatically scaled back Flora's duties because she had been in fragile health. Now, she and Fred were about to have a baby. Fred didn't want to leave her to go sailing, but she assured him that she would be fine and urged him to accompany Dick.

Before they departed for the Caribbean, Dick said he wished

to make Muriel the beneficiary of $200,000 worth of paid up insurance policies, to offer her a little security and to prove his commitment to her. Dick assured Muriel that the policies were only a fraction of the financial security he intended to provide her when they got married. Muriel found the insurance policies a little odd, but grand financial gestures like this were typical of Dick when he was courting a new woman. With Marianne, it was the deed to Sapelo Island on a napkin; to Muriel, it was life insurance.

After Dick finished the paperwork for the policies, they set sail for Nassau. Although Fred and Martin were excellent shrimpers, they were nervous about handling the yacht so far out to sea and didn't really know how to navigate the open water. Fred insisted Dick stay at the bridge and navigate, so Dick couldn't rest all night.

They stopped in Bimini's, Hog Island, and Hope Town on Abaco Island. All along the way, Dick worked on the divorce paperwork. They decided to stay in Hope Town and explore the beaches for a week.

Dick and Muriel would often steal away for picnics on the beach or long walks in the city streets. Sometimes Fred and Martin joined them and sometimes they went off on their own. A few days later, Fred found out that his baby, a healthy son, had been born. He was so thrilled he cried tears of joy. They all toasted Fred on the yacht as the sun set on Hope Town.

The days of exploring, picnicking, sunbathing, and swimming ran into each other. One afternoon, as Dick and Muriel watched the sun go down, Dick spoke both anxiously and wistfully about his early childhood, his family in Winston-Salem, and what a skillful businessman his father had been. Much had changed since those days. Dick could talk about it for only so long before he grew sad and quiet. It was time to change plans again.

Jamaican Adventures

Dick ordered everyone back in the boat so they could set sail for Jamaica. Fred and Martin continued to be afraid of navigating on their own and even got a little seasick. That left Dick to handle the sailing. Dick took the bridge for two full days without a single wink of sleep. Eventually he taught Muriel how to read the autopilot function so he could get some rest. As Dick and Muriel took turns handling the boat, Dick talked with her more about his family's history, the anguish of losing his father and the turmoil he experienced when his mother remarried and died a short time later. It was evident that the pain of these events had stayed with him—perhaps that was why he had such a hard time settling down.

A day later, the men finally had recovered and got themselves on deck, although they were still weary of the sea. Later that afternoon they spotted Cuba, and Fred piped up and said, "Mr. Reynolds, how far is that land over there?"

"Look, Fred," Dick replied, "it's too damned far for you to swim it and you're staying on this boat until we get to Jamaica." Fred burst into laughter, and both he and Martin lightened up after that. Martin even got around to cooking them a delicious Southern dinner.

On the third day, they arrived in Jamaica and Dick dropped anchor at precisely the time he had predicted. Dick sent Fred and Martin home, and brought Peter Barber in to take over the boat. Dick and Muriel went ashore to check into a hotel and spend the week sightseeing. Muriel was sad to leave the boat—in spite of the crew problems, she enjoyed getting to know Dick even better and she had begun to absorb the anguish of his younger years. Dick had tired of talking about his parents, at least for now, and he was ready to party in Jamaica.

From Kingston, Dick and Muriel drove overland to Ocho

Rios, and Peter Barber sailed the *White Heron* to meet them on the other side. Dick had reserved rooms for them, as well as for Strat and his wife, Mackie, who were coming down to join them. Strat had to prepare Dick's spring taxes and it was always easier to join him wherever he was than coax him up to Winston-Salem. Muriel worried that they were there to convince Dick to return to his family and children. But this was not the case—in fact, both of them thought Dick couldn't leave Marianne soon enough.

Over the course of their holiday, the couples took drives through the tropical mountains and went swimming nearly every day. Each evening they dined or went dancing at different establishments together. The more time they spent with her, the more Strat and Mackie liked Muriel and seemed genuinely happy for Dick. It was evident to Muriel how much Strat loved and admired his boss. He knew Dick probably better than anyone, and told Muriel that Winston-Salem wasn't a "large enough orbit" for someone like Dick.

While Dick was avoiding drinking excessively throughout the trip, he couldn't resist the Scotch that was served at lunch one day at their hotel bar. A group of men were sitting next to their table, talking loudly about a mixed race woman who was sitting at the bar. Dick found their language shocking and offensive, and, unable to listen to it, called for the check immediately. Later that night, Dick and Muriel went back to the same bar. The more he drank, the happier he became and Muriel hoped nothing would spoil his mood. Suddenly, he looked up to see the same group of men walking in. They took a seat next to Dick's table.

Dick got up and hurried to the front desk. He asked the clerk who the men were and learned that they were Reynolds engineers.

"What?" Dick asked.

"Yes, sir. Reynolds engineers—they work for the Reynolds bauxite mines."

"Thank you very much, sir." Dick turned on his heel, a wide, mischievous smile spread across his face. He breezed past Muriel, whose face was full of dread. Dick tapped one man's shoulder.

"Excuse me, gentlemen, but who is your manager here?"

"I'm in charge of these boys," one of the men said. "How can I help you?"

"I'm Richard Reynolds, and I'm here to inform you that I found your behavior at lunchtime today reprehensible. I heard the way you discussed a woman in a public restaurant. You're all fired."

The men were in shock. As Dick had hoped, they'd never personally met Richard S. Reynolds Jr., his favorite cousin, who had just built a bauxite mine in Ocho Rios; he turned their credulousness to his advantage. Ignoring their pleas, he whipped out identification to prove his identity. He continued, "Under no circumstances are you to report for work tomorrow." As they protested, Dick turned around, retrieved Muriel, and walked out of the hotel. Once they were out of earshot, Dick doubled over with laughter. He loved pulling pranks.

A year and a half afterward, Dick met his cousin in London, and Muriel watched as Richard told Dick about an incident when one day four of his engineers didn't turn up for work in Jamaica. Dick quietly listened, but never told him that he'd been responsible for their departure. Muriel thought it was hilarious. Poor Richard S. Reynolds had needed those workers, and their disappearance held up business for weeks.

∼ · ∽

A week later, Strat and his wife departed for Winston-Salem, and Dick received news that Marianne knew he was in Jamaica—of course, he felt they should depart at once.

He wanted to go to England immediately to work on the *Aries*, but needed to replace his passport. He'd managed to sail all around the Caribbean without it because authorities rarely checked for the passports of yacht captains in those days. He'd have to apply for a new one and wait for it to come through. Meanwhile, he ordered Muriel to go to London and wait for him. Once Dick got his passport, he would fly to Montreal first where he planned to move large amounts of money out of the country, in anticipation of his divorce from Marianne.

Both Dick and Muriel had many misadventures on their way back to London. Dick had a layover in Chicago and accidentally got on a flight headed for Los Angeles instead of Montreal. Upon his arrival in Los Angeles, he booked another flight to Montreal, again by way of Chicago where he had another long layover. When he arrived in Montreal, he sat down with the president of the Royal Bank of Canada, who helped him transfer his funds and securities there while the divorce was pending. When that was done, Dick booked a flight to London, only to have the plane turn around halfway into the flight due to mechanical problems. Rather than stay another night in Montreal, he booked the next flight to London without sleeping. It was just another week in the life of Dick Reynolds.

At the same time, Muriel took a long, white-knuckle flight from Jamaica to London. She had seen the crew drinking and partying at her hotel the night before until 3:00 A.M. She was mortified to find them operating the plane to London just a few hours later.

When they finally reunited days later, Dick and Muriel collapsed from exhaustion at 15 Grosvenor Square.

Building the *Aries*, March 1952

In London, Dick was exhausted and frustrated with the way the divorce was going. Marianne had apparently just checked into

St. Luke's Hospital after suffering a nervous breakdown. Dick wasn't sure what to think of it, and he was about to have a nervous breakdown himself. Around the same time, newspapers reported that Dick had been seen cruising around the Caribbean with a new woman, which would only complicate the divorce proceedings even more. Dick also felt strongly that he should take care of the two boys, Michael and Patrick, and fought for custody. Although Strat Coyner was still aiding the divorce case, Frank Wells of Courdert Brothers was handling the bulk of the divorce paperwork now. Dick was confident in his attorneys' abilities, but he was annoyed that this case was much less efficient than his divorce from Blitz.

Dick focused on finishing the *Aries*. It had been seven years since the war ended, but it was still difficult to find construction materials. Many of the metal factories made low-quality iron and other metals needed for the yacht. Poorly made machinery and materials often broke or deteriorated, causing delays throughout the process.

To take him back and forth, Dick hired a well-known British chauffeur, Cyril Pollard, who was recommended by the Grosvenor Square doorman. Pollard's résumé included a long assignment at Buckingham Palace, where he'd been the chauffeur to Princess Elizabeth before she became queen. Once she was crowned, he became the chauffeur for Prince Philip. Dick loved Pollard and his entertaining tales of the royal palace. He was fittingly restrained, but when Dick and Muriel begged him, he'd relent and tell them fascinating stories about the royal family. Pollard said he adored Princess Elizabeth and couldn't say enough kind things about her. But he described Prince Philip as a reckless driver who frequently took the wheel and led him on wild-goose chases. Eventually, Pollard tired of his antics and resigned.

Muriel later joined Dick on his trips to Cosport. The work at

Camper & Nicholsons yard, one of the leading yacht builders in England, dragged on—it was as stagnant as Dick's divorce from Marianne. Muriel speculated that they were deliberately working slowly to run up Dick's bills. Dick hoped to launch the *Aries* by April, but it would not happen.

Dick had a devoted longtime employee, Captain Evans, who was set to lead the *Aries* upon its completion, and Evans oversaw the building of the yacht on Dick's behalf. Evans fought in both world wars, and had previously operated the *Zapala* years ago and worked intermittently with Dick when he was in Europe. Captain Evans took great pride in Dick's boats and was honored to work for him.

The other members of the crew did not have as much respect for Dick. Dick's reputation for spending lavishly and picking up drinking buddies often encouraged people to take advantage of him. Captain Evans had noticed that Dick had a "terrible time handling the British crew." Dick would get drunk with them and over-tip them on a regular basis. The unseasoned workmen came to expect these large sums of money, unable to grasp that Dick's generosity was not something to which they were entitled. When it came time to pay their very fair, normal wages, they loudly complained. Captain Evans said Dick was doing a "disservice" to the men because they didn't value their wages, or the work they did anymore.

At times, Muriel couldn't figure out if Dick was naive and vulnerable or if he was the one taking advantage of people. Did people use Dick or did he use them? When Dick was through with employees, he didn't think twice about dumping them and never looking back. In a way, his generosity freed him from any guilt he might have when he dropped people who were no longer of use to him. At the same time, Dick had a habit of being stingy with those close to him, and too generous with perfect strangers. This dynamic was certainly evident with his own children. Dick seemed to buy people's loyalty and then discard it at will—almost like trading relationships the way he traded his stocks.

Muriel would later find out just how harsh this paradox could be.

～ ᵕ ᵔ

Easter was fast approaching, so they took another holiday to Monte Carlo, which would be interrupted by a host of problems. First, Dick found out from Frank Wells that Marianne had attempted to use the $15,000 check she had stolen from him nearly six months before to buy a piece of jewelry at Van Cleef & Arpels. When they refused to honor the check, she filed a lawsuit against Chemical Bank, which issued the check. Dick's lawyers had to handle that lawsuit as well as everything else. Marianne was proving to be a fierce adversary.

Then Dick found out that Republican congressmen had discovered the 1948 IRS ruling that permitted Dick and a few other large Democratic donors to write off their loans as bad business debt. Another investigation was launched, but Dick instructed Coyner to tell them he was out of the country and not to comment. Dick hoped it would blow over.

But the worst was yet to come. Dick received word that Patrick had been diagnosed with polio and was staying at the Crippled Children's Hospital in Miami. Dick contacted the best doctors in Miami to check on Patrick and hired a nurse he knew personally to tend to him. The doctors assured him that the case was mild and they were confident their treatment would be successful. Patrick had to be quarantined because of the polio and couldn't have any visitors, so Dick decided not to go in to see him, but he was in contact every morning and evening.

"Please tell him that Daddy phoned every day," Dick said.

The doctors assured him that if anything happened, they would contact him through his lawyers.

CHAPTER 12

Cracks in the Romance

1952

By the end of the month, Dick received news that Patrick had recovered so well he would soon be released from the hospital. Dick also heard from Frank Wells that there were witnesses prepared to come forward and testify to Marianne's affair with Porfirio Rubirosa.

Dick was jubilant, but hesitant to follow through with this line of attack. Muriel was infuriated. She was tired of waiting for Dick to be divorced so they could marry, and angrily reminded Dick that Marianne was the one who first cheated, not him, and she must take responsibility for that. Dick called Strat Coyner and told him to make sure Rubirosa was named a corespondent in the divorce motion. The divorce motion included Dick's fight for custody of Michael and Patrick, then four and a half and three years old respectively, and additional accusations that Marianne had a "violent and ungovernable temper" (echoing Blitz's divorce), had treated Dick with "extreme cruelty," and that she used profane language in the presence of Dick and the servants. Dick also publicly accused Marianne of drinking too much, which was all too ironic coming from Dick.

Newspapers enthusiastically reported on the scandal, reciting Dick's accusation that Marianne had had an affair with Rubirosa in a Paris hotel. Marianne accused Dick of desertion and said only that she was never "in a hotel" with Rubirosa. Marianne warned Dick that she would contest the divorce unless he withdrew the accusation of "indiscretions with Rubi." Dick did as she said, but the heavy press exposure did motivate Marianne to discuss a settlement.

Dick and Muriel continued to travel incognito. Dick knew that one photo of him and Muriel could sabotage his case. They asked Pollard to meet them at the Hôtel de Paris in Monaco, and they would take a scenic drive up to Provence and Paris, where Muriel had reserved a pair of rooms at the Lancaster Hotel under her maiden name.

Trouble at Hôtel du Nord

One pleasant evening, they stopped for dinner at a restaurant outside Vienne at seven and ordered champagne afterward. The waiter came to their table with a bottle and poured each of them a glass. After taking a sip, Muriel said, "I don't want to drink champagne that's corked. This is corked."

"Why don't we have a new bottle?" Dick motioned to the waiter to replace it. The waiter returned with a new bottle, which was also corked. Muriel instantly detected the faint, moldy smell in the champagne and protested again.

"Why not drink it anyway, Muriel?" Dick said.

Muriel whined, "What if I get sick? Nothing is worse than corked champagne."

"Drink it anyway."

Muriel was unsatisfied. This was supposed to be the best restaurant in town and they were going to spend an absurd amount of money there. Dick used the excuse of corked champagne to start drinking hard liquor.

The waiter finally brought a good bottle, and Dick and Muriel exchanged barbs as the waiter filled their glasses.

But the more Dick drank, the happier he became. The good mood held and spread; the owner and waiter joined Dick and Muriel for liqueurs after their meal.

The good feeling ended when Dick called for the bill and insisted on paying for the two corked bottles of champagne. Muriel's anger flamed anew.

"This shouldn't be the policy of a good restaurant. It's their duty to make the customer happy."

This time, Dick roared with laughter. Muriel did not find it amusing.

"Excuse me, sir!" Muriel called to the owner. She rattled off a few remarks in French to him, and the owner promptly picked up the bill and revised it to remove the two bottles. Dick tried to tell him that he had no problem paying, but the owner insisted.

After he'd paid the bill, Dick refused to leave the restaurant. He forced Muriel to stay with him until 2:00 A.M., while he got sickeningly drunk. Once again Dick would destroy an evening, and probably the day after too, with another drinking jag. Muriel was so angry with him that she said she would walk the four miles into Vienne to check into a hotel. She bolted for the door. Dick happily followed her to the car, tripping over himself along the way. Pollard had been patiently waiting for them the whole time. Dick hopped into the car, but Muriel refused to get in and kept walking. In the dead of night, Muriel walked down the road while Dick and Pollard drove beside her. "Muriel, please get in," Dick pleaded.

She ignored him and kept walking.

"Please, dear," Dick said, patting the seat beside him.

They continued driving alongside Muriel. Pollard was exhausted from having waited for them all night and wanted to get some rest. In frustration he said, "Ma'am, it's getting late. Do get in."

Muriel laughed. "Oh, you poor dear. You must be exhausted. I'll do it for you."

Meanwhile, Dick's temperature was quickly rising. Muriel could by now identify the signs when Dick was about to fall ill. They needed to find a bed as soon as possible, so they checked into the nearest hotel they could find—the Hôtel du Nord—a dump opposite the train station. In the middle of the night they didn't realize how bad it really was. They also had no idea how long they'd have to stay there. It was 3:00 A.M., and the concierge gave them the only room left—a bathroom-less room with a shabby double bed and a collapsible bidet. They'd have to share the bathroom down the hall. They settled into the ugly room and Dick undressed for bed. As soon as he removed all his clothes and dropped the last sock on the floor, he stood up again, pulled all his clothes back on, and headed for the door.

"I'm going to the bar," he said.

"What? Where?" Muriel asked.

"Whatever's open." Dick walked out and shut the door.

Muriel was stunned. What on earth was he doing? What if he injured himself? Surely he was kidding and would return at once. But he didn't. Muriel didn't know it yet, but she was in for a marriage full of nights just like this.

She scrambled to dress herself again and asked the hotel manager where the nearest open bar was located. She got the directions and went searching for Dick. He was already well out of sight, but Muriel eventually found the bar and walked in to find him drinking with some townspeople, happy as ever. The beverage was a raw local brandy. Dick looked horrible, but he was having a great time.

Muriel sauntered up to an amused Dick and took out her

favorite gold lighter to fire up a cigarette and calm her nerves. Dick grabbed the lighter from her hand and offered it to one of the men sitting next to him. Dick was testing her patience and she knew it. Muriel begged the owner to close down the bar and divulged that Dick was too ill to be drinking so much. Twenty minutes later, the owner shut down while Dick picked up the tab for every last person in the bar. Muriel dragged Dick, now feeling as bad as he looked, back to the hotel. To her relief, he passed out.

Dick was terrifyingly sick later that night, vomiting repeatedly in the bidet as the room rattled with the noise of passing trains. Muriel barely slept. The next day, she asked the manager if they could change rooms, and he switched them to the nearest thing he had that resembled a suite, but there was still no bathroom. Since they were in for more vomiting, Muriel hoped she could bribe hotel staff to clean up the mess if necessary. They were still exposed to the noise of trucks, traffic, and trains, and dust and dirt seemed to be everywhere in the small city square below.

Muriel ran out the next day to a local market to buy food, even though Dick still couldn't keep anything down. Pollard waited outside all day for them, from ten in the morning until four in the afternoon, when Muriel finally went out to tell him to take the day off.

Still green-faced, Dick showed no signs of recovery. They were in for more time at the Hôtel du Nord, which made Muriel think of one of those "terrible French movies where people are murdered invariably at the Hôtel du Nord." As Dick begged for forgiveness for his behavior the night before, Muriel squeezed oranges for him, kept cold compresses on his head, and did everything she could to ease his pain.

❦

After two days, Dick was finally able to move on. As always, his recovery was as dramatic as his descent. They skipped their Paris plans and flew to the Netherlands, where they traveled far north to the small beach town of Noordwijk Aan Zee, while Pollard would meet them later in the car.

The North Sea coast was a peaceful contrast to the bustling shores of the French Riviera, but Dick and Muriel found it desolate, and with stuffy company. They hung around for six days in utter boredom and finally called for Pollard to pick them up.

Pollard drove them around Holland, and they marveled at the Dutch spring flower gardens on display. They toured Leiden and heard that Prince Bernhard was lunching at a restaurant in town. Pollard drove them straight there. The prince sat with a group of men and Dick and Muriel ogled them as they ate from their canal-view table. They watched great barges full of tulips, each one filled with a different color, float by.

Dick and Muriel quickly dispatched to the Nederlandic countryside, which they traversed from one end to the other in a matter of hours. They finished their trip with a gastronomic sampling tour of Amsterdam.

Muriel got so comfortable in Holland that she daydreamed about living there indefinitely. Dick interrupted her fantasy abruptly one day with another fit of paranoia and insisted they move again. He suggested Basel, Switzerland.

Dick took Muriel to meet his two Swiss friends, Ellie and Alfonse, who lived in an elegant, art-filled apartment overlooking Basel's central square. Dick had met the couple years earlier with Marianne, when he took her and the kids to Gstaad. Ellie was a hostess at a bar and Ellie's friendship with Dick had evolved when Dick didn't want to leave the bar one night, and Marianne had given up on him and gone to bed. Ellie stayed up with Dick the rest of the night, talking until six in the morning. Muriel could immediately imagine the scene: Dick, on one of his typical drinking binges, picking up another buddy. Also in his typical fashion, Dick gave Ellie and her boyfriend $10,000 so they could start a fur business.

Now here they were, entertaining Dick with Marianne's replacement. They were the first people Muriel met who knew Marianne, and she was surprised to find that Ellie liked her. Ellie said that Marianne appreciated Ellie's keeping Dick company all night so she could get some rest.

For the first time, Muriel felt compassion for Marianne. She'd already had a taste of these difficult nights with Dick, and she could understand what Marianne must have gone through.

After a few days in Basel, Dick surprised Muriel and told her that he was going to set up a trust fund for her, worth hundreds of thousands of dollars. The trust would give Muriel a modest income in case anything should happen to him, and upon her death, the income would go to his two oldest sons. Dick explained that his oldest sons' inheritance had fallen below that of the younger two, because of the way the money had been invested. Dick was very careful to make sure all his children had equal sums, and he was always thinking of their future. The trust was a way to set up some of that money for them in advance, while protecting Muriel at the same time. Dick set up the trust from Basel.

It all sounded fine to Muriel, but she made a grave mistake — she told her mother about it.

Eleanor was one of the most money-obsessed people in Muriel's life, and she always managed to find a way to get money out of Muriel and Muriel's husbands. She did it with Richard Greenough, and also with Muriel's first husband, Harold Allison Laurence. Eleanor saw Muriel as her meal ticket, and it was no secret that she was very pleased that her daughter was spending so much time with R. J. Reynolds Jr. She hoped Muriel wouldn't blow it before they got married. In the meantime, Eleanor was on her best behavior while the courtship progressed.

When Muriel told her mother about the trust, she retorted, "Here you are, prepared to receive hundreds of thousands of dollars, and you've not once considered your dear mother? Do I mean so little to you? Have I not done everything in my power to be a good mother to you?" Eleanor laid it on thick. As always, Muriel was racked with guilt.

Muriel reluctantly went back to Dick. Taking cues from her mother, she wove a manipulative argument. "Because of the way we're traveling…and because of your illnesses, I'm afraid something could happen to both of us. Not just you. Wouldn't it be nice if we set up a trust so my mother could be provided for in case anything happens to us?"

Dick gave it some thought, and eventually agreed to add Eleanor. Although Muriel didn't admit it, Dick could tell that Eleanor was a problem for Muriel, and he didn't want to see her go through the stress of her mother's incessant demands. Dick amended the trust so that Eleanor could have half of it if she outlived Muriel.

~ · ~

After a few nights in Basel, Ellie and Alfonse suggested they all go to Interlaken and stay in a local inn run by friends of theirs. Dick and Muriel drove there in the car with Pollard, trailing Ellie and Alfonse, through perfect scenery and warm May weather. The melting snow in the Alps gave way to green pine trees and plants at the base of the mountains. When they arrived in Interlaken, a festive local fair was in full swing to kick off the year's cheese-making season. Cows were decorated with flowers and bells, and the villagers were dressed in traditional local costumes. The two couples watched the scene over lunch and local wine in the village square.

Dick and Muriel checked into their rooms at the inn as M. Camembert and Mme. Roquefort, giggling as they filled out the log. That evening, the four of them had dinner on the inn's lakeside terrace and watched night fall, while guitarists and pianists played under the moonlight below. The scene was nothing short of idyllic. Even Pollard found friends among some other English speakers in the village.

A few days later, Ellie and Alfonse left them to go back to Basel. Not moments after they left, another roller-coaster drinking rampage began at the inn's bar. After Dick closed down the place, he went back to the hotel room and consumed every colorful vial of liquor in their minibar. His drinking marathon was followed by the usual vomiting and forty-eight hours of bed rest, followed by docile apologies and contrition. Muriel kept telling herself that Dick continued to be under too much stress and occasionally needed these outlets of drinking to relieve the tension. After he got sick, he usually slept for two days straight, and Muriel noticed it was the only time he slept peacefully.

Muriel told herself, *It will all work itself out when we get married.*

Once Dick bounced back, they traveled to Zurich, where Dick heard that there was still controversy over the 1948 IRS rulings, but that it was unlikely he would be called to testify. He was also informed by his lawyers that the divorce was still poking along. Marianne wanted a larger settlement than the one Dick offered. Dick warned her she would risk getting no money at all because of Rubirosa. Nothing worked. Dick's frustration rubbed off on Muriel.

At Marianne's

Marianne O'Brien, the luscious redhead who was the object of so much spite from Dick, struggled with taking care of her two small boys at One Beekman Place. She was furious and saddened by the way Dick was treating her and the horrible things he accused her of in the divorce action. He even went so far as to accuse her of being a poor mother and a drunk. *That is laughable, coming from the world's most notorious drunken heir,* Marianne thought. She deeply regretted the affair with Rubirosa, but she couldn't deny that she needed the affection. Dick's constant drunken tirades and increasing illness over the years had left her a lonely woman. She was starved for the kind of attention Rubirosa showered upon her. He made her feel beautiful and special—something she hadn't felt in ages.

Dick had already left her to deal with Patrick's polio, all on her own, and had made no effort to see him when he was in the hospital. Thankfully, Patrick was only there for six weeks and it hadn't been worse. Her relentless attempts to find Dick, even with the help of private investigators, had more to do with Patrick than anything else, but Dick continued to evade her. Now she was receiving peculiar, anonymous letters in the mail from someone signed "Danger Jones" and "BW." The letters ridiculed her, informed her that she was the laughingstock of New York, and advised that if she wanted to preserve her dignity, she'd better settle with Dick immediately. Marianne wasn't sure who the letters were from, but she heard through the grapevine that Dick was seeing someone in Europe, and she suspected they had come from his lover. The insults in the letter included common accusations Dick made toward her. It made her sick to think that Dick was having an affair, in spite of her own very public infidelity. She was determined to catch Dick in the act in order to level the playing field and get every dime she possibly could out of him. She needed to, for the sake of Patrick and Michael. If that didn't work, she wanted more money—$2 million at least, as well as One Beekman Place, which was worth $350,000 at the time, and their home in Miami. And she wouldn't stop fighting until she got what she wanted.

CHAPTER 13

Le Divorce

1952

Dick and Muriel returned to England so Dick could monitor the *Aries* again. His son Josh wanted to meet up with him because he was finishing a European excursion of his own. Dick offered to let Josh stay at Grosvenor Square for the month of June, which Muriel didn't mind at all. She thought Josh was sweet and they had a good relationship—unlike his unpredictable relationship with Dick. Muriel was in the mood to spoil him.

"Let's take Josh to the best tailors in London. Let's go to Cork Street," said Muriel.

She bought him a complete, custom-made wardrobe over the course of the next month, including several suits, shoes, coats, and hats from Lock & Co. Hatters.

Muriel hoped to set Josh up with a nice British girl while he was in town as well. She put the word out that Dick's son was in town for the summer, and many candidates streamed through their doors over the course of the month.

Josh liked Muriel and repeatedly mentioned that his father seemed more relaxed with her than with anyone else. He told her that his father and mother fought badly during their relationship, and that Blitz couldn't stand it when Dick got drunk. Josh confessed that he'd been worried about his father ever since he was a child and he saw him drink on their family estate, Devotion. Their home was often a party palace in Winston-Salem and Josh grew up with hundreds of people getting hopelessly drunk in his house. He lamented that he and his brothers felt responsible for their parents' unhappiness. Blitz was desperately upset after the divorce, and she later became a heavy drinker herself.

Muriel's heart went out to Josh. She continued to accompany him around the city while Dick stayed in bed and rested, and generally ignored him. The two of them developed a friendship that lasted for many years to come.

By July, it was time for Dick to fly back to America to attend to the divorce. Marianne was prepared to settle—Dick had agreed to give her the apartment in Manhattan and their home on Sunset Island, Florida, as well as the $2 million. Josh took a liner back to America on his own and Muriel stayed in London until she received word from Dick.

Meanwhile, unsubstantiated rumors persisted in America that Dick had left Muriel and was now courting his ex-wife, Blitz. It was probably another clever smoke screen of Dick's to prevent Marianne or anyone else from finding out his intentions to marry Muriel as soon as possible.

Holy Matrimony, August 1952

Finally Muriel got the call she was waiting for: The divorce would soon be finalized and it was time for Muriel to join Dick in Montreal.

Dick treated his premarriage arrangements the way he did

any business. When Muriel arrived in Montreal, they went to the Bank of Montreal to meet the president and discuss the irrevocable trust Dick had set up for Muriel and her mother, and sign the final papers. The trust would deed ten thousand shares of RJR Tobacco, for a total of $100,000, and Muriel and her mother would receive the income from it for their lifetimes. The trust would be held in Winnipeg for tax purposes. Dick had also asked the bank to arrange for a prenuptial agreement, but he would present that to Muriel later. After losing a small fortune to Blitz and Marianne, he wasn't taking any chances.

From there, they took a train to New York, where they would change trains to go to Sapelo and get married on the island as soon as the divorce went through. Dick then took Muriel to obtain Wasserman tests (a test for syphilis required in those days before they could be issued a marriage license) so nothing could hold up their wedding plans when the time came. Muriel brought out a white lace dress for their wedding that she had bought when they were in Mexico in the earlier part of the year.

Finally, after a year of running, hiding, and waiting, Dick was officially divorced from Marianne on August 7, 1952. Marianne got everything she asked for, including custody of Patrick and Michael, the two homes, and two 1952 Cadillacs as well. Muriel could hardly believe it. Her dreams were about to come true.

On the morning of August 8, 1952, Dick and his attorneys, Frank Wells of New York, Paul Varner of Georgia, and Strat Coyner, arrived on Sapelo Island. Dick announced that he and Muriel would get married in the garden that night at nine o'clock.

Muriel pulled out her Mexican-made wedding dress. Dick's pastry chef, Karl Weiss, made a wedding cake for them, and Dick called a local Methodist preacher from Darien, Rev. Gordon C. King, to stand by. The garden in front of South End House twinkled with lights that dangled from the columns and the wisteria trees, now in full bloom and saturated with color. Inside, the main hall and dining room had been cleaned and decorated for the wedding reception. Dick and Muriel picked out an oak tree by the swimming pool that would serve as their 'altar' and made a pact to be buried there together when they passed into the next life.

But there was business to attend to before the festivities began. A few hours before their preceremonial dinner in the Azalea Cottage, Dick pulled Muriel aside for what she thought would be a romantic private moment between them. Instead, without warning, he produced the prenuptial agreement he had prepared. The agreement limited the amount of money Muriel could take from him if they ever got divorced and waived Muriel's right to anything more from Dick than the trusts he had already set up and about $100,000 worth of jewelry that he had already given her. Dick also presented her with a gift of $10,000.

Once she recovered from the surprise of the prenup, Muriel countered with one of her own. She would sign Dick's papers if he signed something for her. Muriel explained that she thought a lot about Dick's drinking in the time she'd known him and it was her opinion that liquor was seriously affecting his health. She asked him to refrain from drinking hard liquor to ensure his health and their happiness. Muriel asked Strat to draw up the agreement right then and there. It included a clause that if Dick broke the agreement, he would have to pay Muriel $15,000, and his prenuptial agreement would be null and void. Dick seemed amused and treated Muriel's prenup the same way he treated the dance contract with Johanna Rischke and the Sapelo deed with Marianne: He didn't take it seriously for a moment.

They both signed.

~ · ~

Strat, Frank, and the rest of Dick's legal entourage popped bottles of champagne and toasted Dick and Muriel on their wedding day. After a round of speeches they sat down for dinner at seven.

After dinner, they all walked to South End House, where Reverend King and the servants were waiting for them. Cushions had been placed at the base of the oak tree, which stood in the shadow of the mansion.

Both Dick and Muriel were touched by the scene. A recording of "Be My Love" by Mario Lanza played over the loudspeakers in the garden as Dick and Muriel knelt down for the service. The moon—the same bright moon that followed their courtship under Italian, Swiss, and English skies—now shone brightly on the eighty guests, most of whom were a congregation of lawyers and Sapelo Island residents. Dick held Muriel's hand throughout the ceremony.

In this remote place on the Georgia coast, the ghosts of the island's past seemed to serenade them as they entered their new life together. At long last they would be married.

Tears streamed down Dick's face. He'd abandoned two wives and two families, and he wanted it to be right this time. He wanted this marriage to be the last one.

When Reverend King pronounced them husband and wife, Dick wrapped his arms around Muriel and kissed her as he wept. Dick helped Muriel to her feet and walked to the oak tree. Using a stick, he carved into the tree, "Muriel and Dick Forever Married Here, August 8, 1952."

After the ceremony, the guests went through the main entrance of the big house for wine and wedding cake. The guests spilled out onto the patio and drank as the night stretched on. Dick and Muriel milled around, chatting with guests. Everyone congratulated them and wished them well, including Dick's lawyers, who seemed happy for Dick after all the romantic mistakes they watched him suffer through. After an hour, Dick and Muriel retreated to Azalea Cottage to be alone for the rest of the night.

The lawyers slept in the big house and left the following morning by private plane, without saying goodbye or disturbing Dick and Muriel. The newlyweds spent the next two weeks anchored at Sapelo, recovering from the exhaustion of being on the run for almost a year. They didn't speak much as Dick drove Muriel around the island in his jeep, showing her all the hidden corners of his private isle that she hadn't seen before.

But all was not as merry as they had hoped on their wedding night. Only three days after the ceremony, Dick went on one of his worst drinking binges. Muriel cried—he had already betrayed his promise. Dick lost his temper and threw a doorstop at her right breast.

Muriel was shocked, but she fired back and pointed out that he had violated the terms of the document he signed for her. Dick dug up the paper, tore it into pieces, and threw them in Muriel's face. Muriel fell into a depression as Dick's alcoholic rampage carried on.

When he came out of it, he begged for forgiveness as usual. Muriel was visibly shaken as she tried to tell Dick she would eventually forgive him, but she couldn't get the words out.

Dick abruptly announced that he'd like his relatives in Winston-Salem to meet Muriel before they departed for their honeymoon. Josh rejoined Dick and Muriel and accompanied them on the drive to Winston-Salem. Dick and Muriel's first visit would be to Blitz's so Dick could see his boys and bring home Josh. Dick intended to talk to Blitz about the younger boys' education. He felt they hadn't had access to good schools in Winston-Salem, and he hoped Blitz would give him an opportunity to make his opinion known.

They would first see Blitz in the morning for a brief visit, after which they were expected for lunch at Roaring Gap, an hour's drive away. Dick warned Muriel that Blitz could be a talker.

∾ · ∾

When they arrived on the huge Surry County acreage in the foothills of the Appalachians, Blitz and the younger boys weren't home, so Josh accompanied Dick and Muriel into the four-story lodge, and showed them the place. It was hard for Dick to be back at Devotion—the first estate he had built for himself— which he had once loved. It hadn't been maintained well and seemed like a ghost of what it had once been. After an hour of waiting, Blitz came in. It was the first time she and Dick had seen each other in years. Because Dick was now with a different woman from the one who broke up her marriage, Blitz could find peace with her ex-husband.

Blitz gave Dick a big hug, briefly shook hands with Muriel, and as Dick predicted, she chatted them up for twenty minutes straight. Dick was nervous because he wanted to broach the subject of schooling, but it didn't look as if he would be able to on this visit. He kept checking his watch. Mary, Dick's sister, was having a celebration for them at Roaring Gap and they were already late. Finally, Dick stood up to leave while Blitz talked on. Muriel and Josh jumped up to join Dick, and Blitz followed them out to the car, still talking. Dick told Blitz he would be back to visit the rest of the boys.

At least the visit had been amicable, and Blitz had been nice to Muriel. They were off to a good start.

Before leaving the estate, which was ten times the size of Dick's second childhood home, Reynolda, Dick squeezed in a few minutes to take Muriel up to a complete shooting range that he had built. Dick had created it himself with an architect's eye.

He informed Muriel that every year they had held the North Carolina State Skeet Shootout, one of Dick's favorite activities, on the estate. The range was used regularly by Winston-Salem residents.

Muriel sensed a hint of sadness on Dick's face since they had pulled up to his tremendous estate. He had put so much work into it, building dams, fishing lakes, the range—all for a love now lost.

Once they got back on the road, Dick's mood improved. When the Roaring Gap country club soon came into view, Dick smiled. He couldn't wait to see his beloved sister. They parked in front of Mary's house and when they got out of the car, Dick was welcomed by many familiar faces.

CHAPTER 14

Winston-Salem Society

1952

M ary's butler, Harvey Miller, opened the door to Dick and burst into tears. The old man had been with the family since the days of R.J. Sr. and he was overwhelmed with emotion at seeing his face. Dick gave him a long hug and Muriel stood by, already liking the place.

Mary's mountain retreat was modest and opposite the scale of Devotion and Sapelo Island. Muriel recalled the time Dick told her that Mary and Nancy had carefully and frugally saved their inheritances, while Dick outspent both of them by far. Mary was very wealthy now, perhaps more so than Dick, because she'd reinvested her money sensibly throughout her adult life.

Mary greeted the couple, and Muriel liked her on the spot. She was elegant, warm, and kind, and it was obvious that Dick and Mary loved each other. Muriel was introduced to her husband, Charles Babcock, and the children, Barbara, Betsy, Mary, and Charles Jr.

Mary planned to throw them a formal evening reception so Muriel would have the chance to meet all of Winston-Salem society. Mary whispered to Muriel, "Blitz is coming. I hope you don't mind." Mary and Nancy both had continued to treat Blitz as a sister-in-law, even after nearly a decade since she divorced Dick.

After lunch, Dick and Muriel went up to the guestroom to rest, but worry permeated Dick's face.

"Mary looks very ill compared to just two years ago when I last saw her. Did you notice that her stomach is large?" asked Dick.

"Perhaps she's having a late baby," replied Muriel.

"Do you mind if I leave you to unpack and go have a word with her alone?"

Muriel assured him that was fine and lay down for a nap.

A couple of hours later, Muriel awoke when Dick came back into the room. He looked even more worried than before. He said that Mary was not, in fact, pregnant, and that her doctor didn't know what was wrong with her and had strongly advised her to see a New York specialist earlier that summer. She hadn't been feeling well all summer, but she was putting it off, which frustrated Dick. Mary wanted to wait until the children went back to school in the fall so she could enjoy the holiday with them.

Dick said he suspected she had a mass in her belly. He vowed to bother Mary about it all weekend, but every time he brought it up, Mary tried to brush it off by saying it might be early menopause. Eventually, Dick let it go when Mary's health seemed to improve during their stay.

They attended the reception that evening. Dick and Muriel stood in the receiving line and it seemed as though the whole town was there to see Dick. Ever since World War II, Dick had been a rare sight in Winston-Salem, but they still spoke of him with pride and claimed him as one of their own.

Blitz approached Muriel after most of the guests had arrived. "It would look nice if we had a long conversation for the sake of all the people here observing us," said Blitz. Muriel agreed and Blitz ushered her to a corner where they talked for a long time. Muriel was surprised by how much she enjoyed Blitz's company and decided she liked her very much. Blitz liked Muriel, too—she was delighted by Muriel's reports that Josh was a perfect gentleman in London, and a great host. Perhaps they would be friends.

Devotion Drama

A few days after the Roaring Gap party, Dick woke early in the morning to spend time with his younger boys, whom he hadn't seen in years. He showed up early, intending to share breakfast with them and Blitz, but when he arrived Blitz wasn't in the mood to wait on him.

Dick hugged his two youngest sons, Will and Zach, and asked one of them to get him breakfast. Dick talked with Blitz cordially for about a half hour until a tray of scrambled eggs arrived. Dick ate from the tray, while Blitz and the boys all lingered awkwardly.

In between bites, Dick asked Blitz if, after all this time, she would mind returning the few valuable personal possessions he had left in the safe at Merry Acres, which he'd never retrieved after their divorce. Of particular importance to him was his pilot's license, his father's Joshua Coin (the ancestral heirloom passed down to male heirs in the family for good luck), and his father's pocket watch and compass, which was an antique nautical navigation timepiece. Dick also wanted all the reels of film he'd shot with the color motion picture production company and lab he'd owned at the time, Precision Films. While he'd been married to Blitz, he also financed a color and sound movie titled *North Carolina: Variety Vacationland,* which was used by the state's Department of Conservation and shown around the country. Dick had once pursued photography as well, and he stored the negatives in filing cabinets at Merry Acres. Dick was eager to take all his films and photos down to the Sapelo theater.

Blitz had little patience for a man who had left her to raise their children on her own and then suddenly showed up years later to demand his things back. She abruptly stood up and shouted, "You will get nothing back from me! You won't get a single thing out of any of the houses. Not so much as a piece of paper!"

Blitz added that Dick could forget about the film footage anyway, because she'd let the younger children play with the reels and they were so unraveled, tangled together, and damaged that no one could get them rewound, let alone view the films again.

Dick and Blitz exchanged venomous looks. Dick was enraged, but he reminded himself that he was there to discuss boarding school. He took a deep breath and poured his third cup of coffee.

Will and Zach were getting restless, so Dick suggested they go out and play. Josh and John sat in on the discussion as Dick broached the subject. Dick said it was time for the two younger boys to go to Virginia's Woodbury Forest, which was one of the best boarding schools in the South and Dick's own childhood school.

"Why don't you mind your own business?" Blitz retorted. "I have custody of them, and if you dare try and do anything about it I'll see you in court."

Dick said again that he felt like they weren't getting a good enough education, and it was time they had an opportunity to be educated like the other boys of their status. Blitz said that public school was good enough for her sons, that they loved the country, and that she wasn't going to pay fees at Woodbury. She only had $5,000 a year for each of the boys. Dick offered to pay their education fees in full.

Blitz refused Dick's offer. She was disgusted by his nerve in telling her what to do with Zach and Will. Instead of bossing her around, he should have been outside spending time with them. They hurled insults at one another just as they had when they were married. Finally, Blitz threw a coffeepot at Dick, narrowly missing him. Dick stormed out of the house, too upset to speak. Josh and John ran out after him. The boys told their father that they would see what they could do to change Blitz's mind. But the message to Dick was clear: too little parenting, too late.

Dick didn't see Blitz again for a long time.

❧ · ❧

Determined to get on with their trip, Dick took Muriel for one more visit to Charles and Mary's and then he went back to Winston-Salem for the day. He wished to show Muriel the bungalow his mother built when he was a kid, the legendary Reynolda.

As they drove down the tree-lined street of the same name, they passed beautiful homes and mansions that had been built up all along the once desolate country road since R.J. Sr. died. The richest people in the area made sure they settled around Reynolda—the prestige of the estate made the neighborhood one of the most valuable sections of the city.

Dick made a slight right turn and abruptly pulled up to an unassuming iron gate. Muriel could see nothing but a large lawn at first. Once Dick drove in a few hundred feet, the estate opened up before them. There it was—the grand Reynolda mansion, poised in the distance at the end of acres and acres of long, rolling, green pasture. It took Muriel's breath away.

Dick was also moved by seeing the house, but in a different way. He regarded it with quiet trepidation as he continued driving down the winding road to the home's entrance. The house and lawn were surrounded by thick woods and the mansion's front garden was adorned with a quiet fountain, flowers, and plants. A wide, windowed porch stretched along the entire width of the back of the house. By now, groves of trees on both sides of the house had grown so thick they hid both wings and made the house look much smaller than it was.

They got out of the car and Dick hastily walked Muriel down the crushed-stone walkway to the back entrance. He seemed unsettled.

The only person in the house at that time was Charles Jr., who greeted them enthusiastically.

Young Charles gave them a tour of the house, which lived up to its magnificent reputation. The main reception hall was a two-tier-wide rectangle—thirty-eight by forty-seven feet—and accented by a marble fireplace in the middle. Velvet sofas sat in the central hall and the windows were covered with silk curtains. A twin staircase trailed up to the second floor balcony, which surrounded the hall and was visible from the ground floor. Both Mary and Nancy had been married at the base of those stairs.

Dick pointed out the Aeolian organ, with its four sets of keyboards, and showed Muriel where he used to play hide-and-seek in the hidden organ chambers. They entertained themselves with the telephones in every room and three dumbwaiters that serviced the house.

Charles briefly left them to take a call. Dick somberly ushered Muriel down a long narrow hall to the wood-paneled library that was meant to be his father's retirement nook and instead served as his sickroom in the final months before his death. The library overlooked a circular garden and fountain near the lake porch on the back of the house. Behind the old desk was a large plate glass picture window with views of Lake Katharine below.

Dick pointed to a long antique sofa by the window and said, "That is the couch on which my father died." His eyes glistened with tears. After all these years, he still missed his father terribly. Dick said they concluded many years after R.J. Sr. died that he likely had pancreatic cancer.

Dick said, "I want you to come upstairs and see the room where Smith died."

Muriel gasped—she hadn't made the connection before. It suddenly occurred to her that Smith was shot in this house. No wonder Dick looked subdued when he first glimpsed the house from the road.

"I don't want to see you upset."

"I want you to see it. I have never understood what happened and I'd like your opinion on it."

Muriel followed him out of the library to the flight of side stairs that led to the master bedroom suite and sleeping porches. The bedroom was intended for Katharine and R.J. Sr. to use, but R.J. Sr. never spent a night in its bed before he died. Muriel hesitated before climbing the stairs. *This house is cursed*, she thought. R.J. Sr. died six months after arriving at Reynolda and even Katharine hadn't had the chance to live there for long before she died tragically prematurely. Then young Smith was shot in the same wing of the house in which R.J. Sr. died. Muriel followed Dick to see where Smith died that fateful night, twenty years earlier.

CHAPTER 15

Smith

1952

They walked up the flight of stairs to the next level. Muriel felt apprehension wash over her as she moved through the ill-fated house.

Dick took her into the east wing sleeping porch and showed her where Smith had been found and where the bullet had landed. He couldn't finish the description, and he sat down on the bed and held his head in his hands.

The room was filled with sadness and regret. Muriel visualized young Smith in that room, with his wife, Libby Holman, and his friend and secretary, Ab Walker.

"I know this is difficult. But we must pull ourselves together for Charles's sake. Your nephew will wonder what happened to us," Muriel said gently.

They shuffled out of the room and Muriel glanced back one more time before closing the door. She imagined what Dick must have gone through upon learning of Smith's death, and how devastating it must have been to never know what really happened. Perhaps the Reynoldses shouldn't have quashed the investigation after all. They would have suffered some embarrassment, but at least they might have gotten some answers.

They rejoined Charles, who had drinks waiting for them in the main hall. They eventually excused themselves and left to eat at a restaurant in town. Dick wanted some quiet time alone. As they settled in with drinks and food, Dick opened up to Muriel about what he knew of Smith's shooting. He explained that while many people felt Smith was suicidal, Dick believed he never intended to carry out a suicide, no matter how desperate he became over Libby. But he had also accepted the fact that it was unlikely that Libby deliberately murdered him. Dick thought maybe Smith threatened to commit suicide and held up the gun, but Libby tried to grab it from him and it went off accidentally. No matter what happened, it was very hard for them all to cope with the uncertainty of it.

Dick told Muriel about the fight they had with Libby over the estate and how Smith's death motivated him to become a philanthropist. The Z. Smith Reynolds Foundation had turned out to be a huge success.

Dick wanted Muriel to see the house, Merry Acres. Dick had designed it with the help of architects from Northup & O'Brien for Blitz and he missed it terribly. When they were building it, Dick flew the architects down to Sapelo to discuss the plans, and Blitz constantly interrupted their meetings to express her ideas. When she left the room, Dick turned to one of the designers, Luther Lashman, and said, "I let Blitz talk all she wants, but when you do the house, do it my way."

The next day they drove to the estate, which sat on several acres on the edge of town, not far from Reynolda. The land was once owned by Dick's Uncle Will, who gave him permission to design his dream house there. When they pulled up, Muriel started laughing. No wonder Dick loved the place. It was built entirely in the shape of *one huge yacht*. It was long, sleek, and as smooth as a sailboat, and looked as if it belonged on a beachfront somewhere. Dick excitedly got out of the car.

He checked the back door and it was open. Muriel followed him inside and he switched on the lights. The house appeared to be unattended.

The inside was as lovely as the outside. Nearly every wall had floor-to-ceiling windows, filling the house with sunlight. Dick told Muriel he had thrown lots of parties at the ship deck-house—he considered it his personal showplace.

Dick lingered a little longer, remembering the many good times he had there. Maybe one day he would buy it back from Blitz, if she was interested.

That evening, Dick and Muriel went to dinner at the Coyner house, and Dick wanted to spend the night there. As they lay down in the guest bedroom, Dick had trouble getting to sleep. Being back in Winston-Salem brought back many feelings.

The following day, Dick took Muriel to the site where his father's old Victorian Fifth Street house once stood; it had recently been torn down. While still married to Marianne, Dick had donated the home, at the time valued at $100,000, and the surrounding land to the city so they could build a public library there. Dick did it on an impulse in celebration of Marianne's birthday in December of 1948. As he stood on the block, he told Muriel stories about his father and his childhood. This spot, unlike Reynolda, was filled with happy memories for Dick. Dick wrapped up the tour by showing Muriel Reynolds Park and the hospitals he and his family had funded.

The Launch at Gosport

When Dick finally had his fill of Winston-Salem, he abruptly changed direction again. It was time for him and Muriel to get back to England to launch the *Aries,* which was finally completed. They planned to fly from Winston-Salem to Miami and then on to England.

Muriel would see one more of Dick's creations before they left. They pulled up to the small municipal airport that Dick had built in his brother's honor just a decade earlier—Z. Smith Reynolds Airport. The airfield was abuzz with small charter planes and aviation enthusiasts, but not many commercial travelers. When they walked in, Muriel thought it looked more like Dick's private hangar. A mural of Z. Smith looking out over Winston-Salem covered the upper half of one wall. Dick had commissioned Charles Augustus Jenkins to paint the image of Smith looking out over the city of Winston-Salem, although the painter never publicly confirmed the identity of the man in the picture. Near the entrance, the marble bust of Z. Smith looked down on them. Muriel read the caption documenting Smith's aviation accomplishments.

Dick glanced up at the bust for a moment before they walked out to meet their private plane. It was time to say goodbye to Winston-Salem.

~ · ~

Once in England, they drove to Gosport for the *Aries* launch party and invited all their friends. The launch was held on an exceptionally beautiful day, and several guests arrived at Camper & Nicholsons' Gosport yard for the party. Muriel's ex-husband Richard Greenough, whom Dick had befriended since his courtship with Muriel, was in attendance, along with Muriel's former *New York Times* friends, Dick and Muriel's London friends, and of course, Muriel's mother, Eleanor. Eleanor brought two friends, a Major Rutherford and Cedric Taylor, who had once worked with Muriel's stepfather in business. The Duke of Edinburgh was also due to show up, but canceled at the last minute.

The launch party doubled as a second wedding reception for those in England who hadn't been able to see Dick and Muriel get married at Sapelo. There were smiles and congratulations all around, and the yard expressed tremendous satisfaction with the ship, which had taken sixty men to build. Dick again joked that he had built the yacht for the express purpose of buoying England's economy.

The unique yacht sat proudly in the shipyard, surrounded by British and American flags, while guests were served food and drinks from Harrod's of London. The one-of-a-kind sailor had a full set of majestic black sails, with the zodiac sign of the ram, Aries, embroidered in gold at the top of the mainsail. Black sails were considered bad luck, but Dick enjoyed going against nautical tradition. The *Aries* was the only sailing yacht registered in the country with black sails.

After a few speeches, it was Muriel's job to break the bottle of champagne against the ship. She had great difficulty cracking it open and had to take three swings before the bottle broke. That was also considered a sign of bad luck in England. They brushed it off as another silly superstition.

~ · ~

While they had been in America, Dick secretly ordered Peter Barber and his crew to take the *White Heron* to Tahiti to wait for them. Dick surprised Muriel with the news that they were going on a honeymoon in the Pacific.

After a month of rare, uneventful normalcy, they left for New York, where they would catch a plane to California, and then be on their way to Tahiti and Fiji. More frenzied adventures were in store.

After a brief passport issue in New York, they flew to San Francisco. When they arrived, thick Bay Area fog had already rolled in and their flight to Hawaii would be delayed until the next day. They caught a cab to the Mark Hopkins Hotel and dined at the Top of the Mark, which had panoramic views of the San Francisco Bay and the Golden Gate Bridge. They toasted the beginning of their honeymoon, and Dick told Muriel more stories of his days in California during the war.

They flew to Honolulu first thing the next morning. They were due to stay at the beautiful Royal Hawaiian Hotel in Wai-kiki and leave for Fiji the following evening. They were flying over the Pacific not more than an hour away from Honolulu when their left engine caught fire. The quick-thinking pilots managed to put out the fire but the plane was gradually losing elevation. Dick had been drinking, but he quickly sobered up in case he'd have to assist in a water landing. The pilots sent out an emergency call over the radio and received word that four destroyers were on their way. The plane continued to drop.

By the time they spotted the ships coming for them, the plane had dropped to a hair-raising two hundred feet above water. The plane was able to land on one of the ships and they were taken safely to Honolulu.

It was nine at night when they arrived. There was only one way to cap off the night. Dick and Muriel were so happy to be alive, they went straight to Trader Vic's for rum punch, and enveloped themselves in the romance of steamy Hawaii as if it were their last night on earth.

Muriel eventually dragged Dick to the Royal Hawaiian at three in the morning, when he turned around and pulled another "Hôtel du Nord." Just as he was settling down to bed, he got up, put his clothes on, walked out the door, and disappeared for the night. This time Muriel wasn't going to look for him.

Dick turned up at the hotel at eleven the next morning. They weren't scheduled to catch their next plane until that evening, so Muriel helped Dick get into his pajamas. He looked so haggard and desperate, Muriel couldn't get mad at him. She thought it was funny. She was starting to get used to this.

After Dick rested awhile, they got ready for the next leg of the trip. Because of the delays they had suffered, they decided to skip Tahiti and go straight to Fiji, where Dick had chartered a yacht to take them to the Yasawa Islands.

Dick still looked terrible. Luckily, they had reserved a sleeper suite with their own bunk beds and bathrooms on the transpacific flight. Muriel tucked Dick in as soon as they boarded and he slept all the way to Wake Island, where they had a brief layover before continuing on to Fiji.

After all of the delays and the agonizing travel, they finally arrived in Fiji that night. Hopefully, they would have the chance to enjoy their honeymoon at last.

CHAPTER 16

Things Fall Apart

1953–1959

As Dick's personal life spiraled downward in the final decade of his life, his increasingly irrational behavior reflected the sentiment of the times. The country was in a state of heightened Cold War paranoia with espionage and nuclear deadlock haunting the public consciousness. The number of millionaires in the world was skyrocketing but they were nervous. Fellow tycoons like Stavros Niarchos and J. Paul Getty were increasingly fearful of threats to their families due to their wealth. Technology was all the rage—space exploration was budding, commercial aviation was becoming a way of life, and Dick's primal passion, yachting, became more and more sophisticated, not without the help of Dick's advancements in the field.

It was also a time when people refused to accept that alcoholism was a disease or that smoking wreaked havoc on the body. To the contrary, these comforts were welcomed and indulged. Dick was still a dangerous drunk, emptying entire bottles of liquor in a day, even while taking medication for emphysema. Tobacco's harm had been documented but largely ignored, particularly by tobacco companies and their producers. Dick fell ill about once a week starting in the mid-1950s. As his illness and alcoholism progressed, so did his erratic behavior.

Dick and Muriel's marriage continued at the same frenetic pace as their courtship. The next seven years would move very quickly. Dick's health continued to falter, and in spite of the warning signs, he drank and smoked heavily every day. Rarely could he be seen without a drink and an unfiltered Camel.

In 1953, less than a year after Dick and Muriel visited her, Mary died of stomach cancer. Dick's instincts had been right— she had been seriously ill and had waited too long to be treated. Mary had no idea how grave her situation was; she had accepted an invitation to see Dick and Muriel right before she died.

That same year, Nancy divorced her husband, Henry Bagley, after twenty-three years of marriage and four children. With the loss of Mary and her husband, Nancy grew closer to Dick.

Dick and Muriel attended the funeral at Reynolda and continued to visit Winston-Salem periodically over the next few years. Soon Muriel became a prominent member of Roaring Gap's country club and was on everyone's lunch invitation list, including Blitz's parties at Merry Acres. She spent time with Mackie, Strat Coyner's wife, and a variety of other society women regularly. She loved buying gifts for them and often had custom-made clothing sent down from New York, making her a very popular society wife. They visited the four oldest sons much more often than Dick had before.

The Copenhagen Debacle

In May of 1954, Dick and Muriel set sail from Brunswick, Georgia, in the *Aries*, the yacht they had worked so hard to complete, on a trip to Europe. This trip would be no different from Dick and Muriel's usual escapades, except that it threatened their marriage for the first time.

Dick had hired a new, experienced skipper, Arved Jeannot Rosing, to be master of the *Aries*. Dick also hired Arved's Estonian wife, Irma Orras, to clean. Karl Weiss was brought along to cook.

They got as far as Bermuda when the radar and the gyroscope failed, causing a delay of ten days. While mechanics flew down from New York, Dick started drinking—mainly because he was extremely irritated by the machinery holding up their well-laid plans.

One evening he and Muriel went ashore and hopped from bar to bar, and came back to the boat to find that the repairmen had fallen asleep in the deckhouse and the yacht was drifting out to sea. It was 2:00 A.M., and Dick was furious. There was a fast and dangerous tide, but Dick got undressed and said he was going to swim to the yacht.

Dick jumped in the water and pulled Muriel in behind him, even though she was still in her evening clothes. As they splashed and flailed in the water, Muriel pleaded with Dick to get back on the dock, but he replied with an angry "no." Muriel grabbed hold of the dock and struggled to pull herself out of the water. She hailed a taxi and begged the driver to help her retrieve Dick. The driver ran over to the dock and shouted at Dick, who was still treading water, to get out. He finally gave in and the driver hoisted him up on the dock. With the help of the taxi driver, Muriel got Dick to a hotel by four.

When they returned the next night to the now anchored yacht, Dick stumbled down the steep gangplank, slipped, hit the stanchion, and injured himself. Muriel covered him with a raincoat and called two local doctors for help—a Dr. Fulton and Dr. Leon Fox, who rushed to the dock to examine Dick. Fulton advised him to rest and strongly suggested they X-ray his ribs, which he thought might have been fractured. But Dick insisted that he wanted to sail the next day and refused to have it treated. Dick admitted to the doctors that he had a history of falling down and injuring his chest, but he had always been fine in the past. The doctors noted on their medical report that Dick was "obviously drunk." Muriel threw up her hands, exasperated by Dick's stubborn refusal to get the help he needed.

Meanwhile, Dick was exasperated by the way he had let Muriel alter the yacht when it was being designed. He said if he had never met Muriel, eight feet of the yacht would have been entirely different, and that she'd taken up too much valuable space for unnecessary luxuries like deck chairs. He even blamed her when machinery broke down. Muriel said, "You should have thought of that before you proposed."

After her anger, Muriel always found excuses for Dick's behavior, no matter what he did. She still told herself that he was sweet and kind and generous at heart, if she could just get him to lay off the bottle.

～ · ～

The next day, they sailed across the Atlantic to the Azores Islands, en route to Lisbon. By now it was June 1954, and there was a terrible storm that lasted the entire crossing. Muriel thought for sure she wouldn't live to see the Azores port of Horta.

Muriel had also developed a habit of taking out her anger toward Dick on the servants. Muriel and Irma, the skipper's wife, weren't getting along so well. Irma was upset because Muriel changed her wishes too often and was rude to her and Karl. Muriel ridiculed Karl's knowledge of cooking, and Irma hated that they could never make Muriel happy. Every morning, she insisted she have a tablecloth at breakfast, and if Irma forgot to bring it Muriel would have a fit. In a typical morning,

Muriel would buzz Irma for a cup of coffee; Irma would bring it and leave. Moments later, Muriel would buzz Irma again. "This coffee is cold." Irma would retrieve the cup, warm it, return it to Muriel, and leave. Moments later, another buzz. "This coffee is too hot." And so it went.

Karl was having terrible bouts of seasickness, so Irma had to cook for everyone most of the time. Muriel insisted she have her breakfast at 7:30, and the crew was to have breakfast at eight. But Irma was usually so busy heating and cooling Muriel's coffee and tending to her every need, she was always late serving the crew. She concluded that Muriel simply ordered everyone around just to make everyone as miserable as she was.

When they arrived in Europe, an old acquaintance of Dick's, Christian Nissen, who was recommended to him by Sparkman & Stephens, joined them to sail. Nissen had met Dick during the British Fastnet race in the 1930s, when Dick raced with the *Lizzie McCaw*. Nissen was known among the yachting set by his captain nickname, "Hein Muck," named for the famed World War I shipyard carpenter, Hein Muck of Bremerhaven.

When they arrived in Hamburg, Germany, Dick disappeared from their room at the Atlantic Hotel and was out all night. Having grown accustomed to Dick's disappearances and "Hotel du Nords," Muriel didn't worry about it until six in the morning when he still hadn't shown up. She went out looking for him and finally discovered him at the Reeperbahn—Hamburg's red-light district—with a dozen "derelicts." Dick pretended not to know who she was, so she sat in the corner of the bar until nine to make sure he was safe. She finally asked a manager and head waiter to help her get him home. Dick wouldn't budge, so she called Nissen and asked him to retrieve Dick for her. At noon, Nissen pulled Dick out of the bar, and discovered that he'd spent $4,000 at the establishment.

After Dick recovered on the yacht, they sailed to the Baltic

Sea, stopping at the Kiel Yacht Club where Dick's sister Nancy and his niece Susan joined them. After everyone had gone to bed, Dick stayed up all night again in another drunken binge, and Muriel had to stay up with him until morning, trying to prevent him from embarrassing himself in front of his family. The next morning, Dick was bedridden, so Muriel helped Nancy and Susan get breakfast and catch a train out of town without having a wink of sleep herself.

Muriel was angry. Nissen noticed the tension. Now in a terrible mood, Muriel saw a grocery bill that Captain Rosing had brought back to them, and she flew into a rage when she saw that he'd purchased eggs for a dollar a dozen. "I just saw eggs in town for seventy-five cents!" Muriel screamed. Dick retorted, "If you don't like it, you do the shopping." So Muriel called Hamburg and ordered a Mercedes 300 with a chauffeur to come 125 miles to Kiel to take her two miles into town.

While she was gone, a German reporter came onboard to interview Dick about his yachting activities in the area. She brought with her a sixteen-year-old American exchange student to translate, and Dick invited them to stay awhile. They were there all afternoon and into the night while Muriel was away. When photos of Dick and the teenager showed up in the newspaper, Muriel accused him of sleeping with her. Dick never said one way or the other, but Muriel started to worry that Dick was having affairs.

From Kiel, they sailed to the port of Travemünde, where Muriel developed an abscessed tooth. Dick was so anxious to keep sailing, he asked her if she could get it removed locally. So as not to disappoint Dick, Muriel found a dentist, who removed her tooth using very little anesthesia. In the process, the dentist damaged her root, and she had to get a root canal on top of it.

A couple of hours later, Nissen met her at the dentist and took her back to the yacht. Dick greeted her with disdain.

"You're late. I've been waiting to sail for the last hour." Muriel couldn't believe his reaction—after all the times she had nursed him to health, this was all he had to say to her after her ordeal.

By now it was August, and they sailed from Travemünde to Copenhagen. They had acquired an English engineer and a Danish boatswain, whom Muriel liked a lot—finally some hired help Muriel could get along with. Nissen's wife, Eureka, had also joined them at Dick's invitation.

They got off the boat and traveled to Helsinger because Dick wanted to see the castles. They went to a fine restaurant, and Dick and Muriel began arguing and shouting in front of the patrons. Afterward, they went to Kronborg Castle, still fighting. Dick had met up with a Navy friend who was in charge of a shipping museum there, and Muriel purposely made derogatory comments about Danish shipping in front of him. Dick said, "Muriel, shut up, don't be an idiot. They can hear us." But she wouldn't stop.

By dinnertime that night, they were still arguing and bickering—about what, no one could remember. Dick enjoyed arguing with Muriel most of the time. He just didn't like it when she won. He and Blitz had the same dynamic in their marriage, but Muriel could quickly turn mean. At one point, Dick turned to Eureka for support and said, "Am I not right?" to which Muriel replied, "Oh, she is dumb, she doesn't speak any English anyway." Eureka said she had a headache and excused herself. Dick screamed at Muriel, "Get off the boat! I don't want to see you anymore." Muriel said, "Fine, I will."

It was August 15, and Muriel sauntered off the boat without any of her belongings, not realizing that Dick was serious.

When Dick pulled up anchor and sailed off without her, she panicked. She immediately called the Royal Bank of Canada and asked for a transfer of $550,000 from Dick's account at the RBC to their joint bank account.

Meanwhile, Dick sailed back to Travemünde and into the

Elbe River at Cuxhaven. He intended to go to Stockholm but didn't make it because the boat needed repairs. As he sailed back to the shipyard at Bremen, he found out about the money transfer and he became enraged. He was so angry he called up his lawyers to talk to them for the first time about divorcing Muriel.

Muriel, meanwhile, had ended up in Paris, and she called Irma and Nissen to bring her belongings. Nissen jumped on a train in Bremen and took them to her personally in Paris and stayed with her for two days, but he refused to tell her where Dick was. Then Muriel dropped a bomb. "I'm pregnant," she said. Nissen's jaw dropped. Muriel went on to explain that because of her hormones, she was having a hard time controlling her temper. She apologized for transferring the money and begged Nissen to convince Dick to forgive her.

Once Dick heard the news he immediately went down to Paris to meet Muriel. In spite of an apparent lack of interest in parenting, he was desperate to have a baby with Muriel and was very excited. He got over the money transfer pretty quickly, sending a jovial note to the Royal Bank of Canada and asking them to stop the transfer. It had just been a result of a "domestic spat" that was long since forgiven, according to Dick.

While Muriel rested at the hotel, Dick went out to Fred Payne's bar for the night to let off steam. Marianne O'Brien happened to be in town and strolled into the same establishment. Dick hadn't seen Marianne since the divorce and he thought it would be fun to catch up. He invited her to sit and talk with him and they chatted amicably for some time. Marianne realized how much she'd missed Dick. She was still lonely after their divorce and was looking for love. She mistook Dick's drunken friendliness for renewed interest in her. When Dick made an insulting remark about her looks to the bartender, Marianne flew into a rage, screaming at Dick all the things she had wanted to say to him during the divorce. Then she got physical. Marianne not only struck Dick in the head with a shoe, she threw glasses and bottles all over the bar, causing 40,000 francs in damage. Marianne's tendency to resort to violence had not changed—at least when it came to Dick. She was ordered to leave the premises in shame.

Meanwhile, Dick picked up another "human collectible"—a French girl named Gabrielle—and had the nerve to bring her back to Muriel's hotel at dawn. Muriel was humiliated and hurt, especially in light of her recent news. Of course, once Dick sobered up, he begged her forgiveness, and all was forgiven.

In October 1954, Dick and Muriel flew back to York, England, to attend the wedding of Richard Greenough to his third wife, which was being held at Claxton Hall. Richard, who had met Dick only a few times with Muriel, surprisingly asked Dick to be his best man. Christian Nissen brought the rest of Dick's formal clothing from the yacht so he would have something to wear at the wedding. Muriel thanked Nissen for all he did and rewarded him with money she had won gambling in Travemünde. She even bought the Nissens a new car and a new apartment in Hamburg.

Richard Greenough and his new wife, and Muriel and Dick continued to be good friends throughout the years. Dick even suggested Muriel sell her old Seventy-ninth Street apartment in New York to Richard so they could live nearby.

Before they departed England, Dick and Muriel consulted with a doctor who confirmed Muriel's pregnancy. Dick was elated by the news. She had been trying to get pregnant since the first day of their marriage.

~ · ~

Dick was due to return to the *Aries* and sail to Tangiers to test the yacht, so he instructed Muriel to go to New York, get some rest, and wait for him. The Rosings had fallen ill during sailing, and

Dick replaced them with a new crew. He invited John Walter Gates to be the new master of the *Aries* and also hired a young German man named Guenther Lehman to be his personal secretary. They sailed to Tangiers first, and then made their way back across the Atlantic toward St. Thomas in the Virgin Islands.

When Muriel returned to New York, it was November 1954. One night when she was out at the movies with a friend, she was attacked and mugged on the street. She was in such a state of shock and nervousness that she went home and called a doctor to examine her. The doctor confirmed that she was fine and healthy, but that she seemed exhausted and should relax as much as possible. That was hard for Muriel to do—Dick wasn't around and she was deeply shaken by the ordeal. Three days later in her hotel room, she suffered a miscarriage in the bathtub. She had been three months along.

Dick was in the Caribbean when Muriel told him what happened. He gently assured her they would keep trying, and at least now they knew it was possible. Dick asked Muriel to fly to Palm Beach and meet him there, where they could be reunited for Christmas. Christian Nissen would join them for the holiday, along with Karl Weiss and Martin Hall from Sapelo.

Once they were reunited, it didn't take long for Dick and Muriel's reconciliation to turn sour. They spent the holiday arguing and Muriel was back to complaining about the servants once again.

~ · ~

The marriage was strained more and more as time went on. Dick's drinking continued to be extreme—every morning he had brandy, crème de cacao, and milk for breakfast, and the drinking increased throughout the day. Each time he recovered, Muriel followed the usual routine—nursing him back to health and calling hosts of doctors wherever in the world they happened to be. But Muriel never complained about the work she had to do to help him through it, and she never asked any of Dick's family for help.

In spite of spending almost a million dollars a year, Dick couldn't help making money hand over fist. He managed to earn big capital gains on his investments each year and was still one of the richest men in America. Dick and Muriel continued to spend that cash and be dizzyingly extravagant and adventurous, no matter how often Dick was bedridden. He never slowed down for long before he caught his second wind. In addition to Sapelo, they kept homes in Palm Beach, in New York on East Sixty-sixth Street, in Monte Carlo, and in Tahiti, and they traveled between them often. They spent four months out of the year on the *Aries,* which had a crew of seven permanent employees, as well as a new yacht, the *Scarlett O'Hara,* with a permanent crew of two. They also kept a twin-engine Beechcraft airplane and numerous island boats at Sapelo.

Dick and Muriel's wild adventures continued to draw national attention. In 1955, they were sailing off the coast of Miami when their fastest boat, the *Scarlett O'Hara*, caught fire. They jumped into a dinghy and rowed to shore, where they tried to catch a taxi. Looking haggard and disheveled, they tried to convince a driver that they'd abandoned a burning ship and needed to be taken to a hotel. The driver didn't believe them but finally agreed to take them where they needed to go. The incident made headlines.

In 1956, Dick and Muriel went back to Winston-Salem to attend the dedication ceremony for Wake Forest's new campus. Dick was credited for being the "motivating force" behind the college's relocation to Winston-Salem. That same year, Dick invited all the North Carolinians who were in Chicago for the Democratic National Convention to come and celebrate with him and Muriel after the convention was over. Hundreds of people streamed to Sapelo on chartered planes at Dick's expense.

Around the same time, Dick worked on developing Sapelo. He had visions of Sapelo being a great resort island, much like Sea Island. Dick had almost finished migrating all of Sapelo Island's residents into an enclave called Hog Hammock. Previously, the residents had been scattered throughout several coastal hamlets around the island, and Dick and his farm managers bought them all up for a fraction of what their land was worth. In exchange, Dick paid for their new homes in the central hammock on the island. This angered some of the island's residents, but they felt powerless. Unbeknownst to Dick, Frank Durant even threatened some, telling them they would lose their jobs if they didn't take the offer. To make matters worse, Dick never did finish developing the coast as he'd intended. The movement of all those residents for a half-hearted project that was never completed caused a lot of grief that continues to this day.

In August 1956, Dick and Muriel spent their anniversary in Bremen working on the *Aries,* which again had to be repaired. They met Christian Nissen in Kiev and they all traveled to Berlin for a week's vacation. Dick, Muriel, and Nissen went out to a club on their own one night, and there was a beautiful singer with whom Dick became infatuated. He kept throwing hundred-dollar bills at her so she would keep singing, even as the club closed. Muriel, still feeling insecure about the Gabrielle incident a couple of years prior, turned to Nissen. "What do you think about giving Dick this?" Muriel said as she stuck $200 worth of bills in Nissen's hand. "Get the singer to go to bed with him tonight."

Nissen refused, saying, "Muriel, you ought to be ashamed of yourself to do such a thing." Muriel shrugged her shoulders and put the money back in her purse. It was clear that being married to Dick had desensitized Muriel to such scandalous behavior.

By the fall of 1957, Muriel was seasoned at summoning doctors for Dick whenever he drank too much. During one examination, Dick was informed that he had a low, nearly inactive sperm count, and their hopes for a child were gone.

On another occasion while they were in New York, Dick turned unusually gray and pale after a drinking binge, and Muriel called Dr. Mark O'Vickie, who rushed to their apartment. O'Vickie determined that Dick had "a touch of dropsy" and ordered him to stop drinking if he wanted to save his life. Dick asked to be sent to Winston-Salem to see his old family friend Dr. Henry Valk, and Muriel drove him down in October of 1957. Valk reiterated what O'Vickie had said in New York. Dick was on the verge of destroying himself, and if he intended to live a minute longer he had to stop drinking at once. Afterward, they flew to Palm Beach so Dick could recuperate.

Around the same time, Dick's third son, Zach, became engaged to a nice Winston-Salem girl, Linda Lee Tise. Dick had spent so little time with Zach throughout his life that Zach admitted that he deliberately hid from his father when he came to Winston-Salem because he didn't know what to say to him. Linda, whom Dick loved, provided an opportunity for them to reconnect. Zach and Linda were soon spending more time with Dick and Muriel in Palm Beach and Sapelo. After one visit in Florida, Linda was in a bad car accident on her way to meet friends. She had nearly severed her leg and was fighting for her life, but because she was underage, she couldn't receive surgery without her parents' permission, and they were out of state. Dick rushed to the hospital and immediately took responsibility for her. She said she never saw a medical bill and that Dick was instrumental in saving her life, and she was forever grateful to him. When she later married Zach, Dick was overjoyed.

Zach and Linda weren't Dick's only regular guests in Palm Beach and Sapelo. Dick and Muriel, and sometimes only Dick, spent a lot of time with Muriel's brother, Tony Marston, and his family. Dick loved skeet shooting with Tony and eating his wife's cooking. Dick also took a liking to his son Clay, whom he treated more like a son than his own boys. Dick delighted Clay with bowling games at Sapelo and generous toys and gifts during the holidays. Sometimes the Marstons spent months at a time with Dick, whether or not Muriel was around. Dick had a rapport with the Marstons that he did not have with his own family, and their impression of Dick was very different. They perceived Dick as one of the kindest, most generous, and cheerful individuals they had ever met. They never saw his outbursts of anger or the dark side of his drinking. All they saw was a man who appreciated each new day and lived for the moment. They saw a man who always had a smile on his face and would do anything for them.

This was in stark contrast to the man Dick's sons saw. Dick complained that the boys were too spoiled and undisciplined, and that their behavior was increasingly out of control. He felt they weren't being raised right by their mother, but he did little to take responsibility for them himself. While Dick bought gifts for nonfamily members, it was usually left to Muriel to shop for Dick's sons. It seemed that Dick couldn't bring himself to give his attention and his unconditional generosity to his family the way he did for everyone else. Only his worsening health would temporarily break this pattern.

By the time Dick and Muriel attended the Georgetown Regatta in the spring of 1958, Dick drank again, and disrupted his health once again. He would go through several more bouts of sickness, but for him it was better than going through alcohol withdrawal.

In April 1958, Dick and Muriel went back to Winston-Salem for the Founders' Day Celebration at Wake Forest, and Muriel was on hand with a $11,000 bust of Dick she had made for the university. Dick wasn't at the ceremony because he was sick in bed.

Dick's Rapid Decline

In May of 1958, Dick and Muriel were at their Palm Beach house having lunch when Dick became very ill again. He had the same gray look he had in New York the year before. Muriel knew this was bad. She chartered a plane for him to fly to Winston-Salem's Baptist Hospital, where he recuperated again under Dr. Valk's care. Valk again said that if he didn't stop drinking, he would probably have only five more years to live. At the same time, Dick was diagnosed with pulmonary emphysema, which was believed to be caused by a genetic disorder, and which was exacerbated by Dick's hard living. For the first time in his life, Dick took his health seriously. He was going to quit drinking for good.

Following Dick's hospital stay, he and Muriel went up to Fancy Gap, Virginia, for a holiday and to spend more time with the family. Dick bought Zach a mountain lodge there, which Muriel fully furnished for him. Nancy's children also visited for days at a time.

At that time, Dick made the decision to sell his RJR stock. The price had soared to almost twice its value and everyone in town was selling. Dick made over $2 million on the stock that he had originally purchased in 1929 during the Great Depression. It was Muriel's idea after she noticed they had changed the label on the Camel brand. As a gesture of gratitude, Dick wished to set up a new trust for Muriel with the proceeds.

Money had been on his mind because of his health problems, and the trust would be a good place to stuff all this new cash. While still sojourning at Fancy Gap, Dick arranged for a trust worth $6,113,000, which he felt "should become my wife's share of my estate," and made Muriel the beneficiary. Dick also sent

$50,000 to each of his sons as a "just because" gift. He had his sons on his mind too.

Twenty-five-year-old Josh had become somewhat unstable and had a nervous breakdown before he was hospitalized in Detroit. Dick let him stay in their apartment in New York, and Josh lived with Dick and Muriel on and off for a year. He became very close to Muriel especially, and she coached him through his low periods.

When Dick returned from Fancy Gap in September, he had given up drinking completely and suffered from severe alcohol withdrawal again. The lack of alcohol was taking its toll and he was probably enduring a mild case of delirium tremens. He grew increasingly paranoid and later became convinced that his son, Muriel, and his longtime employees were all trying to kill him and take his money. He angrily accused them all of wanting him dead and in the next breath offered them gifts, money, and apologies. It was a sign that Dick's ill health was starting to affect his mind.

Nevertheless, he handed out more money. He set up a $45,000 checking account for Muriel for Christmas, along with a note saying, "May this Christmas and birthday gift bring you happiness whenever you sign your name. This is better than jewels. A big, big kiss, Buck."

That same Christmas, they hosted a party and hunting trip on Sapelo and invited local dignitaries, including Judge Stephen Scarlett of Brunswick, who was newly appointed to a federal judgeship. Muriel wasn't impressed with the judge's promotion and told him, "How can a little country lawyer like you be a federal judge when you have not traveled? You were born and raised in this backward section of Georgia and have never seen the world."

Dick flew into a rage, ordering her to "shut up." Judge Scarlett was offended and asked to be excused. Muriel's elitism and directness was clearly at odds with the genteel ways of the American South.

At another party over the holidays, Dick was ill and couldn't attend, so Muriel hosted on his behalf. When she announced to the guests that Dick would be unable to join them, she remarked that Dick would be "better off dead." Karl Weiss told Dick about it, which further convinced him that Muriel really did want him dead. Karl and Muriel continued to fight. Muriel made menus for him to follow every day and often produced them one hour before he was supposed to serve the meal. No matter how hard he worked, it was never good enough for Muriel. Once he was scrubbing the kitchen with sweat pouring down his cheeks, and Muriel came in and said, "That's right. Whoever wants to work for me has to sweat."

In spite of the fact that Dick constantly accused Muriel of trying to kill him, he bought Muriel a handmade rifle in the early part of 1959 so she could participate in turkey shoots. When they weren't out shooting birds, they were befriending them. Dick had a flock of geese on the island and he decided to keep one of them in the house. He named her Gretel. Dick let Gretel have baths in his bathtub and kept her in his bedroom, even when she relieved herself all over the floor. It didn't take long before Gretel knew the sound of Dick's voice and followed him all over the house.

Dick then became paranoid that the world markets were on the verge of collapsing, so he kept millions of dollars in bearer bonds in Muriel's locked closet and buried gold around the island.

Muriel was not without her own eccentricities. She carried a six-inch knife around with her at all times, at Dick's suggestion, to cut flowers in the garden. Muriel had been intensely interested in gardens her entire life and throughout their marriage, and she felt the servants on the island did a terrible job of maintaining them. So she trimmed them herself, almost obsessively, every day. Her knife-wielding frightened the servants.

The island residents soon noticed that all was not well in Dick and Muriel's land. Once, Dick and Muriel visited Sapelo's school and Muriel refused to smile at the kids, who thought she was snobby and cold. On another occasion, when Dick and Muriel had an argument, he placed dynamite all around a turkey-shaped fountain in the center of the farm complex. BOOM! When the smoke cleared, he had blown all the windows in the surrounding buildings. The turkey statue was still intact.

When Dick wasn't fighting with Muriel, he was in bed, getting worse by the day. The tobacco heir had danced with death several times as a youngster and managed to survive his wild habits. Now, his breathing problems were so serious that he had to have oxygen administered regularly and was heavily medicated most days. After years of world-class jet-setting, the couple now spent nearly all their time on Sapelo Island. Gone were the days when they would visit Pompeii, convinced they were lovers there in previous lives. There were no more outrageous side parties at the Kentucky Derby, one of their favorite events.

These days Dick wanted to spend all his time on Sapelo, his private empire. But Dick was Muriel's only real companion on the remote island and she had grown increasingly ill at ease under the circumstances. They deliberately irritated each other with their oddball behaviors, day in and day out. Dick built a pond on the estate to represent the world's oceans and continents, just because Muriel hated the idea. Muriel read books on voodoo, burned incense in honor of Buddha, and performed witchcraft rituals in Dick's presence, just to make him nervous.

Muriel wrote to her friends that Dick was "still very weak" during March of 1959 and said she'd only been able to take him on two drives around the island. In three months he had been outdoors only twice, and up to dinner only four times. Dick was still interested in developing the island and never gave up on the idea of building a golf course or a resort, which he discussed with Muriel often to keep his mind occupied. His sons visited, including Will, Patrick, and Michael, whom Dick hadn't seen in years.

When Muriel told Dick she thought Michael was a little terror, he claimed that she hated his kids. That wasn't true—she loved his boys and always encouraged Dick to spend more time with them—she just didn't like this one. But Dick was offended and ordered her to leave them alone.

Muriel left for Palm Beach to get away. Her mother, who was also in Florida, was nagging her to visit anyway. Eleanor still pressured Muriel to visit her as much as possible and managed to keep a hold on her all these years.

❧ · ☙

Muriel expressed her exhaustion with taking care of Dick when she wrote to a friend of hers that she needed a long vacation. She'd been away for only twenty days in six months, and by her standards, that was too much time spent on Sapelo Island.

Dick required close monitoring and a strict health plan, which he rarely followed when Muriel was around. The plan was undercut by his continued smoking. Dick had given up the bottle but couldn't shake the cigarettes. He kept his oxygen tank in his bedroom at Sapelo and had a dehumidifier installed in his sitting room.

While Muriel was gone, Dick complained about her constantly. When a servant mistakenly salted Dick's food and blamed Muriel for telling her to do it, Dick once again became convinced that she was trying to kill him. The truth was that no one was killing Dick faster than he himself. On another occasion, Fred Johnson couldn't find Dick's oxygen mask and Dick started to black out. Fred managed to find it under a pile of dirty clothes in the closet. Dick concluded that Muriel had deliberately hidden it.

His rants echoed the past. When Dick was getting tired of Marianne, he fantasized that she had hired a former Mafia boyfriend to murder him. Dick turned on Muriel the same way, taking bits of information and arriving at histrionic conclusions—mainly because he was sick of the marriage.

When Muriel returned from Palm Beach, they argued incessantly. It was worse than before. Dick complained that Muriel ran into his room at three in the morning just to berate him and curse at him—likely because he refused her advances. Dick's attraction to Muriel had steadily waned along with his health, leaving Muriel in need of affection. Dick also accused Muriel of being anti-American, and said she mocked the American way of life even around his friends and guests. Muriel thought Americans were uncultured and she didn't like the commercialism of American television. She had a special loathing for the South, saying, "The average Southern worker is quite good, but a Spanish mañana is like a LeMans racer compared to the mañana of the South." Muriel especially rankled Dick when she made fun of the U.S. Navy. When Dick expressed dismay at her statements, she promised never to repeat them. But she always did, especially after she had a few drinks.

Dick and Muriel had been married for seven years, and together for eight. Although they were from two different worlds, they were equals in intellect and passion, and the pair could have been riding the highs of a marvelous life together. But Dick's drinking and mood swings were more than Muriel could bear, and Dick, who was very down-to-earth in spite of his wealth, grew to loathe Muriel's high-handed snobbery. Soon, Muriel's rude demeanor and constant complaining, along with Dick's inability to make a sustained commitment to love, family, and his health prevailed.

∼ · ∾

In 1959, Dick resigned as director of Delta. He had held the post since 1949 and didn't have the energy for it anymore. The company credited Dick for making it a world-class airline, rivaling all the top airlines in the United States. Dick nominated his old friend and widower of Ella Cannon, Emory Flinn, to take his place. Dick also made moves to sell most of his Delta stock. He had been the largest stockholder his whole life, but it was time to close that chapter as well.

Although Dick had given up many of his business interests—he sold American Mail Line in 1957 and had resigned from most of the business posts he had held throughout his life—he kept himself busy in other ways. He donated money to the New York Maritime College in the Bronx for a new planetarium. He became a permanent resident of Sapelo, and established research programs at the University of Georgia. For years, Dick had experimented with marsh crops before making the decision to turn over large chunks of the island to marine biology research. They had their inaugural salt marsh conference in 1958, and the program would be called the University of Georgia Marine Institute. The program would receive funding from his own Georgia Agricultural and Forestry Foundation, as well as the Sapelo Foundation/Sapelo Island Research Foundation, which Dick had established and financed since 1952, and of which he and Muriel were trustees. In a ceremony at Sapelo, university president O. C. Aderhold recognized him for his generosity. The program and its access to Sapelo Island's unique saltwater marsh wildlife would give the university a huge scientific advantage in marine biology.

Later that year, the North Carolina State College alumni association presented Dick with a meritorious services award and an honorary Ph.D. for his work for the Democratic Party and his funding of agriculture and industry programs at the college. In addition, Dick was credited for establishing the Department of Aeronautical Engineering at the college.

Dick had also been hard at work developing Golden Isles

Airlines, which would merge with the islands' Baker Flying Service and provide service from Georgia's coastal islands to other Southern cities. Dick's goal with Golden Isles was to provide feeder service from small cities and communities in the Southeast that weren't large enough to receive regular airline services. Although Dick had long since given up flying on his own, he enjoyed keeping himself involved in aviation through business interests like this one.

Dick appointed all the officers for the new feeder service and financed the merger. The airline would operate from McKinnon Airport on St. Simon's Island after they built more offices and a hangar for the airline. Dick purchased four twin-engine, nine-seat De Havilland Doves and planned to begin service later in 1959.

In addition, Dick made plans to help build a much-needed $70,000 gymnasium at Darien's local black school. The town was deeply grateful to Dick for making the offer, and the gesture further cemented Dick's reputation in the town. The gym would be called the Richard J. Reynolds Gymnasium.

While Dick earned more fans around town, Muriel earned more enemies. Muriel still felt helpless and trapped on the island and longed for their jet-setting days. The servants continued to bear the brunt of her unhappiness.

After years of putting up with her, Dick's servants couldn't stand Muriel. She wouldn't let them eat the same food she and Dick ate, even if there were leftovers. She ordered them around imperiously. And she still couldn't get along with Karl Weiss. He found her demands outrageous and indefensible, and they butted heads nearly every day. In spite of this, Muriel also confided in Karl and told him where she kept many of her personal effects and private papers in her room. Muriel admitted that Karl's personality got on her nerves, but she always maintained that she had compassion for him because he'd had a difficult life. While

Muriel may have simply been eccentric, complex, and emotionally unstable, it was hard for the victims of her verbal abuse to see it that way.

Summer 1959

Although Dick drove her crazy, Muriel did listen to Dick's medical advisers. His primary caretakers included Dr. Harry Rollings of Atlanta and a nurse named Miss Waxman. Both Rollings and Waxman were appointed by Dr. Valk. Dr. Rollings, a native of Hattiesburg, Mississippi, had been the chief surgeon of Hunter Air Force Base during the war. In June of 1959, Dick convinced Dr. Rollings to order Muriel off the island and give them both a much needed break. Rollings wrote letters to Muriel, saying that her own smoking and the arguing between them was harming Dick's health and encouraged her to get away. Muriel was reluctant—something didn't feel right about it. But she did need a vacation, and her mother, now back in England, was begging her to visit. Perhaps Dick needed the space, Muriel reasoned. He had just sent his sons off on a long trip to Nairobi as well, so maybe everyone needed to be kicked out for a while.

On June 17, the morning of her departure, Muriel woke up early and Dick came to her bedroom for a couple of hours. They had breakfast together, and Muriel gave Dick a bath with the help of his servant, James Banks. She washed his hair and styled it, and cut his fingernails, as she always did. She put him in fresh pajamas and they sat and talked until 11:30 while she finished packing. Her plane was leaving at four that day, so after she put Dick to bed for his afternoon nap, she held his hand until he drifted off. Before he fell asleep, he said, "You don't mind, darling, if I don't go to the airport?"

"Not at all. Tom Durant will take me . . . are you sure you want me to leave you?" Muriel asked as she kissed him goodbye.

Dick insisted she take the trip and assured her that he would be all right, saying, "Write me very long letters every week. Put all the local news in the world in it," and sweet-talked her all the way out his bedroom door.

Before she left, she took $200,000 in bearer bonds out of her locked closet to take on the trip. Dick always left her in charge of the bonds and Muriel considered them joint property.

Muriel said goodbye to nurse Waxman and the staff and boarded her private plane at the Sapelo hangar with enough luggage to last her the rest of the summer. She waved goodbye to Tom Durant.

Muriel arrived in New York, where she would tend to some business for a few weeks before going to Europe. For months, Muriel had been working with Strat Coyner on setting up a new will. On July 2, she received her new will from Coyner and executed it in New York. She made Dick the beneficiary but added provisions for charity. Coyner was in constant contact with her while she finalized it.

Before she left for Europe, she went to Cartier and picked up a $100,000 bracelet—just a little something to dress up her evening wear on the French Riviera.

Finally, she flew to Paris, where a car and chauffeur that Dick had arranged met her at the airport. Muriel made her way to the Riviera, spending most of her time in Monte Carlo where she played her favorite game of chemin de fer. Gambling was always a great weakness.

She wrote Dick gossipy, colorful letters and sent him gifts along the way, including records she thought he would enjoy. On July 15, Dick sent her a telegram saying he was playing the records she sent at five that morning. Throughout the trip, Muriel stayed in touch with Dick constantly, checking on his health and general status. He sent her lovely letters at each hotel she stayed in and expressed how much he missed her. He even sent her $200 worth of flowers on their anniversary. It had been the first extended amount of time they'd spent apart since their marriage.

On August 15, Dick called and they talked for an hour and a half. He asked where she was going to stay and suggested she go to London. Muriel said she'd go to Biarritz first, and then on the 1st of September she'd go to London and stay until the 15th, at which time she would return to Sapelo. "Which hotel are you staying at again?" Dick asked. Muriel said, "The Hôtel Le Café de Paris in Biarritz."

"What's the exact address? Can you spell it?" Dick asked. Muriel recited the address. Dick went on to say he couldn't wait for her return and sent her a telegram later that day repeating the same.

The morning of August 16, Muriel received a call from Dick's lawyer, Frank Wells. Frank said he was in Biarritz. "What are you doing here?" Muriel asked. Frank said, "I've got something serious to discuss."

After years of Dick's drinking, illness, and brushes with death, Muriel panicked. "Oh my God, is Dick all right?"

"Yes, yes. Dick is all right. But I need to discuss something with you at your hotel." Unconvinced, Muriel said that was fine. Half an hour later, he showed up, along with his Paris associate Charles Torem.

"Come in, come in," Muriel said anxiously. "Have a cup of coffee."

Frank declined and abruptly said, "We have come to tell you that your husband is through."

"What?" Muriel asked. "I don't understand."

Frank handed her divorce papers and the two disappeared. It was the coup de grâce.

Muriel thought, *Is this a joke?* It must have been a joke. She had just spoken to Dick yesterday. The file accused Muriel of stealing the bearer bonds, buying an expensive bracelet for herself, infidelity as discovered in her personal diaries, and changing her will without telling Dick. The grounds for divorce were mental cruelty.

Muriel had just become the next victim of Dick's complete doorstopping technique: the smoke screen, the dispatch of lawyers, the residency trick (which she didn't yet know), and the final blow. She didn't believe it at first, thinking Dick was simply sick or drunk and was throwing another temper tantrum, although she was furious that he had been reading her diaries. Many of them dated from 1937, well before she knew Dick, but they were still personal and intimate. Muriel would return to America right away and find out what was going on.

It wasn't until she flew to New York and Dick's lawyers converged on her again that she realized the preposterous divorce papers were real.

Muriel was devastated.

CHAPTER 17

Darien

1959–1963

Muriel's initial reaction was to fly back to Sapelo immediately and get Frank Wells, Dick's sister Nancy, and her own brother, Tony, who was still a very good friend of Dick's, to help her persuade Dick to rethink his move. She wrote a desperate letter to Nancy, begging her to intervene and telling her not to believe the things Dick said. But she received an "icy reply" in return.

Then Muriel appealed to Dick directly. She begged him to reconsider and accused the doctors and the nurse of conspiring to turn him against her. Her letters were mixed with anger, sadness, and demands. When she tried to call Dick and he hung up on her, she fought back. She wrote him a letter warning that she would fight him to the bitter end and if he wanted to get rid of her, they could get a quick divorce in Reno and settle right then for $2 million.

Dick refused. He wasn't about to give Muriel a dime. There

was already a lot of talk around town of Muriel's diaries and her supposed infidelity, and Dick was furious about it. Muriel wrote to Nancy saying she kept those diaries unlocked for a reason—there was nothing to hide.

Then Muriel wondered if Dick had found another woman. She had certainly witnessed his shenanigans when he was trying to divorce Marianne. Maybe he was up to his old tricks again.

Muriel appealed to Dick directly yet again. She wrote him saying, "The medicine is affecting your judgment. The accusations are absurd. You have always let me cut the bonds...they are part of the trust...you told me to keep them in the box. I didn't steal them. As for the bracelet, you never used to have problems with things like this. Cartier gave me a great price... that was two months ago and you never said anything...love does not turn off and on like an electric light bulb....Your broken hearted wife."

Muriel also defended her changing her will, saying she never disinherited Dick and even used his lawyer to make the changes. What was so wrong with that? Strat Coyner had reported the change of will to Dick, she pointed out. She wasn't trying to hide it. It also occurred to Muriel that Karl, who knew where her diaries were kept, must have directed Dick to the chest in her room. She wondered who else had betrayed her at Sapelo.

Dick's complaints about the bonds continued to perplex her. They were right there in her closet, in the safe, she reasoned. She had always been in charge of them. Muriel even sent Dick the coupons and receipts from New York after she cashed them. Did he not receive the box? And what of all the letters he sent her all summer, signed "with a heart full of love from ole Buck Rabbit"? Muriel continued to suspect that Dick was out of his mind when he filed for this divorce. Maybe he would come around.

While she shopped for lawyers, Muriel consoled herself at El Morocco, the Key Club, the Stork Club, and "21" with her friends. But she felt she was living her worst nightmare. After all she had done for Dick, this was the thanks she got. Of course, Eleanor made things worse—she demanded that Muriel find a way to hang on to Dick, or at the very least, take him for all he was worth. Muriel sadly told reporters, "If this man doesn't like me anymore, all he has to do is meet me with my brother or my family like a gentleman, tell me the truth, instead of which the divorce was thrown in my face."

Muriel's society friends in Winston-Salem also expressed shock at Dick's actions. No one saw it coming. They told Muriel how excited they had been when Dick found her—"someone he could converse intelligently with after his two other great mistakes. Who would either gamble with him at Monte Carlo or run the vacuum cleaner at Fancy Gap! Could have twenty for a formal dinner or steak sandwiches in the trailer," wrote Dr. Valk's wife, Bungy.

~ · ~

Meanwhile, Dick moved to dump as many assets as he could. He was tired of living with Muriel's constant complaining, he was sick, and he wanted to live in peace for once in his life. In fact, he wanted to be rid of everyone, including his sons, who he now felt were nothing more than leeches, too. Dick got into an argument with his son Zach when he asked to buy a Sapelo jeep. Dick inexplicably grew furious, accused him of trying to take his money like Muriel, and kicked him out of the house. Dick wanted to be alone for good.

He gave $442,000 to his agricultural foundation, $10,000 to the local Presbyterian Hospital, nearly $2 million to the University of Georgia, and he donated the *Aries,* which had too many memories with Muriel, to the Woods Hole Oceanographic Institute. He also revoked the $6 million trust he had set up for Muriel.

Fearing Muriel would try to get to Sapelo, Dick stationed

guards all over the island—the Meridian Dock, the Salt Marsh Dock, and at the house. He advised his servants to "shoot first and ask questions later." Then Dick had his lawyers serve Muriel with a restraining order at her apartment at the Ritz Tower. The order said that Muriel had threatened him, his nurse, and his doctor, citing her letters to them all, and said they all feared for their lives.

Her little Ritz flat, room 503, would soon be the site of many more servings of motions. Private investigators from the Schindler Bureau of Investigation, including Walter Russell and Shelby Williams, followed Muriel all over town. They served her in front of Fortieth Street, Madison Avenue, Seventy-ninth Street (Richard Greenough's place), the Hotel Astor at Broadway, the Park Sheraton, and more.

Muriel hired one of the best lawyers she could find, Smythe Gambrell of Atlanta, on recommendation from Louis Nizer, renowned attorney to the stars. Nizer had been Marianne's lawyer when she divorced Dick in 1952. Gambrell was one of the best lawyers in the South and he was also counsel for Eastern Airlines, Dick's former investment and rival to Delta.

～ · ～

Throughout the fall, depositions and subpoenas were taken from and issued to Dick and Muriel, and Dick subpoenaed his witnesses—Irma and Arved Rosing, Captain Evans in Gosport, Dr. Harry Rollings, Dr. Henry Valk, jeweler Louis Cartier, Charles Torem, the representatives of the Montreal Trust Company and the Royal Bank of Canada, and Strat Coyner—and that was only the beginning. Muriel concluded that Dick meant to highlight every negative incident in their marriage—the spats with the servants and the workers at Gosport, the disagreements with his doctors, the time she wired the half million to herself after Copenhagen, and the disputed bracelet from Cartier—all to prove his claim of mental cruelty.

Once Muriel realized the case was definitely going forward, she turned up the attacks as well. No more tears, no more grief. She was going to take Dick for all he was worth. Once again, Dick had underestimated his opponent.

Muriel knew Dick's strategy, and she would use it to her advantage. She realized that Dick had been tricking her all along—the letters, the flowers, encouraging her to take a holiday. He always tricked his soon-to-be ex-wives in order to catch them off guard right before he filed for divorce. Muriel had seen it firsthand during his divorce from Marianne.

They went back and forth for months, filing hundreds of motions to produce. Muriel's lawyers were going to tell the jury all about Dick's drinking. They wanted all of Dick's booze bills for the last seven years. For every incident of Muriel's alleged cruelty, she was going to match it with an incident of Dick's drinking.

The exchange of motions, written interrogatories, and subpoenas that were exchanged throughout late 1959 and early 1960 seemed to last forever. In the spring of 1960, it was finally time to go to trial.

~ · ~

The divorce proceedings were held at the Darien, Georgia, courthouse, which served as the seat of McIntosh County, and were launched on May 2, 1960. Sixty local jurors, including members of the politically connected Poppell family and Frank Durant, were selected for the trial. Witnesses from Europe and all over the United States would provide testimony in support of Dick's charges that Muriel's cruelty exacerbated his pulmonary emphysema and threatened his health.

Muriel was still in shock over Dick's actions and stupefied by her own inability to see it coming. Muriel was only in her mid-forties and thought she would spend the rest of her life with

Dick. She should have known this would happen. Sooner or later, Dick always left his wives.

Muriel's lawyers opened with the position that "mental cruelty" was not grounds for divorce in Georgia. Muriel angrily denied the accusations anyway—what Dick perceived as nagging, Muriel said, was simply her insistence that he take his medicine and continue treatment for alcoholism. Muriel's attorney, Smythe Gambrell, opened by stating that he was trying to find the reason for the "baffling mystery" of Mr Reynolds's suit against Muriel, as well as the paranoid restraining order he issued. Gambrell also pointed out that Dick had been writing and phoning Muriel almost daily throughout her summer vacation, leading them to believe he deliberately tricked her. If he had, this would also be grounds to refuse a divorce to Dick.

Dick's Savannah lawyer, Paul Varner, whom Muriel knew well, said in his opening statement, "We're going to lay it on her and we're going to tear her to pieces, piece by piece and thread by thread. We're going to tear her to pieces in this courtroom and throw her out the window." With that, Varner set the tone.

Both Dick and Muriel had an army of lawyers, and both sides engaged in vicious attacks. Dick's lawyers paraded the prenuptial agreement that Muriel had signed in 1952, warning the jury that if they found favor with Dick in this case, they should consider giving Muriel no alimony because of it. Muriel's lawyers accused Dick of being a sadist.

Witness depositions were soon recited. Irma and Arved Rosing testified to Muriel's meanness toward them and the chef, Karl Weiss, on the *Aries*. Drs. Harry Rollings and Henry Valk testified that Muriel made Dick's health worse. Admiral Durgin and Price Gilbert, from Dick's wartime days, testified to Dick's character, and Nancy testified that she received desperate letters from Muriel.

Dick's financial life became an important issue. As Strat

Coyner, Dick's ever-present cleanup guy, served as a witness for Dick, he had a hard time looking Muriel in the eye. Under examination by one of Muriel's lawyers, Robert Richardson, Strat disclosed that Dick owned a company called Netherlands Meade that was a foreign corporation. Dick had created it for the express purpose of making foreign investments, including fine gold, which he kept in Switzerland. This piece of information was to become important in just a few years. Richardson went on to question Coyner about Dick's income and expenses in an attempt to show what Dick was worth, how extravagantly he lived, and his standard of living while he was married to Muriel.

Coyner also testified that he knew Dick was talking about divorce after Muriel left the summer before, but he didn't tell her—even as he was working on her will. Coyner was forced to admit that Muriel was very good to his own wife, having bought her clothing and gifts, and that she was popular among Winston-Salem society.

John Gates, current master of the *Aries,* testified as to Dick's and Muriel's conduct on their yachts over the years. Gates also told the court that Muriel cursed too much and encouraged Dick's drinking, even when he was trying to quit.

Muriel Takes the Stand

On direct examination, Muriel talked about her marriage with Dick and recalled their wedding. "Karl Weiss baked a cake, the housekeeper made a lovely hat of gardenias to wear, Karl put lanterns in the garden," she said. Muriel pointed out that all of Dick's attorneys, now there fighting her, had witnessed Dick's signing of the drinking agreement, which trumped the prenuptial agreement of 1952.

On cross-examination, Muriel was criticized for going to El

Morocco and spending hundreds of dollars while trying to portray herself as the poor victimized wife. She countered that it cost four times as much to have a meal shipped in to Sapelo.

To obtain some sort of settlement, Muriel had a fight on her hands. Even a fraction of Blitz's and Marianne's settlements would be difficult because of the prenuptial agreement and the fact that she and Dick had no children. Dick had settled with his previous two wives for around $11 million. Even though Dick had almost instantly broken his alcohol contract, no one took that document seriously. Muriel was asking for $2 million, and in spite of Dick's large settlements in the past, the press was heavily publicizing the sum.

Muriel had lost the battle before she'd even begun when Gambrell failed to get a relocation of the trial. Muriel's legal team argued it was impossible for Muriel to get a fair trial in McIntosh County, where Dick was one of the county's most prominent citizens as well as one of its largest employers and benefactors. Dick owned one quarter of the land in the county, and his many lavish gifts would undoubtedly sway public opinion in his favor.

Dick had conveniently and cleverly established legal residency on Sapelo—the residency trick—which he had owned for almost twenty-five years, just six months before he filed for divorce. The entire town of Darien was either directly employed by, or benefited from, Dick Reynolds. Even the city's energy was supplied by Dick. The sheriff had just received a handsome donation from Dick, and the judges and lawyers were all Dick's friends or business partners. Muriel's legal team requested a change in location. But the judge denied the motion. Now Muriel would be at the mercy of those "backwoods" Southerners she used to mock.

Throughout the interrogation, Muriel managed to stay calm and even maintain her sense of humor, even though she was dying inside. She swore to the jury that she would have loved Dick if he had no money at all.

The half-million-dollar money transfer after the Copenhagen incident came up in court. Muriel testified that Dick pulled anchor and left her stranded without funds or even clothes, which was why she had withdrawn the money. It came out that in order to make the transfer, Muriel had to forge Dick's hand. Muriel said this was normal. She had done it "thousands of times during Dick's seven years' intoxication" and claimed she had done nothing wrong because she didn't even spend the money. It was fully intact two weeks later, "as safe in a joint account with me as it would be in Fort Knox."

~ · ~

As the court heard hundreds of pages of depositions and testimony and the tedious trial continued, one thing was missing: Dick. The presiding judge, Henry Durrence, ruled that Dick was too ill to appear in court. Instead, an oral deposition was taken from Dick on Sapelo by a court-appointed reporter, Mrs. Minnie Lee Johnson, and all of his accusations were read in court by his attorneys. Dick was supposedly living alone in paranoia with his servants and Nancy, who was on Sapelo during Dick's depositions. When Dick claimed to be too sick to come to court, Muriel's lawyers said that being impaired by excessive use of whiskey and tobacco did not constitute an inability to answer questions. Gambrell said Dick was being allowed to hide out from Muriel and demanded the right to question Dick personally.

When Gambrell finally had the chance to interview Dick on Sapelo Island, he was flippant and sarcastic, sometimes refusing to answer questions altogether. Dick dismissed questions about his foundations and their worth, saying, "It has nothing to do with the case." He refused to answer questions or submit evidence of how much he drank. When Gambrell pressed him about his net worth, Dick finally admitted he was worth about $25 million—far less than he really was. Gambrell asked him questions about his divorces from Blitz and Marianne, trying to get him to admit that he used trickery and a change in residency in all his divorces. Finally caught using his old tricks, Dick refused to answer.

Gambrell turned to the possibility of other women. When asked if he had any intention of reconciling with Marianne, Dick said "NO, with a capital N and O." When he was asked if he ever wished to marry again, he said, "NO with a capital N and O, underscored."

Dick reported that Muriel had a "fiendish temper," and he lived in constant terror. She frequently mentioned that she wished he were dead and asked doctors how long he had to live. Dick brought up the voodoo and witchcraft, saying, "She had a way of shuffling cards." He said Muriel had people to do her bidding, and that she was a Gypsy who could see the future. He claimed he kept his bedroom door locked at night because Muriel boasted of her underworld connections.

Underworld connections? Muriel felt she was in a dream—reliving what must have been Marianne's ordeal with Dick. How could he be so predictable?

When Gambrell asked about their sex life, Dick said he hadn't slept in the same bed with Muriel since January 1, 1959. Dick repeated his claim that Muriel's diaries revealed that she was with former lovers throughout their marriage. Muriel countered that both she and Dick were friends with many of her exes, including Richard Greenough, who was mentioned in the diaries, and whenever she was with him, she never did anything wrong. Muriel said many of the diary entries dated back to 1937, long before she met Dick.

Muriel's lawyers asked why the diaries weren't entered into

evidence if there was damning information in them. Dick's camp claimed that they did not expose the diaries because international society was very worried about who and what was in them, and they didn't want to offend anyone. In the end, most observers concluded the diaries likely never had anything of interest in them—Dick could have easily presented them and saved himself a lot of time and money.

It turned out that Muriel was guilty of one thing—gambling away her money in Monte Carlo. Dick revealed that he had private detectives follow her during her entire vacation—one of the men who Muriel thought was her chauffeur was actually a private investigator, and Dick had spent $56,000 just to have her followed. None of the investigators caught Muriel doing anything wrong.

Then Dick accused Muriel of sending her mother's friend Cedric Taylor to spy on him at Sapelo. In fact, Dick had flown Cedric down to Sapelo, at his expense, to show him her diaries after he cracked them open. He wanted to turn Cedric against her. Dick even told Cedric that he would kill Muriel with a pistol if he saw her.

The trial dragged on. Numerous letters were entered into evidence on both sides, including letters from Muriel to Dick's friends and associates after he sued her for divorce, and letters between Muriel and Dick throughout 1959, affectionately written and signed by Dick's and Muriel's pet names for each other, "Buck Rabbit" and "Doe."

As headlines portrayed Dick as a "hard-living heir now confined by ill health to his private island," "sick" Dick was on a cruise in England with his sister.

In the end, the jurors, many of whom benefited from Dick's spending habits serving as the county's biggest industry, ruled in Dick's favor. On May 16, 1960, the jury awarded Dick his divorce and granted Muriel $1,042 per month in alimony. It was a fraction of what Muriel felt Dick owed her.

A New Love

Far away from it all, Christian Nissen joined Dick onboard the *Natalie* along with Nancy and her new husband, expert yachts-man Gilbert Verney, as well as her kids. Nancy had also become good friends with Nissen in 1957, shortly after she divorced Henry Bagley.

On the cruise, Nissen noted Dick's failing health and recommended a doctor he knew in Bad Harzburg, East Germany—a man named Hans Lindemann. Dick went to the clinic on his advice. During his stay, Dr. Lindemann's wife, Ilsa, introduced Dick to a young woman, Annemarie Schmitt, who had a doctorate in philosophy. According to Dick, he fell in love with Annemarie in a matter of weeks. With the ink barely dry on his divorce, Dick proposed. He had obviously changed his mind about never marrying again.

Back in America, society circles had already written the obituary on Dick and Muriel's marriage. Friends and associates who had once thought that Dick and Muriel had finally found lasting love after two divorces each, feverishly discussed the trial details. Muriel went from gifts of $125,000 in spending money, $40,000 worth of jewels, the $6 million–dollar revocable trust fund, and a $45,000 checking account to a measly $1,000-a-month alimony check. Muriel poured her dwindling funds into an appeal.

Gambrell and company spent the next year putting together motions for a new trial. Their first appeal, with Judge Durrence, was denied in the fall of 1960. Meanwhile, Dick courted his new lover while his lawyers kept him up to date on the chances of an appeal. Gambrell appealed again the following spring, March of 1961. Muriel was denied a new trial. Dick was waiting for that call.

When Dick got news that there was little chance an appeal would ever be granted, he did what he always did when he was officially a free man—he immediately made moves to wed his new lover. He and Annemarie were sailing in the South China Sea on the SS *Rotterdam,* and Dick had a reverend onboard, ready for that moment. On March 15, 1961, the ceremony took place without delay.

Dick boldly brought Annemarie to Sapelo for their honeymoon, as the news of his new marriage to a pretty young German woman reached America. Annemarie would soon be sleeping in Muriel's bed.

Dick issued a four-page statement through an Atlanta public relations firm explaining his new marriage and the circumstances of his divorce, in coded language meant for Muriel's lawyers. In it he said something strange that many believed was untrue: "I'm not the wealthy individual that some people seem to think I am, having given away the bulk of my fortune to various charities and universities and having only enough of my money to live comfortably after paying taxes."

Muriel was stunned by Dick's new marriage, telling reporters, "I am shocked. The world, no doubt, is beginning to understand what I have been made to endure. I have every confidence that the courts of Georgia in which our case is still pending will see that justice is done." Her lawyers announced that Dick had no right to marry, and that he was improperly living with a woman when he knew his divorce decree was still being challenged. Muriel immediately hired spies of her own.

The Appeal

On September 8, 1961, Justice Grady Head of the Georgia Supreme Court ruled that Muriel would get her appeal, based on several mistakes—thirty-nine errors to be exact—made by both Judge Durrence and Dick's lawyers in the first trial. Justice Head stated the trial contained "numerous errors of procedure and evidence" and that some of the evidence was irrelevant and prejudicial to Muriel. Muriel's team was jubilant. The divorce decree was immediately nullified and a retrial ordered. Dick heard the news while he was in Friedrichshafen, Germany, with Annemarie, now officially, or unofficially, his fourth wife. Some things never changed in Dick's world. There he was, again, with major "unfinished business" getting in the way of a new love. He had underestimated Blitz and Marianne, but he was in for the fight of his life with Muriel.

Having already been humiliated, publicly and privately, by Dick's attempts to dispose of her, Muriel vowed to fight harder. She wanted the entire $6 million from the trust Dick set up for her and had since revoked, and she wouldn't settle until she got it. Dick said this request was ridiculous since they had no children. Muriel didn't care.

Muriel's team of lawyers tried again to get a change of venue to another county in the opening hours of the trial. The concerns about bias in the first trial were supported by several revelations. One juror from the first trial admitted to favoring Dick. Sheriff Poppell, who handled all the subpoenas, had gone out of his jurisdiction and joined Dick's Savannah attorney, Paul Varner, on a trip to New York to serve Muriel with divorce papers. Poppell had also proudly testified to being a loyal supporter of Reynolds, admitted dining with witnesses, and conceded he probably wasn't fit to handle divorce proceedings. Gambrell cited nearly $69,000 in local government and civic bonds in 1960 alone as well as Dick's $60,000 donation to the R. J. Reynolds Gymnasium at Todd Grant High School, and the tens of thousands of dollars he had given to the city since he'd been married to Muriel. Gambrell said there was no way Muriel could have an unbiased trial in the little town.

The presiding Superior Court judge, J. K. Whaley, again denied the motion for a change of venue but promised Muriel she'd get a fair trial. However, Muriel's legal team was successful in requiring that Dick be present this time.

Dick and Annemarie

During the fall of 1961, Dick and Annemarie, a modest, conservative-looking young woman, took long walks at night along the peaceful lakeside of Locarno, Switzerland. They strolled the narrow streets, lined with flower boxes, as the little village sparkled and twinkled with lights. It was a place one would never expect to find an American millionaire now engaged in bigamy with a young German scholar. Neatly parked streetcars lined the roadways, rugged Alps dotted the horizon, small rowboats bobbed up and down as the lake water lapped along the boardwalk. A dainty wrought iron fence protected passersby. Locarno was clean, organized, meticulous, and quiet. Their hotel was boxy, stale, safe, and uncontroversial. So unlike Dick's exotic locales and fancy homes during his marriage to Muriel. This was a new era for Dick—the age of Annemarie.

As they strolled along one evening, Annemarie walked submissively behind Dick, bundled up in a white coat. Dick's oxygen tank was notably absent, and they held hands on their way to dinner. At a quiet, empty restaurant, they sat side by side in a booth. They talked more like old friends. Dick's voice often dropped off as he stared out into the distance. Dick had a lot on his mind, and he didn't feel well. Annemarie gently tried to get Dick's attention before giving up and staring off into space herself.

On the way back, they didn't hold hands. Perhaps they knew they were being followed—by now Dick had heard about Muriel's new appeal. Annemarie lugged her heavy purse by herself. Dick carried papers of some sort in his hand. The street was virtually empty except for the occasional streetcar or shop owner. Just Dick and his bride, living in isolation. Gone were the days of Dick's partying and jet-setting. Gone was the fun-loving, full-of-life Dick Reynolds.

The Second Trial

On May 6, 1962, the Darien courthouse was packed with reporters and columnists. Darien locals streamed in to hear the gossipy details of Dick and Muriel's life, and everyone was eager to get a glimpse of poor, dear Dick Reynolds. He came in with his entourage of assistants, doctors, and lawyers, and his oxygen mask firmly attached to his wheezing face, for which he gained a significant amount of sympathy. Muriel's lawyers began to wonder if they'd been better off if he hadn't shown up. Just a week before, Dick had been photographed smiling broadly at the courthouse for a deposition where Muriel's attorneys grilled him. Muriel, who hadn't seen Dick in two and a half years, couldn't even look at him without tearing up, nor could he look at her. He had a new life and a new wife now, and this was the last place on earth he wanted to be. The trial got underway.

Graphic and riveting details of Dick and Muriel's life together were revealed once again. This trial was almost identical to the first: It had all the same drama, viciousness, and legal maneu-vering—plus Dick and an oxygen tank. The epic divorce was quickly becoming the stuff of legend, and the testimony, which was at some times dramatic and at others downright funny, was fit for the big screen.

Christian Nissen had flown to Georgia and volunteered to testify against Muriel for both trials. He recounted the Copen-hagen incident and implied that Dick was forced to fire the Rosings because of Muriel. He also testified that Muriel never wanted American citizenship as proof of her anti-American sen-timent. She complained that the American Navy was worthless, which upset Dick, and said Americans had no culture, didn't eat properly, and couldn't dress.

"Dick would get so mad," Nissen said.

Under cross-examination, Nissen was forced to admit that Dick didn't like the British either, especially because of his prison time. He also admitted that the Rosings were discharged mainly because they were ill, not because of Muriel, who was not on the ship when they left. Muriel's lawyers asked if he listened to Dick's playing tapes of the first trial as he often did with his friends for his own amusement. Nissen claimed that he did not participate in such activities, but courtroom observers were nonetheless disturbed by the knowledge that Dick was replaying the tapes. Then Muriel's lawyers revealed to the court that Nissen was once a Nazi spy and had received the Iron Cross for his service. Dick's witnesses weren't looking too good.

Guenther Lehman, who had just returned from a brief period of service in the Navy, testified to Muriel's rudeness on the yacht. He said Muriel was disgusted by how everything in America was mass-produced. But Lehman admitted that he got along well with her. She used to order him around at first, and one time she put a big sign in the yacht's galley that said, "THINK." Lehman confronted her about it and tore down the sign. Muriel just "had a terrible desire to manage people," Lehman said.

Dick Takes the Stand

After several of Dick's witnesses testified, Dick finally took the stand, wheezing into his oxygen mask. As he sat in the box, he again accused Muriel of vicious cruelty and of trying to kill him. He brought up the time Muriel had allegedly ordered the servants to salt his food and said she blew smoke in his face when he was trying to quit smoking. He dramatically emphasized the garden knife and the occult activities. Muriel's lawyers challenged him, saying Dick told her to use the knife for gardening and had never complained about it till now.

Dick then claimed Muriel was really trying to kill him with

cruelty. He said that Muriel got him so upset he threw up his lunches. "Two months prior to her leaving, I had lunch brought in on a tray, and she'd say, 'This food is slop, it's trash, the cook is no good, you ought to throw it all in the garbage can.' I'd say, 'Please leave this room. Let me eat in peace for god's sake.' And she wouldn't leave." Dick recounted all of the times Muriel mocked his friends and associates, which he said traumatized him. When he got upset, she always promised she would never say mean things again, but she always did.

Then Dick accused Muriel of forcing him to sell his 25,000 shares of RJR Tobacco stock too early. He said if he would have waited, he would have made millions more. Dick entered into evidence the yellow paper tablet showing the 1958 sale and said Muriel had a fit when she bought a pack of Camels and saw that the camel illustration was removed. She convinced Dick to sell based on that. On cross-examination, Dick was forced to admit that he also was mad that they had changed the logo without consulting him, and he had made millions of dollars on that sale. Later, Strat Coyner testified that lots of people sold at that time, and it was unlikely that Muriel was the only one who influenced Dick. "He just thought it was a good time to sell," Coyner said.

Meanwhile, the court learned, Dick had fired Coyner, his lawyer of thirty years, over his dealings with Muriel and her will. Ledyard Staples handled the paperwork now. Muriel was stunned. *What has gotten into Dick?* Muriel thought. *He's losing his mind.*

Muriel's lawyers reminded the court of Dick's pet, Gretel the goose, to show that Dick had, in fact, lost his mind. Frank Durant took the stand and defended Dick's love for the goose, saying, "He likes animals."

Dick expressed resentment over Muriel having a "whopping good time" with her mother and there were hints of Dick's exhaustion with regard to Eleanor. As Muriel listened, she quietly cursed her mother for helping to ruin yet another marriage

Then Dick charged Muriel with the oddest claim yet—he said Muriel had faked her pregnancy to stop him from divorcing her in 1954 after she took the half million dollars in Copenhagen. Dick said there was never any proof that she was pregnant or miscarried and it was evidence of her deceiving ways. Dick's claims were never proven, and Muriel produced all of the doctor's reports and the certificate of fetal death in response.

Muriel continued to present herself as the poor, penniless wife in her effort to get more alimony. This seemed ridiculous, as she surrounded herself with lawyers worth hundreds of thousands of dollars. Jurors didn't believe she was suffering in New York either—her Park Avenue address alone was synonymous with luxury. But Muriel did a good job of pointing out that compared to Dick's standards and the way she was accustomed to living, it was a significant downgrade. Dick's lawyers protested by showing the jury pictures of the lobby. Muriel said, "I don't own the building and I don't live in the lobby. I live in a fifteen-by-fifteen room." Aaron Kravitch, one of Dick's eight lawyers, reminded her that she had entered pictures of Dick's lobby into evidence the day before. Muriel said, "He owns his lobby." She went on to note that Dick owned a hotel in Tennessee that was the same size as the whole Park Avenue building in which she lived.

When Dick accused Muriel of extravagance, it seemed preposterous in light of the way he lived. Muriel's lawyers tracked down evidence of Dick's own extravagance, and his extensive travel while he was supposedly sick—Dick ordered tickets to the Kentucky Derby just two months before the trial and had tens of thousands of dollars' worth of filet mignon, assorted steaks, lobster, frog legs, and king crab delivered to Sapelo via Delta Air Freight.

Dick then accused Muriel of hating his kids. She replied that she had been close to his older sons during their marriage. She admitted to complaining about Michael, but he was the only one. Dick said that she hated "the little brats."

Dick's lawyers then delivered a special surprise. They entered letters, courtesy of Marianne O'Brien, into evidence—all sealed with the red wax that Muriel used on all her letters, and signed, "Danger Jones" and "BW." The 1952 letters from Danger Jones to Marianne accused her of sleeping with everyone, including Frank Sinatra, and called her a penniless, failed Hollywood actress and "a hard-boiled gangster's moll with a foul mouth who never lifted a finger to care for Dick." Marianne, eager for revenge against Muriel, brought them to Dick's lawyers the same day Muriel left the island in 1959. Handwriting experts confirmed they were Muriel's letters. While they were an attempt to prove Muriel's cruelty, they also worked against Dick—further proving he had tricked Muriel off the island and was planning the divorce all along.

Dick's lawyers accused Muriel of hoping he would die before the divorce was final and dragging out the divorce proceedings for that purpose. Muriel's lawyers responded that Dick could have easily settled with Muriel, but he was trying to starve her out until she ran out of money. Gambrell went on to say that Dick's entire mental cruelty charge was a sham. The bearer bonds and money didn't work, the servants' arguments were weak, and the alleged infidelity didn't work. Torem collected reports from the private investigators the entire time Muriel was in Paris, and when nothing else worked, Dick drummed up the not-so-original idea of mental cruelty.

As Gambrell then accused Dick of adultery and bigamy, the trial took a new turn.

Adultery with Annemarie

Muriel produced dozens of exhibits: envelopes and stationery monogrammed "Dr. Annemarie Schmitt Reynolds," huge checks written out to Annemarie in 1960, their *Rotterdam* itinerary, photos of the two of them together, and statements from Berg-dorf Goodman — they had mistakenly sent receipts for items for Annemarie to Muriel's house.

The exhibits, which included his passport, made a mockery of Dick's claims that he was too sick to go to court — he had obtained visas for Nepal and actually traveled to Canada, Hong Kong, Bombay, Holland, Thailand, Japan, France, Norway, Egypt, and other countries. The couple was caught at the Park Hotel in Bremen, where Muriel's private investigators snapped photos of the floors they occupied. There were photos of their mailbox at the La Palma resort in Locarno, Switzerland, and photos of them eating at various restaurants together. There they were, romancing each other, just as Dick had done with Muriel not so long ago during his divorce with Marianne.

Muriel produced airline stubs, their marriage certificate, and a statement by Rev. Charles Nabers, who married them in the South China Sea. Their official witnesses were Hans and Ilsa Lindemann.

Muriel's lawyers also revealed that Annemarie had refused a subpoena that was delivered to her on May 26, 1961, and had continued to evade their requests to take her deposition. This didn't look good. Dick's attorneys took action.

～·～

Finally, the court would hear from the mystery woman. Annemarie never did appear in court, but she delivered a stipu-lation. The lengthy explanation stated that she and Dick met in the fall of 1960, spent time in Paris, and traveled to Tucson where they registered at a hotel under the false name "A. B. Car-ling." She said Dick paid for everything and gave her $200,000 in jewels, furs, and gifts. In November 1960, she went to Sapelo, stayed in Florida for a week, quit her job in Europe, and took a trip on the *Rotterdam* with Dick, where they got married in March. She lived on Sapelo afterward and then moved with

Dick to Locarno, where they stayed from June till November 1961. While on Sapelo, the sheriff served her and Dick with the subpoena but Dick told her she didn't have to obey it.

She then went to Nassau on November 30, 1961, while Dick went to Georgia to testify, and he joined her in Nassau in December. Dick paid for a two-year lease at the La Palma Hotel in Locarno in Annemarie's name.

She admitted influencing Dick to transfer more than $1 million to European investments and persuaded him to make more investments in Germany and other European spots in the future. Annemarie said that Dick gave her additional gifts in excess of $400,000 since November 1960, which included a Mercedes-Benz, a Porsche, stock in her former company, diamonds, and furs.

Muriel's lawyers asked the jurors to take note of the amount of money Dick gave Annemarie in this short amount of time, proving how much Dick could spend on a woman who wasn't even his legal wife. Muriel knew all too well how much Dick spoiled his mistresses.

Closing Arguments

Muriel's attorneys laid out the facts for a case that should have been easy for them to win.

Dick's marriage was proof of bigamy and adultery and Dick's divorce trial against Muriel should have been terminated. Dick's bigamy automatically should have prevented him, the now guilty party, from further action against Muriel, who, because of the appeal, was still considered innocent of the charges Dick brought against her.

While they were on the *Rotterdam* cruise, Dick had been cabled by his lawyers that Muriel's motion for a new trial had been denied, so he felt free to marry Annemarie. He moved too quickly after the appeal denial for the marriage to be in "good faith," and his lawyers had informed them that Muriel would likely appeal again.

Dick claimed that since he learned of the divorce decree, he had stopped living with Annemarie as his wife and had been unable to consummate the marriage due to his illness. Everyone in the courtroom believed this was a lie.

Gambrell repeated an example of Dick's deposition during the first trial, when he was asked about "the usual incidents of man and wife" and, becoming belligerent, he said, "Put it in blunt words, she had her bedroom and I have mine, and if you're trying to ask if we have intercourse or not . . . is that what you're trying to ask? I refuse to answer." Gambrell pressed him and Dick said, "Remember, I am a very ill man." Then he said, "I'm not saying I never went to bed with her."

"How many times?" Gambrell asked.

"I have been to bed with her," Dick said.

"Pardon?" Gambrell asked.

"Of course I have been to bed with her, but I didn't say it was done immediately, though." Dick argued that he was embarrassed and was just trying to get rid of him—he didn't realize what he was saying. Rollings tried to help by testifying that Dick's sexual capacity was limited.

Gambrell asked why they wouldn't release Muriel's diaries to her. Kravitch said they were open for them to read in the clerk of court's office. Gambrell said, "It was like trying to read and memorize *Gone with the Wind* in the office hours of the clerk in Darien." Gambrell went on to say the real reason they wouldn't enter the diaries into evidence was because they would prove that "Dick is not the Prince of Sapelo as the newspaper article said he was. He would be the common drunk of Sapelo community which Muriel's been living with for seven years, because it's in there."

Gambrell also said the court didn't make much of Dick being quoted as saying, "Sapelo is a wonderful place to shuck a wife" and also didn't seem to be concerned with Dick's constant travel. During the first trial, Dick took trips to Knoxville, Lookout Mountain, and the graduation exercises at Wake Forest School of Medicine within three weeks of the first trial's conclusion. Muriel's lawyers found out that Dick had paid $45,000 to charter the *Natalie* six weeks before the first trial even started. Then on June 7, 1960, Dick took a BOAC flight from Idlewild Airport in New York for a flight to England, stayed at the International Hotel, and then went to Gosport to take his cruise. The cruise took him to the Baltic Sea, Germany, Sweden, Norway, and Denmark. Muriel's lawyers said, "He's laughing up his sleeve. So is Dr. Rollings and everybody. He goes to Rotterdam, Miami, Hamburg, Bremen, Heidelberg…all of these places somehow suddenly become good places for emphysema patients. To try to sell you on the idea that all he's done has been aimed at his health is hogwash," they said.

Robert Richardson, another of Muriel's lawyers, stated, "Annemarie Schmitt may be a fine person—we've never seen her. She didn't come here to testify." He noted that Dick asked her to marry him after five days' acquaintance, and had kept her hidden since then—in Europe, on Sapelo, and in the Bahamas.

They brought up the dozens of times Dick had lied to the court. He claimed that he "almost died" during his fall deposition in the second trial, which Muriel's attorneys said he staged to escape his deposition and run off for a prearranged tryst with Annemarie in Nassau. Dick repeatedly committed perjury and whined that the cross-examination was "grueling" and "merciless." But Dick had his way throughout the trial and managed to evade the toughest questions.

The court heard again the letter Dick wrote to get Muriel off the island in 1959. Dick wrote, "You have been here on Sapelo, for long periods, isolated with a sick man who is cross and irritable over the least trifle. You have stood it like a Roman soldier but it's getting you down. I urge you to leave and come back and find your old Buck strong and more reasonable. With all my love, Dick (Cross Buck)."

Muriel's lawyers said, "It was a loving letter he slyly used as he was planning a perfidious scheme to traduce and cast her off like a worn out garment. He was acting the solicitous husband, keeping in touch with her on the trans-Atlantic telephone, so as to direct activities to his French detectives." He was "framing his middle-aged wife, who was no longer appealing to him," and he was trying to "steal a march" on the court by marrying Annemarie the day Muriel's appeal was denied, and before the court had an opportunity to say whether the decree he obtained was or was not final.

Robert Richardson continued, "Did anyone at Fancy Gap say Muriel was not attentive, religious in her efforts while Dick was in the mountains recuperating? Karl Weiss says it, she babied him and cooked for him — she did not make him sick. Maybe a man withdrawing from cigarettes and alcohol is what's making him an irritable man, so says his doctors. The minute she left she was under surveillance, Dick admits she wasn't following his plan. He went to the trouble of getting an adjoining apartment to keep an eye on her. Dick said 'Of course I was tricking her.' . . . Dick was flitting all over the place in private airlines, paying for laymen, doctors, medical students, the Lindemanns, whoever they are, all flitting around somewhere."

Richardson said Dick wanted more than justice and was willing to pay to get it. He "organized an armada of strategically located legal talent" and "purposely filed appeals on the alimony and cross appeals to keep Muriel's money draining." Richardson finished by saying the jury had better not forgive him for his "open and notorious adultery" with Annemarie.

One of Dick's attorneys, Mr. White, concluded his closing arguments with a simple message that Muriel was nothing more than a money-hungry beast. He said: "If ever there was a hen-pecked, devil-driven, hag-ridden poor specimen of humanity it was Mr. Richard Reynolds on Sapelo island" during his life with Muriel. "You saw how she twisted and turned, wiggled and squirmed and slithered round there on that stand like an eel on a slick rock. This wife as a result of her unholy lust for money has destroyed within herself, within her own breast every symbolance of womanly virtue that she may have had."

That was all the town of Darien needed to hear. After Muriel spent $500,000 in legal fees and Dick spent $1 million, and the court had documented a record eight thousand pages of testimony—the jury ruled, again, in Dick's favor after only six hours of deliberation. This time they denied Muriel any alimony whatsoever and revoked the roughly $12,500 per year she was supposed to receive before. The prenuptial agreement would prevail.

Muriel was devastated. Her lawyers were convinced the county was the single most biased, prejudicial jurisdiction they had ever served.

In early January 1963, Muriel filed another appeal with the state Supreme Court in Atlanta and won a new hearing. Her divorce from Dick, now going into its fourth year, was setting precedents in Georgia law.

❧ · ❧

In May of 1963, Muriel abruptly dropped her second appeal. Dick had finally moved to settle the bitter case. Muriel flew down to Atlanta for the settlement. Surprisingly, Dick agreed to pay $2,142,624 in alimony, the largest recorded in Georgia history, including $500,000 for Muriel's legal fees and a written guarantee to not disturb the old Canadian trust, which would bring Muriel and her mother, Eleanor, $32,000 a year for life. Muriel would get an immediate cash payment of $681,250 and $60,000 per year for the next twenty years. She had already received $94,072 and $177,301 under court orders. Muriel's mother was pleased. Muriel was exhausted.

One of Dick's attorneys, William H. Schroder Jr. of Atlanta, issued a statement saying that Dick's "physical well being requires that a halt be brought to litigation." Schroder also stated that Dick had been vindicated by two juries but they had to do this because "Mrs. Reynolds also is dismissing two lawsuits she instituted against Reynolds in the New York Supreme Court. In one she sought to recover $1,800,000 from Reynolds because of an alleged misunderstanding about some bonds she claims he gave her. In the other case she sought to have herself declared the owner of insurance policies on Reynolds' life with a face value of $325,000." Schroder explained the details with disgust. At this point, Muriel and her lawyers, Gambrell and the others, didn't care what they said. Dick had gone to the trouble to publicly humiliate her and she figured he deserved the fight he got.

Dick was ordered to return Muriel's controversial diaries and her personal belongings from Sapelo as well. There was one more part of their settlement agreement: Upon their deaths, neither of them would be entitled to interest in the other's estate.

~ · ~

After the exhausting trials with Muriel, Dick prepared to leave America. He wanted little to do with her or his boys — whom he perceived as freeloaders — for a while, until they had "straightened out." Before Dick left Sapelo for Switzerland to live with his new wife, he called his four older sons together to tell them his plans. They were now age twenty-nine, twenty-six, twenty-four, and twenty-two. He asked them to bring his Orville Wright pilot's license and the ancestral Joshua Coin, which had been with Blitz all these years. He remembered the Reynolds family superstition that the piece would confer good luck upon the male heirs of the coin. Dick, whose health was getting worse, was in need of good luck again.

Blitz had passed away from cancer the year before, in 1961, and the boys had been very lonely. They were eager to see their father, who remained elusive except for the occasional vacations in Europe, hunting trips on Sapelo Island, and reunions in Winston-Salem. Since meeting Annemarie, he had gone back to ignoring them completely. Dick told the boys he was moving to Europe, which didn't surprise them. Dick always went where his wives wanted him, and Annemarie probably wanted to live there. As they stood on the beach, Dick examined the coin and when he saw that Blitz had a diamond placed in it, he became enraged and threw the diamond, and possibly the coin, into the ocean.

Dick had severely neglected his boys their whole lives and he had little to say to them, except to scold them for living off of his money instead of getting jobs. It seemed an odd way to say goodbye.

~ · ~

Dick remained a master at constructing grand schemes, even as he suffered from emphysema. No one could figure out what drove him to orchestrate the whole mess — the abrupt divorce from Muriel, the marriage to the young, foreign Annemarie, the continued abandonment of his sons. Perhaps he had been suffering too much from his illness, and it really had affected his mind. All anyone knew for certain was that Dick seemed content with his new German friends: Annemarie, the Lindemanns, Christian Nissen, and the secretary, Guenther Lehman.

Before Dick left for Europe, he had a few last items of business to take care of. He gave more land to the Sapelo Island Research Foundation and sold most of his American assets. He also rounded up his servants and dug up several bags of gold that he had previously hidden in the woods when he thought the world markets would collapse. They never knew exactly what he did with those bags.

CHAPTER 18

North Carolina's Prince of Wales: The Mystery

1964–1966

On December 14, 1964, R. J. Reynolds Jr., who had been living with his new wife in seclusion in the tiny mountain village of Emmetten, Switzerland, was rushed to the hospital as he lost consciousness. By the time he arrived at the hospital, he was dead. Muriel heard the news while traveling with her mother.

Annemarie immediately ordered Dick's body to be cremated, against his previously stated wishes. When Dick's six sons found out about it, they sent a telegram to Switzerland to have the cremation stopped. Only two of Dick's older sons made it to Europe in time for the quickly assembled funeral and when they arrived, the coffin was closed. They never saw their father's body.

The boys were also shocked to find that Annemarie couldn't attend the ceremony because she was about to deliver a baby. No one knew she had been pregnant. Thirty-six hours after

Dick died, she delivered a baby girl, Irene Sabina, in the maternity ward of the same hospital where Dick died.

It had only been a year and a half since Dick had settled with Muriel and remarried Annemarie on July 10, 1963, in Muralto, Switzerland, at the La Palma Hotel. The wedding was conducted in their small suite of rooms without any witnesses or guests—Muralto was situated in a canton in Switzerland where unwitnessed marriages were permitted. Dick was feeling ill that day, so the registrar who married the couple didn't actually see his face. Dick's back was to the registrar as he signed the necessary marriage certificates. There was no public announcement of the marriage.

After Muriel heard this, she wished she would have never settled or freed up the love of her life to marry this woman— even after she got all that money. What she really wanted was Dick back in her life.

Muriel had continued to feel emotionally bankrupt after her divorce from Dick. It left a hole in her heart that wouldn't seem to mend. She went through the details of the case in her mind daily and couldn't believe it had all happened. She hated this new wife and blamed her for stealing Dick from her. She became convinced that Dick was having an affair with Annemarie when she left during the summer of 1959, and she was the reason Dick divorced Muriel.

~·~

Annemarie and Dick carried out their quiet life together, building a large villa in Emmetten in the remote Swiss countryside, where they planned to settle down. Dick, still only fifty-eight years old, was in even worse health than before. In spite of this, he told reporters in North Carolina, "Contrary to what you may have heard in Winston-Salem, I plan to go on living for quite a while."

Now Dick was gone.

At first Swiss authorities and hospital officials didn't reveal the details. Dick had collapsed suddenly, and they weren't sure what happened. Nancy Reynolds told reporters that she thought he had a heart attack.

Hugo Frey, Dick and Annemarie's attorney, acted as the family's press spokesman and funneled reports to the American media. He said Dick had been using a pressure breathing apparatus for years with a face mask and motor that pumped oxygen into his lungs, and that he was dying of emphysema, but that they thought the immediate cause of death might have been a heart seizure brought on by the strain of the disease. As soon as Dick began having trouble that Sunday, they had called Dr. Rosier of the University of Zurich, a leading medical specialist in Europe, but Dick succumbed in the presence of Rosier and two other doctors. Dr. Heinrich Holtz, the physician who treated Dick at the clinic, said an autopsy would be performed prior to the memorial service. Frey reported that Dick had used the oxygen tank only briefly before living in Switzerland and had moved to Europe when his condition became worse. He had recently been using the oxygen pump every three minutes. Until the spring of 1964, he and Annemarie had been living in Locarno on the sunny side of the Swiss Alps. Now they were living in Emmetten near Mount Bürgenstock, Switzerland's "magic mountain" (made famous by Thomas Mann's 1924 book), where they built a home that was completed during the spring.

A few days later, the attending physician at St. Anna Clinic reported that Dick entered the hospital Sunday afternoon and that he'd been suffering a long time from emphysema. The immediate cause of death appeared to be "too much oxygen to the brain."

Too much oxygen?

The physician went on to say that Dick had been "in an oxygen tent" but wouldn't give any further details. Dick had spent a lot of time with oxygen tanks in recent years and was never without his oxygen tank administrator, Sergio Amati. Reporters recalled how he was excused from court during his first trial with Muriel because of his ill health. Even at that time, Dr. Henry Valk had told the Darien judge that Dick's life expectancy was only five to seven years, although few took his claims seriously.

∽ · ∾

Back at Sapelo and Darien, the entire community seemed to be in mourning. Dick's former employees, Sapelo residents, Darien friends, and city officials expressed shock and grief upon hearing the news of Dick's passing. Karl Weiss, Dick's attorneys, and the president of the University of Georgia all expressed regret and sadness. Most had expected to never see Dick again when he had departed for Switzerland a year and a half earlier.

Karl, Dick's chef of thirty years, said he'd just returned from Switzerland where he found Dick to be "well again and then sick again." Karl said Dick suffered a relapse recently and he feared the end was coming. Paul Varner said residents of McIntosh County were shocked by his death, including some of those who served on the jury during his divorce trial from Muriel. Others had heard about or visited the Sapelo Island mansion and its extensive guest quarters since they were kids, and said it was hard to imagine Sapelo without Dick. Varner also noted all of the contributions Dick had made to the city, including the millions of dollars for research and charity through the Sapelo Island Research Foundation for the last ten years.

From Athens, Georgia, University of Georgia president O. C. Aderhold expressed sadness over "the death of a great friend and benefactor, R. J. Reynolds." Delta Airlines president and general manager C. E. Woolman of Atlanta said that Delta considered Dick "an ally, a friend, and a valued member of the board of directors…we are most regretful of his death." Woolman said that

"Dick was always interested in aviation and his interest affected the right side and the progressive side" of the company and that he was a "cooperator—the kind of fellow a friend is. I never called on him to do something that he didn't do." Woolman said Dick was a "partner...he worked with all of us. I was very fond of him."

Dick was remembered in Winston-Salem as a colorful, flamboyant, warmhearted man who loved people and loved to be generous with friends, strangers, the Winston-Salem community, and the state of North Carolina. He was recognized as an expert businessman in his own right, who greatly influenced aviation and shipping, and the city was grateful to have the attention of such a charitable former citizen. In addition to his celebrated gifts to Wake Forest, Reynolds Park, Z. Smith Reynolds Airport, and the library, Dick had most recently made large gifts to Winston-Salem's Baptist Hospital and the University of Georgia.

The *Winston-Salem Journal* called Dick North Carolina's Prince of Wales. Writer Roy Thompson said, "Edward VIII gave up the English crown for a woman he loved and Dick Reynolds gave up his place in the tobacco empire for the life he loved." He wrote that Dick would be remembered "as an often-married international playboy" and "a maverick, a loner who went his own way" even as he was the life of the party and the gossip columnists everywhere he went. While the tobacco fortune made Dick rich and famous, he spent much of his life trying to find himself outside of it.

The flag on top of the R. J. Reynolds Tobacco building flew at half-mast to pay tribute to Dick. Friends said Dick never had a big enough ego to carry on with his father's tobacco company. Dick always said, "They seem to be getting along all right without me."

❧ · ❧

Dick's son John was the first of four sons to fly from Winston-Salem to Switzerland as soon as he could. Funeral plans for the only surviving and firstborn son of the R. J. Reynolds tobacco empire and magnate, R. J. Reynolds Sr., were underway. The boys brought attorneys with them, just in case anything was amiss.

On December 17, 1964, the funeral services were held at a local chapel in Lucerne, and Dick's body was brought to the tiny cemetery in the local churchyard of Emmetten, high in the Swiss Alps. The church could be seen from Annemarie's villa.

Annemarie was still in the hospital, having just given birth to her six-pound baby, Dick's first and only daughter. Annemarie had a difficult labor and delivery and had to receive blood transfusions but was recovering well. Staff at Dick and Annemarie's villa, Schyn-boedeli, including Sergio Amati, said Annemarie needed time to recover from the shock of Dick's death and the birth of the baby.

The boys attended the 11:00 A.M. funeral along with Nancy, who flew in from Greenwich, Connecticut. They learned that Annemarie had intended to have Dick's ashes spread in the same churchyard and they were glad to have stopped it. But the boys were frustrated by not being able to see their father's body and irritated that he had not been brought to Winston-Salem to be buried. Marianne was also on her way to the funeral with Michael and Patrick, who had seen their father only five times in their entire lives, but they didn't arrive in time for the service. Dick had only one surviving granddaughter—Linda Lee Reynolds—who was just born to Zach and his wife. The four boys from Dick's first marriage were now orphaned.

~ · ~

The boys also found the circumstances of Dick's death by what appeared to be an oxygen overdose highly suspicious. No one in the family had seen Dick in nearly two years, except Nancy, who had been to Switzerland on business to discuss the transition of the Z. Smith Reynolds Foundation to her control. Emory Flinn had also stopped by to discuss Delta business, as well as

Dr. Rollings, who strongly disapproved of Dr. Lindemann's overseeing Dick's health because he was not a pulmonary specialist. Lindemann was actually a spiritual healer who practiced the same eccentric religious rituals as Muriel, which Dick used to loathe so much. Dick apparently had not wanted any visitors— the one time his son Will trekked all the way to the remote Swiss town to see him, he was turned away at the door. Otherwise, Dick would see only Christian Nissen, the Lindemanns, Guenther Lehman, Karl Weiss, and of course Annemarie and Sergio Amati.

On top of everything else, Dick's sons could never understand why Dick, whose heart belonged to the ocean and who cherished his beloved Sapelo Island so much, would end up in landlocked Switzerland, surrounded by the towering Alps. It was as if Dick abandoned the sea and had lost himself in the process.

∿ ∿

Since Dick's Swiss burial caused an uproar, Annemarie had a stone laid in the cemetery in Winston-Salem after she recuperated. But Dick's odd burial arrangements were only the beginning.

Speculation began almost immediately on the size of the estate Dick left behind. Most estimated his worth at around $25 million, which was the figure named in the divorce trial.

At the time of the funeral there was no information on Dick's will, except that it would be domiciled in Switzerland.

In January of 1965, the representatives of the family were called into the little probate office in Emmetten for the reading of the will. Dick had nine wills registered there, most of them dated in the past decade. The last will, dated and executed August of 1964, named Annemarie the sole heir to all of his wealth and declared all previous wills null and void. This was the will that prevailed. Not one of Dick's six sons would receive a penny from his estate.

The boys were stunned. How could this be possible? Why would Dick disinherit them all? Marianne was livid on behalf of her boys. Muriel got word of it, too. Something didn't seem right.

They were also shocked to learn that Dick's worth was estimated to be only $10 to $12 million, less than half of what he was worth just as recently as his divorce from Muriel. At the time, the $25 million quoted during his divorce was already considered a gross underestimate.

This sum caused considerable surprise back in North Carolina too. Unnamed sources tried to explain it by pointing out the large sums of money Dick had given away as well as the large amounts of money that went to his ex-wives in their settlements.

Dick had supposedly made a statement in his estate papers about his boys, too. He said his six sons had already received "directly and indirectly" substantial sums of money and that receipt of more money would "deprive them of the will to work," although this statement couldn't be found in the estate papers that arrived in the United States. Now the thirty-five-year-old new mother, Annemarie, would get everything.

Annemarie said that she planned to stay in Emmetten in the villa Dick bought for her with her five-week-old daughter. According to local sources, she was actually in need of therapeutic care for some time following Dick's death and stayed at St. Anna Clinic with the baby for extended periods of time. Now that Dick was gone, she would have to care for her daughter alone.

The boys had little sympathy for Annemarie's circumstances. They had all been alone and abandoned their whole lives. And they had just received the final slap in the face from Dick—the ultimate coup de grâce.

~ · ~

Dick's will was said to have been a short holographic will that also named Annemarie sole executrix. Dick had supposedly made a more formal will but hadn't signed it.

The will was written in Dick's scrawl, crooked and running off the page. For a man with so many projects, investments, property, and money in his lifetime, it was amazing that this should be his final will. When the boys' lawyers brought back a copy, they noted that it was written on Dick's personal stationery, with "Richard J. Reynolds" in the upper left corner. It read:

Emmetten N.W.
Aug. 15, 1964

My Last Will
I the undersigned, Richard Joshua Reynolds being of sound mind hereby declare this to be my last will:

1) My succession, my inheritance, my estate should be governed and ruled by the law of my nationality and particularly by the law of my birthplace (i.e.) by the law of the State of North Carolina
2) I direct that my only heir should be my dear wife Annemarie Reynolds born Schmitt. Accordingly she will have the only and exclusive rights to my whole estate.
3) I name as my executor, my wife Annemarie Reynolds, born Schmitt.
4) I hereby revoke and declare null and void *all* previous wills and testaments complete with all codicils.

This last will has been executed by me pursuant to the requirements of the form appropriate in Switzerland.

Emmetten, N.W. Aug. 15, 1964
Richard J. Reynolds

The will contained the seal of the Swiss registrar and was listed as domiciled in Dick and Annemarie's villa, Im Schyn. The registrar and the Council of the Community of Emmetten went to establish a "Certificate of Heirship," which stated that the will, along with all the previously registered wills, had been opened on January 18, 1965. They included wills dating from October 21, 1952, November 22, 1961, April 25, 1962, August 14, 1963, and the last will of August 15, 1964. Annemarie accepted her appointment as executrix on February 2, 1965.

Not long after the will was read, Nancy contacted the boys. She offered each $500,000 as a gift from Dick's estate, but they had to promise not to contest the will and to never publicly question Dick's death. They also had to promise not to question the paternity of Irene. Why would they question her paternity in the first place? they wondered. The mere existence of such a statement caused them to question it. In order to pressure them further, all six boys had to sign off on Annemarie's application as permanent administrator of Dick's estate, or none of them would receive anything. Paul Varner, who had so successfully quashed Muriel a few years earlier, handled the paperwork.

The four oldest boys already had a considerable amount of wealth from Blitz's settlement with Dick in 1946, and they weren't about to deny their two younger brothers (from Marianne), who had not received as much money. As far as they were concerned, the damage had already been done. This was about Dick's choice to disinherit them. This was about the absence of love and attention from an absentee father. It wasn't about the money.

Eventually all four of the older boys signed the agreement on December 12, 1965.

Both Michael and Patrick were teenagers at the time, so Marianne had to make the decision for them. She hated everything about the agreement, but she didn't want to make problems for the four older boys, so she gave in and signed, too. Later in life, Patrick Reynolds contemplated this controversial offer. He wondered, in his family memoir, *Why give away money if there was nothing to hide? And how cheaply had they all been bought?*

Meanwhile Annemarie, who just a year before was the modest, seemingly unsophisticated new wife of a millionaire, certainly knew what she was doing now. She set about finalizing the estate as quickly and efficiently as possible. She dumped Golden Isles Airlines, donated the Sapelo Island furniture, and gave more shares of Sapelo Island to the Sapelo Island Research Foundation via a company set up for her called American Properties, Inc. She paid tens of thousands of dollars in inheritance tax, paid herself $50,000 for executrix work, and paid off numerous debts and bills owed in the process.

In Baltimore, Maryland, the trust that Katharine Reynolds had established decades before, amounting to $11 million and including Reynolds stock, was dissolved and distributed among the seven children. The inheritance from their grandmother, which grew to $2.5 million each, would be the only inheritance the boys would see from the Reynolds family. While they were grateful for the money, it hardly compared to the hundreds of millions of dollars their aunts, uncles, and cousins held for the next several decades.

When word of this reached Muriel, she was deeply shaken. She had a hard time believing the boys were intentionally disinherited, and she had serious doubts about Irene. In 1957, Dick had been diagnosed with an inactive sperm count due to his alcoholism.

Muriel also seriously doubted the value of Dick's wealth. She remembered Annemarie's stipulation in the divorce trial—Dick invested large amounts of money in European stocks, at Annemarie's request. And what happened to all that gold he had buried on the island? Muriel recalled Strat's testimony that Dick had Swiss gold accounts. How convenient that he'd ended up in Switzerland.

Muriel had not signed anything and had no legal obligation to the Reynolds family. Partly out of a vengeful attitude toward Annemarie, and partly out of her own delusion that Dick had never really wanted to divorce her and was forced into it by his handlers, she immediately launched an investigation. That same month, February 1965, Muriel sent a private investigator, Frederick Sands, to Switzerland, where he retraced Dick's footsteps over the past few years. He first spent time in Muralto where Dick and Annemarie had gotten married the second time. He interviewed the registrar who married them and learned that the wedding had been odd in many ways. The registrar said he had no idea of the prominence of the man he was marrying and confirmed that there were no guests, no wedding party, no meal, and no flowers. He also mentioned that the marriage license was actually signed a few days before the marriage—also unusual. They discovered that Annemarie had signed a document forfeiting all her rights to Dick's estate for a settlement of $300,000, which had been set up by a bank called Mercantile Safe Deposit and Trust in Baltimore in 1961. It seemed that Annemarie had also been a short-term victim of Dick's paranoid suspicion that everyone was trying to steal from him. This document was also brought to the registrar along with the marriage license by Guenther Lehman. Lehman swore to the registrar that the signatures on the documents belonged to Dick, and that he was too ill to appear in person.

An additional permit from the US consulate was also required for them to marry, and again Dick did not appear in person to obtain that permit. The consul stated that he accepted Dick's divorce document from Muriel, which was required to obtain the permit, and that the document was sworn to by Dick's lawyers in Atlanta. The consul assumed it was valid. Guenther Lehman again carried out this task and presented a typewritten letter from Dick with his signature.

According to the investigator's report, two days later, the registrar was called to perform the marriage in Dick and Annemarie's suite. He told the investigator, Sands, that he'd never performed a marriage under such strange conditions. Annemarie took the marriage document to the small sitting room and the registrar saw a man with his back to him. Annemarie placed the document in front of the man and said, "Sign here." He didn't turn around, and Annemarie came back and told the registrar, "He has a bad cold today. We would like you to stay for a drink, but I must get him to bed." The registrar said it all took ten minutes, and he assumed it was an old invalid wanting to marry his mistress before he died. He also confirmed that it was not against the law to marry in Muralto without any witnesses.

~ · ~

At this point Humphrey "Hutch" Hutchins came into the picture. Hutch was a friend of Muriel's whom she had initially hired to write her life story after her divorce. That didn't happen, but Hutch became one of her best friends and a fellow investigator of Dick's death. Muriel, Hutch, and private detectives searched the Swiss countryside, Sapelo Island, and various other stops in between, and made many important discoveries.

The team discovered that large amounts of Dick's paperwork, investment papers, and other documents on Sapelo Island had been destroyed and burned by Strat Coyner, Dick's accountant Ledyard Staples, and possibly Nancy, who had been taking care of the island when Dick moved to Europe. Nearly all of Dick's staff, some of whom had worked for him for over twenty years, were fired once Annemarie arrived. The only employees who remained were Karl Weiss and Guenther Lehman. Nancy brought in some of her staff from nearby Musgrove Plantation on St. Simon's Island to take over. It began to look like Dick had lost control of the estate ever since Muriel had left. Christian Nissen also reappeared in Dick's life the summer Muriel went on vacation, and one of Dick's sons later claimed that he had seen Annemarie on the island in 1959.

Fred Johnson confirmed that before Dick left for Switzerland, he had helped him move several bags of gold to various hiding spots on the island. This gold, which Dick may have smuggled into Europe before he left, wasn't mentioned in any of the wills. Dick's European stock and countless other assets were missing, as well as an estimated $15 million in his bank accounts. And in a cruel twist of fate, the residents of Hog Hammock were left with nothing, in spite of the fact that Dick had always promised that they would be provided for when he died. The destruction of records on the island after Dick's death made it impossible for the loyal old servants to prove that they had been employees of Dick's for so many years. They were not even able to collect Social Security benefits. Dick's most trusted assistant, Fred Johnson, said, "Dick would still be here if it wasn't for that German woman."

Some handwriting experts Muriel hired concluded that the penmanship in Dick's last informal written will was not Dick's. Muriel remembered that Christian Nissen had served as a forgery expert for the Nazis, for which Hitler presented him with the Iron Cross, and speculated that he could have forged Dick's will. Investigators discovered that "Dr." Hans Lindemann was listed in no medical directories. When Muriel's investigators tried to interview Lindemann, he initially avoided them, but finally gave in to a meeting and became nervous and pale when confronted with questions about Dick. He said that Lehman "has all the answers" about Dick's death, but when they tried to interview

Lehman he wouldn't talk. Muriel's suspicions that they'd all had something to do with Dick's death deepened when she received an anonymous letter saying that Dick had actually died in the summer of 1964. The postmark was Bad Godesburg, Germany, which happened to be Dr. Lindemann's hometown.

It also turned out that under Swiss law, it was illegal to disinherit one's children. Although Dick requested that his will be domiciled under North Carolina law—another residency trick of Dick's, so he could legally disinherit them—this might have explained the reasoning behind the peculiar disbursement of funds among all of Dick's boys. But would Annemarie have done it if there wasn't a legal risk?

❧ ⋅ ☙

Every trail leading up to Annemarie appeared suspicious to outsiders, including Dick's isolation in his last years, their hasty and unwitnessed marriage, and her entourage of German friends who were the only people to see Dick regularly during the last two years of his life. They all seemed to know more about Dick's death and final will than anyone else. Outsiders wondered whether they were all part of some plot to steal Dick's millions. Annemarie had been introduced to Dick by Ilsa Lindemann (who had been introduced by Nissen) and claimed not to have known Dick until they met in East Germany. But Dick's Sapelo Island servants said that Annemarie had been on the island much earlier. Dick had obviously hidden this fact because he was still married to Muriel, but why were they flown in all the way from Germany and under what pretenses? If that was true, Dick and many others had committed perjury in his divorce trial from Muriel.

Finally, no one could attest to the birth of Irene. Both her birth certificate and Dick's death certificate were filed in one of the cantons of Switzerland where unwitnessed documents can be formally registered.

∾ · ∾

Muriel believed she had made enough of a case to at least charge Annemarie and company with conspiracy and fraud in the forgery of Dick's last will and the willful destruction of his documents, and to contest Irene's paternity. Dick's son Patrick even suggested they should have Dick's body exhumed for a proper autopsy as well—to make sure he really died the way they said he did.

However, following her lawyer's counsel, Muriel did not make these claims part of her case. Muriel's famous Washington, D.C., attorneys, including Paul R. Connelly, and a criminal investigator, Thomas Lavenia, advised her to take the angle of contesting Annemarie's marriage to Dick instead, in which she had more of a case.

In April of 1966, Muriel filed a $10 million damage suit in U.S. federal court claiming that she was Dick's lawful widow and had rights to his estate. She claimed that she was forced by a Georgia Supreme Court justice to accept a divorce granted to Dick, and named Annemarie and the Bankers Trust Company of New York as defendants. Muriel claimed that Annemarie "purports to be the surviving wife" of Dick and that she obtained an order from the Surrogate Court in Manhattan allowing her to act as executrix of Dick's "many millions of dollars of assets within New York."

Muriel's suit described the two divorce cases she had with Dick and said that when she appealed the case a second time, Chief Justice William Duckworth of the Georgia Supreme Court forced her attorney to settle the case without a third trial and that she signed the settlement and withdrew the appeal under duress. The goal of the suit was to reinstate Dick's older will, which included Muriel and the boys.

However, the court wasn't buying it, and as hard as Muriel

tried, she couldn't make the case that Annemarie was not Dick's lawful widow. Muriel could think of no other way to go after Annemarie or seek revenge on behalf of herself or Dick's boys, and she was making herself out to be a money-hungry ex-wife again.

❧ · ❧

Were Muriel's instincts right? Was she on to something? It was a climate in which wealthy men like J. Paul Getty's family faced kidnapping, maiming, and threats in exchange for money. Conspiracy theories abounded as the Cold War and the Vietnam War dragged on and the world dealt with the assassinations of John Kennedy, Robert Kennedy, and Martin Luther King. Did Dick Reynolds join a long line of prominent men caught up in a conspiracy?

Muriel would never give up trying to save her ex-husband's disappearing patrimony and uncover the truth. But she was consistently blocked by the rest of the Reynolds family and could never prove it in a court of law.

Epilogue

A lawsuit this week claiming R.J. (Dick) Reynolds was murdered...was filed by Marianne O'Brien Reynolds, second wife of the tobacco heir.... The suit alleged that Reynolds' death in 1964 "was willfully and feloniously caused" by his fourth wife, Annemarie Schmitt Reynolds, who inherited the bulk of Reynolds' estate.... The lawsuit claimed Reynolds was "kept drugged and incapacitated...in various clinics" until "a forged will" could be prepared.

— *Winston-Salem Journal*, January 2, 1976

Patrick panned the camera across the crowd. He wanted to reject the idea of a conspiracy that had done away with his father's millions—but, in these circumstances, it was hard to do.
— *The Gilded Leaf*, Patrick Reynolds and Tom Schactman, 1989

Muriel's friend Hutch Hutchins wasn't her only collaborator. Dick's second wife, Marianne, who was once Muriel's archenemy, also contributed tens of thousands of dollars to a decade-long quest to find out what happened to their mutual ex-husband and his fortune. Both of them believed almost twice as much money had been unaccounted for when Dick died, and they suspected he had smuggled millions in gold into Switzerland. After Muriel's failed attempts to bring the case to justice, Marianne took the conspiracy case to court on her own. She wanted to see justice done for her disinherited sons.

It was 1975 and Dick had been dead for over ten years, but the fight over his estate raged on. On December 19, Marianne filed suit in McIntosh County Superior Court against Dick's estate, Annemarie, Nancy Reynolds, the board of directors of the Sapelo Island Research Foundation, Sapelo Plantation, Inc., Strat Coyner, Ledyard Staples, and other associates. Marianne claimed that she owned part of Sapelo Island, based on the note scribbled on a piece of calendar notebook paper in Dick's handwriting, which read:

"Received of Marianne O'Brien the sum of $10 and other valuables considered as payment in full for the common stock of Sapelo Plantation, Inc.—said stock to be delivered by sunset Saturday October 20, 1945."

It was signed Richard J. Reynolds—twice.

The paper was, of course, another one of Dick's jokes, like the alcohol clause he once signed for Muriel. Apparently it wasn't enough of a joke to keep lawyers off the case. Dick could never have dreamed that another of his broken promises would end up in court again, ten years after his death.

Marianne brought several counts against the defendants. She claimed that she was entitled to all the common stock of Sapelo Island. Then she claimed the estate was being fraudulently probated in Switzerland when Dick was a U.S. citizen and resident at the time of his death. Marianne explained that Sapelo Plantation, Inc., which owned Sapelo Island, was dissolved on January 21, 1950. Marianne sought to show that the dissolution was improper and designed to defraud Marianne of her rights. She accused Strat Coyner—the "cleaner"—of being a conspirator in the dissolution, along with the others named in her suit.

According to Marianne, on October 20, 1945, Dick acquired the sixteen thousand acres of Sapelo under the Sapelo Foundation. At the time he proposed, Dick asked Marianne to give up her movie career to marry him upon his discharge from the Navy, and asked her to live at Sapelo with him. Marianne was hesitant to completely give up her career, so to further entice her, Dick offered her the handwritten agreement to give her that piece of land. Marianne accepted the offer, and Dick promised that the common stock in question would be placed in Marianne's name. One could imagine the twinkle in Dick's eye as he made this promise. Then, on October 1, 1949, Dick dissolved Sapelo Plantation, Inc., stating that all the stockholders agreed to the dissolution. This wasn't true because Marianne never knew about it. The arrangement was handled by Dick's usual entourage of Paul Varner, Strat Coyner, and Ledyard Staples, and Marianne stated that they knew about the existence of Dick and Marianne's agreement at the time.

On August 7, 1952, when the final divorce between Marianne and R.J. was granted, the decree made no mention of the property and, based on this handwritten scrawl on a tiny piece of paper, Marianne would argue that she still held the title.

∾ · ∾

Then Marianne alleged in court papers that Annemarie conspired to acquire Sapelo for herself. When Dick died and Annemarie inherited everything, Annemarie later sold the 13,750 acres of the property, as well as Meridian Dock and the riverside tract on June 27, 1969, to the Sapelo Island Research Foundation for $835,000, far less than the land was worth. Marianne estimated that because of the excessive beachfront access and what was believed to be valuable, minable titanium underneath, the land was worth more like a whopping $100 million. She also stated that during his lifetime and marriage to Marianne, Dick smuggled large quantities of gold bullion—private ownership of which was illegal at the time—and jewels on private vessels to and from the island and buried it there, never to be seen again. Marianne stated this was common knowledge among Strat, Nancy, Annemarie, and Ledyard.

Then Marianne spelled out what was on a lot of people's minds, including Muriel's. She stated in the suit that Dick's death was willfully and feloniously caused by Annemarie and that she should not be allowed to inherit any portion of his estate, much of which was physically located in Georgia, and which, by law, must pass by intestate succession to Dick's heirs. Marianne said that Nancy acted in concert with Annemarie, along with Christian Nissen, Guenther Lehman, and Hans Lindemann, who conspired together to remove Dick from his home on Sapelo and get him to Germany, where he was kept drugged and incapacitated by "German nationals at various clinics." That, she said, was when they prepared a fraudulent marriage to Annemarie and forged the holographic last will. Marianne stated that Dick lacked the mental capacity to change his domicile at the time of the last will, and that his removal was involuntary. Marianne claimed that Dick actually died at the hands of the conspirators in Bad Godesburg in July 1964 and she ordered Dick's body exhumed for examination.

Marianne asserted that the will was the work of a professional forger, Christian Nissen, at the instance of Nancy and Annemarie for the purpose of defrauding Marianne and Dick's heirs. Marianne asked the McIntosh probate court to set aside the forged will, declare Annemarie and Nancy trustees ex maleficio, and readminister the will to the rightful heirs.

Finally, Marianne accused Irene of not being Dick's child, but an imposter procured for the purpose of defrauding Dick's sons.

In Winston-Salem, people were shocked by the headlines.

Gene Whitman of the *Twin City Sentinel* reported, "Most members of the Reynolds family were not in Winston-Salem today, but one who could be reached said the lawsuit this week claiming R. J. Reynolds was murdered came as a complete surprise." Reporters recalled how difficult it was to obtain details of Dick's death when he died in 1964, and how it took them two days of calling overseas to secure information. Some family members suspected that Dick's oxygen tank administrator, Sergio Amati, was to blame for Dick's accidental oxygen overdose and Annemarie chose not to bring a suit, but this was pure speculation. Now with these new claims, some wondered: Would they ever know exactly what happened to Dick when he died?

Eventually Marianne's case was dismissed on almost all counts, but not before it went to the Georgia Supreme Court. The handwritten document Dick wrote before they were married was an issue. Ultimately the courts concluded that Marianne had forfeited her rights when she divorced Dick, and again when she signed off on her sons' inheritance in 1965. Marianne's charges against Annemarie were never fully investigated—they were thrown out due to lack of evidence, and Marianne had to remove them if she stood a chance of winning the land grant portion of the suit.

Both Muriel and Marianne continued to believe that Annemarie had pillaged Dick's estate, hoarded his money in foreign accounts, and purposely cut out his sons, and may have even forged his will, had a baby by another man and claimed it was Dick's, and faked the timing of Dick's death to achieve it all.

In the end, the details of Dick's dubiously managed estate were hidden behind an impenetrable curtain of secrecy. His heritage would be swallowed up into Swiss accounts, vanished gold, and a new European child. Dick's whole-scale abandonment of his sons proved to be a magnified version of his own sense of abandonment by the early deaths of his parents. His dis-inheritance of his own children, and the entire group's failed crusade to find the answers to the mystery around Dick's death and estate, would ultimately mean death to Dick's legacy.

Dick's sons would never be allowed on any boards or in any of the companies he founded and funded. They were even forbidden access to the family documents and had to purchase their father's heirlooms at an auction. To visit the family estates, the boys had to go through the same channels as the general public. In a heated moment in 1975, Patrick confronted Nancy on the absurdity of this, and she claimed she had no control over the island or Dick's estates. That was nonsense—her son, Smith Bagley, had been hosting grand parties at Sapelo whenever he wished. Patrick Reynolds noted how much of his father had all but disappeared from the family-run institutions that remained.

In the early part of 1995, Michael Reynolds also conducted an investigation into the estate, and obtained a court order to gain access to sealed papers belonging to his father and to determine if he had received his fair share of his father's estate. He investigated portions of Dick's stockholdings that were never accounted for, and he also investigated his cousins' relationship to Dick—including the ones who appeared as officers on all of Dick's foundations. It's unclear what he discovered, but he didn't appear to receive any more from the estate as a result of his efforts.

❧ · ❧

Despite a glamorous Hollywood lifestyle of her own filled with dazzling parties with the likes of Joan Fontaine and Elizabeth Taylor, Muriel remained obsessed with her dear ex-husband till the end. Muriel always claimed that R. J. Reynolds Sr. came to her in her dreams, begging her to solve his son's mysterious end. She continued to whip around the globe, spending most of her time in New York, Palm Beach, and London.

At the end of her years, Muriel wrote melodramatic letters to her friend Hutch, having fallen into a serious depression that left her drifting from one aimless venture to another. She often tormented her servants with unreasonable demands and wasted her resources on travel and gambling. Muriel never got over Dick and talked about him endlessly for the rest of her life.

On October 10, 1981, Muriel died at 12:15 A.M. of respiratory failure in West Palm Beach at the age of sixty-two. She had been battling lung cancer for ten years and was admitted to the hospital one month before she died. Hard living caught up with both Muriel and her ex-husband, and their lives had ended much earlier than they should have. Muriel's death certificate stated that she was "widowed."

⁓ · ⁓

Nancy has also since passed away, but, unlike Dick's boys, her children have benefited richly from their access to the family funds, foundations, and legacies. Nancy spent much of her life donating money to charities and managing several foundations in her family's name, including the Katharine Reynolds Foundation and the Acra Foundation. She was a committed Democrat like the rest of the family, even allowing her good friend Jimmy Carter, a Georgia native, to hold his preinaugural cabinet meeting at her home on Musgrove Plantation. *Town & Country* magazine named her one of the ten most generous living Americans in 1985. Nancy's accomplishments and contributions to society through the Reynolds family foundations were immeasurable. However, Nancy the individual remained elusive, even to her own nephews and nieces. Ironically, she was giving and selfless to the community around her but failed to extend the same generosity to her blood relatives.

Nancy, who remained very close to Dick later in his life, was the only blood relative to see Dick in his last year, and her behavior toward Dick's children was at best cold and oblivious and at worst deliberately harmful. They never knew exactly what motivated her, except that she viewed the boys as living symbols of Dick's embarrassing mistakes. It was easier to preserve the family image by shutting them out.

After Dick died, Nancy took control of the wealthy Z. Smith Reynolds Foundation and the Sapelo Foundation, both of which were founded by Dick. Throughout the rest of her life, Nancy seemed obsessed with controlling the family's image in the media and used money and bribery to silence family members from releasing information to the public, particularly after Dick died. Her efforts were almost completely successful — the family received little press from the 1960s to the 1980s, until after Nancy passed away.

The elusive Annemarie has never been more mysterious or well hidden, and she still lives in the same tiny Swiss mountain town where Dick died. Annemarie still has a view of Dick's grave in the little churchyard in Emmetten, although his plot has been turned over and reoccupied twice since he died.

Neighbors who are acquainted with Annemarie and her daughter seem unaware that the two women are the heirs of a deceased American millionaire, with the exception of the staff at St. Anna Clinic, who still remember Dick and Annemarie fondly. According to the general public in Winston-Salem and the residents of Sapelo Island, Annemarie is friendly and good to them but keeps herself distanced from most Reynolds family affairs.

Annemarie's introduction into Dick's life continues to be inexplicable to many who knew him. She became a huge influence over the last two years of Dick's life and ultimately retained all of the power over the estate of a man she had known for only a few years, causing her to become the target of suspicion that continues today. She never remarried while she quietly raised her daughter and is a large benefactor of many charitable institutions in Switzerland.

Annemarie reportedly does little business in the United States, except to tend to the Sapelo Foundation in Georgia, of which she is honorary president, and to donate funds to the Reynolda House Museum of American Art and other stateside institutions for the Reynolds family.

Today, the Sapelo Island Research Foundation, still presided over by Annemarie, Irene, and Nancy's children, is a respectable institution that continues to fund marine biology, oceanography, and limnology (the study of inland waters) research in conjunction with the University of Georgia. The University of Georgia Marine Institute facilities are housed on the island and maintained by the Georgia Department of Natural Resources. The lovely South End House is now a park museum, and large groups can rent the mansion for the weekend to sample the multimillionaire's life. Wake Forest University, which still owns the marble bust of Dick that Muriel purchased for them in the 1950s, remains an excellent school today. The Z. Smith Reynolds Foundation, which is run by Nancy's family, continues to fund charitable programs throughout North Carolina.

Patrick Reynolds, that young twentysomething who once entertained the idea of raising his father's coffin with Muriel, didn't go away quietly. In 1989 he published a multigenerational family history titled *The Gilded Leaf*. The book was received with trepidation by most of his brothers and outright anger by his cousins. But it was clear that Patrick shared many of his mother's and Muriel's suspicions, although he tried to be fair. It was also evident that Patrick had not quite forgiven his father for disinheriting him and sought answers he was never able to find.

Irene is Dick's only other living child. The older she grew, the more she looked like Dick, even sharing his distinctive dimpled chin. It looked like Irene wasn't an "impostor" child after all, and that Dick had missed out on the life of his only daughter. Zachary Taylor, an eccentric young man who was a living legend in North Carolina and renowned for motorcycle racing, ham radio operations, and aerobatic flying, died tragically in a plane crash in 1979. John died in 1990, Josh in 1995, Michael in 2004, and Will in 2009. Of all the children, only Irene presumably understood Dick's actions before he died. And only Irene would reap the benefits of his fortune and his legacy.

∾ · ∽

Dick Reynolds, the yachtsman, the aviator, the philanthropist, the businessman, grappled with the tragedy of his parents' deaths as a teenager, and then grew into an unsupervised, daring young adult who took great gambles with his life and money. He had everything he could ever want except discipline and restraint. When the excitement of his youth tapered off, so did his ability to stick with any one enterprise for long. Seized by the thrill of new technology, Dick would peak into intense periods of entrepreneurship, and then ditch the whole endeavor when the buzz wore off.

Throughout his years as a generous, friendly, carefree playboy, partying at posh clubs like El Morocco, "21," and Harry's New York Bar in Paris, Dick would marry four times in all and produce six sons and one daughter, leaving each set of children to pursue a relationship with the next wife. He partied too much to devote any meaningful time to his family members—his love of the sea and the bottle and his desire to escape would reign over them all.

Dick, who behind the jovial façade was a lonely, sad, and private man, consistently yearned for the solitude of his boats. When all else came and went, Dick closely guarded his yachts, building them larger and grander with each passing year. He would put up with life-threatening adventures to stay on a boat, but he wouldn't put up with the hardships of a relationship and parenthood. It was too painful and too difficult to face his own failures, and his cherished vessels became his primary escape route when those failures caught up with him. But Dick loved alcohol just as he loved the sea—and he ultimately drowned his destiny in alcohol instead of giving the promises of his life a chance.

Dick had been born amid great fanfare and opportunity and died in bitter, cold obscurity. His suddenly landlocked and suspicious end seemed indicative of a life that was no longer his own, and his dreams died with him. How would things have been different if Dick had lived up to his legacy? How many more opportunities could his boys have had? RJR Tobacco is now almost completely out of the Reynolds family's hands—did it have to be that way? And how many more lives would have been changed if Dick's boys could have carried on his generosity? Instead, Dick's family would live out the rest of their lives with their pain and outrage, silenced by their own blood relatives for reasons they would never understand. Just as Dick before them, they would carry the scars of a fatherless childhood that would never heal. Their own children would start virtually from scratch instead of enjoying the legacy of R. J. Sr., a hardworking ancestor who surely never dreamed that the fruits of his labor would be removed from his own grandchildren.

❧ · ❧

To this day, Dick's heirs and observers can't account for his actions toward his family in his final years. The man he once was—the kind, generous philanthropist, the brilliant businessman, the merry, one-of-a-kind sailor—vanished too soon like a cloud of Camel cigarette smoke, forever.

But in their hearts and minds, the unforgettable spirit of R. J. "Dick" Reynolds Jr.—aka Kid Carolina—lives on.

AUTHOR'S NOTE

During the course of writing this book, my research evolved from being introduced to Dick Reynolds by Muriel's papers to my own quest to find the most objective sources I could. This was no easy task. Considering the fame of the family, very little has been written about Dick or the first-generation Reynolds tobacco heirs, apart from the countless news stories of their era and Patrick Reynolds's admirable, but at times biased, account in *The Gilded Leaf*. I spent hundreds of hours cross-checking often conflicting accounts in news stories, interviews, books, and other publications. Information I received from individual interviews also frequently conflicted with other sources—so much so that I relied very little on interviews in my final draft. I have concluded that because so much secrecy surrounds the legacy of the Reynolds family, not even the descendants and acquaintances know or understand the complete details of the family's history, apart from censored accounts.

Because Dick spent so much time in his life involved in litigation, I often turned to court documents to help me analyze and conclude the likely facts of any given event to offset the conflicts in other sources. Dick and Muriel's two divorce trials alone included eight thousand pages of detailed testimony about their lives. I believe that if my readers followed my research and analytical footsteps, they would reach similar conclusions about the story of Dick Reynolds.

Muriel Reynolds's compilation of letters, papers, diaries, transcripts, and manuscripts, which are based on her recollection of Dick's life story as he shared it with her during their marriage, is one of the largest known original collections of documentation about the Reynolds family, going back as far as Hardin Reynolds. To honor her monumental efforts and work, I centralized Muriel's perspective and her marriage to Dick in this story. I was well aware that Muriel had her own biases as well, and her memories of events, dates, and times were sometimes in conflict with other sources. At other times, her memory of events was stunning in its accuracy, scope, and detail. I cross-checked Muriel's accounts using the same analytical exercises, and where there were no other sources to confirm Muriel's memory, especially during her courtship with Dick, I took her at her word when it was reasonable and made sense contextually.

I also made a point to tell the story of Dick and Muriel's divorce from Muriel's perspective. Muriel was vilified in numerous accounts of the trial at the time, but the court transcripts tell a very different story—one in which Dick's actions were just as irresponsible, scheming, and often vicious. I thought this was important to relay, because Dick was normally a good-natured and giving man, and his turn toward extreme vengeance in the trial set the tone of the final years of his life and provided clues to his state of mind when he married Annemarie, escaped to Switzerland, and ultimately disinherited his six sons.

When Dick died of "too much oxygen to the brain" it inspired confusion that continues in some circles today. Most have accepted that Dick died of emphysema, since he had fallen so ill from the disease in the last few years of his life, but Dick said himself only months before he died that he expected to go on quite a bit longer, and his servants agreed with him.

Marianne O'Brien and Muriel felt certain there was more to the murky story of his death, and these suspicions only grew when the boys were disinherited. The actions of Nancy Reynolds and Annemarie didn't help. Nancy had likely intervened quickly because she was fixated on keeping scandal out of the family name. Many who knew her in Winston-Salem have confirmed that she was obsessed with sanitizing the family's image and that she considered Dick's womanizing and drinking a family embarrassment. His divorce from Muriel, double marriage to Annemarie, disinheritance of his sons, his obscure death by too much oxygen, and the birth of a daughter he never knew were likely more scandal than Nancy could bear.

Annemarie was said to be traumatized by her wild ride with Dick from the start. First she dealt with the contentious divorce from Muriel, in which she played the part of the shameful other woman and was a focal point of the bloodthirsty second trial. Next, Annemarie would rapidly learn the stress of Dick's on-again, off-again health problems, ailments, and tobacco and alcohol withdrawal. The final blow was Dick's unexpected death at a time when she was due to deliver her first child. Annemarie's difficult birth of her daughter just three days later sent her into a whirlwind of emotion. She gained a beautiful baby girl and lost a new husband she had left everything for—a career, her family, and her own autonomy—just a few years earlier.

Her troubles didn't end there. When the news broke that the boys were disinherited, Annemarie became the subject of hatred and rage. Her only ally, Nancy, likely made the situation worse by her secrecy and suspicious proposals to silence the boys. Presumably only Annemarie, Dick's oxygen therapist, Sergio Amati, Dick's longtime assistant, Guenther Lehman, and possibly other medical assistants knew exactly what happened to Dick in that oxygen tent. Was it an accident, did someone cause his death, or was there even more to the story?

There were allegations that Annemarie kept Dick "drugged and incapacitated," that she "willfully and feloniously" caused his death six months earlier and his death was concealed, and that his last will was forged. The circumstances of Dick's death were unusual and it was unlike Dick to handwrite an unwitnessed will and let it stand. Therefore, the suspicions of Dick's family members weren't unreasonable. That said, I have found no proof of wrongdoing on the part of Annemarie or anyone else.

Annemarie would continue to be sued for years to come. Her defenders say she was blindsided by the Reynolds family drama from the beginning and never sought the wealth or trouble that marrying Dick brought her. Dick's descendants have little sympathy and say she could have done more to reach out to them if she had really cared about Dick or the family and if she was innocent of any wrongdoing. They say she knows more about Dick's death and his disinheritance of his sons than she has revealed, and she need only break the silence to mend the family wounds. To this day, Dick's heirs in Winston-Salem regard her as "the one who got everything" as they live with pint-sized coffers that are less than 10 percent of the size of their cousins'.

In the end, I conclude that Dick deliberately chose to disinherit his sons in a moment of illness-induced hostility and cruel disdain for them. He never approved of their lifestyles and failed to acknowledge his own responsibility for their shortcomings. Annemarie may or may not have been an influence in his choice, but I do believe both Annemarie and Nancy were always insensitive to Dick's sons and poorly handled the aftermath of the disinheritance. I remain uncertain about Dick's death. I suspect Dick's death by too much oxygen to his brain was an accident that could have been prevented if he had more competent medical attention, much like Smith Reynolds's death in 1932 was probably a preventable accident. As in the case of Smith's death, I believe that the secretive, reticent behavior by those who surrounded Dick created even more controversy and suspicion than the situation warranted. I don't believe Annemarie deliberately caused his death or kept him "drugged and incapacitated," but I don't necessarily trust everyone who surrounded her and Dick in the last few years of his life. I believe there is more to the story than has been told. I do believe that Annemarie willingly and without regret accepted her full inheritance, which she has kept and is rumored to have expanded considerably since Dick's death. I also believe Annemarie knows more than anyone about Dick's other assets, such as the offshore accounts and buried gold that Dick likely smuggled into Europe. In Switzerland, reporters speculate that Dick's untaxed and unaccounted-for millions at the time of his death were stored in Swiss numbered accounts and have ballooned into the billions by now.

Annemarie might have been more generous had she been more welcomed into her American husband's family. The more she was the subject of harassment and suits, the less she probably cared what happened to Dick's sons and other descendants. Perhaps Annemarie really was the nice, modest German lady who fell into the claws of a rich and troubled American family, or perhaps she was savvier than people realize. Either way, she "got everything" and the damage Dick did to his children by disinheriting them was already done.

Dick's story can teach the rest of us how money can corrupt a family but it also teaches us how fatherlessness can be even worse. Had Dick reaped the benefits of his own father's love a while longer, perhaps he would have been a better father to his sons. There is no doubt that Dick had a big-hearted side to him and was loved by many. But Dick ultimately had a choice and he chose his desires, his money, his yachts, his women, and himself over his relationships with the boys. Had he picked a different path and committed himself to his sons' lives, his descendants would have a very different story to tell today.

ACKNOWLEDGMENTS

No biography is possible without an armada of people who believe in the project, the subject, and the author. Without the following individuals this book would not be possible.

First, I thank my Aunt Clara Smith for initiating this project, conducting research along the way, and resolutely believing in me as only an aunt could. Thank you to her friend Jeanette Scotton, for sharing Muriel's wild, entertaining, and moving stories with me. I don't know if we've satisfied the ghost, but I hope it's a strong start.

My sincerest thanks to my dedicated agent, Farley Chase, for taking on this project with me, and helping me develop the story in its early stages. I do believe you are the most patient agent in the business. Thank you to my acquiring editors, Sarah Sper and Harry Helm, for their keen interest in this story and commitment to the project. My sincerest thanks to Michelle Rapkin, Adlai Yeomans, Whitney Luken, Jody Waldrup, Bob Castillo, Peggy Boelke, and everyone at Center Street. To my editor, Holly Halverson—thank you for your enthusiasm, patience, and skill. You helped me shape this book with speed and grace, and you carried me through to the finish line. I'm forever grateful to you.

At times in everyone's life, there are certain individuals who are so supportive and steadfast during challenging endeavors, they leave you speechless with gratitude.

When it comes to work, I've always been a loner, but those times ended the day Joan Maltese became my friend and colleague. Joan, this book is as much yours as it is mine. You have not only taught me everything I know as a writer, you never say no when I need a hand, you always teach me something new, and you are a terrific friend. Thank you for being my editor, researcher, teacher, philosopher, coach, babysitter, friend...I could go on. I couldn't have done this without you. Thank you.

To my darling husband, Victor Navarro: No one leaves me more speechless than you. If there were an award for the most patient, loving man on earth, it would go to you. You are my inspiration, my rock, and my best friend. I know there is no one in the world who believes in me the way you do, and when I push myself to accomplish a feat and be successful, I do it because I want to make you proud. I know you mean it when you tell me that I've already won. I know it because I have you.

I am forever indebted to you for your graciousness, kindness, and love throughout all of my endeavors, and every day I am stunned by how lucky I am to have your support. So many times, only your strength, wisdom, and optimism kept my fingers to the keyboard. This book would have been impossible without you and I share it with you. Thank you from the bottom of my heart.

Finally, I thank my son, Karl. You shared your first year and a half of life with this book, and you rarely complained. When you flash that bright smile, it's like a dose of vitamin C each time, and it kept me going on some of my longest days. Thank you for teaching me how to be a good mother to you, and with such patience and forgiveness. I know I've said it a thousand times, but I will make up for all those play dates we missed. You're my little treasure and my good luck charm, and I would do anything for you. This one's for you.

∿ · ∾

I also share this book with the following individuals whose assistance, support, and contributions shaped this story in some form since its conception.

I thank Cheryl Adams, Cornelia Walker Bailey, Melynda Bissmeyer, Fam Brownlee, Fred Chase, Brenda Concepcion, Amanda Cothren, Theresa Croll, Liz Deery, Maggie Faircloth-Gersham, Jade Galston, Bootie Goodrich, Yvonne Grosvenor, Matthew Hanson, David Hardy, Thomas Haughton, Susan James, Alison Jordan, Maurice Klapwald, Sarah Lynch, Cristy Maltese, Jeanette Maltese, Ludwig Marek, Elisa Marquez, Clay Marston, Steve Metcalfe, Dawn Milici, Jeff Miller, Mickey Olsen, Gerrie Pitt, Molly Grogan Rawls, Linda Lee Reynolds, Marina Rodriguez, Emily Hart Roth, Henry Schnakenberg, Rachel Schnakenberg, Sarah Scott, Randy Sowell, Leslie Stauffer, Lindsay Sutton, Maura Wogan, and Nadia Yakoob. I'd also like to thank members of the Reynolds family who contributed to this book on the condition of anonymity.

In addition to these individuals, I thank the staff at the Associated Press, Beekman Place Association, Bibliotek of Lucerne, Carvasso's in London, Central Bibliotek of Zurich, Central Intelligence Agency, Corbis, Dorchester Collection, Federal Bureau of Investigation, Forsyth County Public Library, Fortnum & Mason, Franklin D. Roosevelt Presidential Library, Fulton County Courthouse, Fulton County Public Library, Georgia Probate Court, Georgia Supreme Court Archives, Getty Images, Harry S. Truman Presidential Library, Hertfordshire Archives and Local Studies, Jimmy Carter Presidential Library, Library of

Congress, McIntosh County Courthouse, National Archives—England, Mossiman's Belfry, National Archives and Records Administration, New York County Courthouse, New York Public Library, Old Bailey Courthouse, Palm Beach Courthouse, Photo Response Studio, Quaglino's, Reynolda House Museum of American Art, The Ritz London, RJR Tobacco Company, San Diego Law Library, Sapelo Island Tourist Center, Schweizer Illustrierte, SICARS, St. Anna Clinic, Tanglewood Park, Wake Forest University, Winston-Salem Visitor Center, Women's Library at London Metropolitan University, HM Prison Wormwood Scrubs, Zivilstandswesen of Lucerne, Z. Smith Reynolds Airport, Z. Smith Reynolds Library, University of Zurich Library.

SOURCE NOTES

This is a partial list of sources for each section or scene in the story. A complete list of sources can be found in the Bibliography. While some of the dialogue in this book has been created, the facts contained in the dialogue are true and accurate.

INTRODUCTION

Ghost of Muriel: Interviews with Jeanette Scotton, March 2005; H. W. Hutchins, personal papers, letters from Muriel M. Reynolds to H. W. Hutchins, courtesy Jeanette Scotton.

Reynolds influence, Winston-Salem: Frank V. Tursi, *Winston-Salem: A History* (Winston-Salem: John F. Blair, 1994); Bryan Burrough and John Helyar, *Barbarians at the Gate: The Fall of RJR Nabisco* (New York: Harper-Collins, 1990).

1. THE PATRIARCH

Reynolds homestead at Critz: Nannie Tilley, *The R.J. Reynolds Tobacco Company* (Chapel Hill: University of North Carolina Press, 1985); Barbara Mayer, *Reynolda: A History of an American House* (Winston-Salem: John F. Blair, 1997); "Winston-Salem Saddened by Reynolds Shift," *New York Times*, February 1, 1987.

A businessman is born: Molly Grogan Rawls, *Winston-Salem in Vintage Postcards* (Charleston: Arcadia, 2004); Burrough and Helyar, *Barbarians at the Gate*; Tilley, *The R.J. Reynolds Tobacco Company*.

R.J. at work: Susan E. White, Frank V. Tursi, and Steve McQuilkin, *Lost Empire: The Fall of R.J. Reynolds Tobacco Company* (Winston-Salem: Winston-Salem Journal, 2000); Catherine Howett, *A World of Her Own Making: Katharine Smith Reynolds and the Landscape of Reynolda* (Amherst: University of Massachusetts Press, 2007); Milton Ready, *The Tar Heel State: A History of North Carolina* (Columbia: University of South Carolina Press, 2005); Rawls, *Winston-Salem in Vintage Postcards*; Eric J. Elliot, *Winston-Salem's Historic West End* (Charleston: Arcadia, 2004); Michael P. Gleason and Andrew McCutcheon, *Sarge Reynolds: In the Time of His Life* (Gwynn, VA: Gleason, 1996).

R.J. finds love: Howett, *A World of Her Own Making*; Tursi, *Winston-Salem*; Mayer, *Reynolda*.

2. FAVORITE SON

Dick's first room: Muriel Reynolds papers; Recollections of family accounts as relayed to Muriel Reynolds by R. J. Reynolds Jr., 1951–1959, courtesy Jeanette Scotton.

Dick's idyllic early childhood: Tursi, *Winston-Salem*; Howett, *A World of Her Own Making*; Mayer, *Reynolda*.

Richard S. Reynolds: Gleason and McCutcheon, *Sarge Reynolds*; John A. Garraty and Mark C. Carnes, *American National Biography* (New York: Oxford University Press, 1999); Patrick Reynolds and Tom Shachtman, *The Gilded Leaf: Triumph, Tragedy, and Tobacco: Three Generations of the R.J. Reynolds Family and Fortune* (Boston: Little, Brown, 1989).

RJR Tobacco flourishes: Tilley, *The R.J. Reynolds Tobacco Company*; Elliot, *Winston-Salem's Historic West End*; Burrough and Helyar, *Barbarians at the Gate*; Ready, *The Tar Heel State*; White et al., *Lost Empire*; "The Controversial Princess," *Time*, April 11, 1960; Howett, *A World of Her Own Making*.

Dick's early business ventures: Howett, *A World of Her Own Making*; Mayer, *Reynolda*; Muriel Reynolds papers; Bill East, "Young Reynolds' Newspaper Was Neighborhood Success," *Twin City Sentinel*, December 16, 1964.

Katharine builds Reynolda: Mayer, *Reynolda*; "Reynolda Farm" (Winston-Salem: Twin-City Sentinel, 1917); Howett, *A World of Her Own Making*.

Dick learns the tobacco trade: Howett, *A World of Her Own Making*. Muriel Reynolds papers.

Death of a legend: Mayer, *Reynolda*; Elliot, *Winston-Salem's Historic West End*; Tilley, *The R.J. Reynolds Tobacco Company*; Rawls, *Winston-Salem in Vintage Postcards*.

3. LIFE AFTER R.J.

Katharine mourning, Dick's schools: Howett, *A World of Her Own Making*; Rollin Smith, *The Reynolda House Aeolian Organ* (Winston-Salem: Reynolda House Museum of Art, 1997); Sheila M. Dow, *Business Leader Profiles for Students* (Florence, KY: Gale Research, 1999); Muriel Reynolds papers; Mayer, *Reynolda*.

Katharine falls in love: Howett, *A World of Her Own Making*; Patrick Reynolds and Shachtman, *The Gilded Leaf*; Muriel Reynolds papers.

Escape to sea: Robert Erwin, "Dick Reynolds," *State Magazine*, August 16, 1941; Muriel Reynolds papers.

Punishing Katharine: Tilley, *The R.J. Reynolds Tobacco Company*; Howett, *A World of Her Own Making*.

Orphans: Howett, *A World of Her Own Making*; Mayer, *Reynolda*; Muriel Reynolds papers.

After Katharine: Howett, *A World of Her Own Making*; Patrick Reynolds and Shachtman, *The Gilded Leaf*.

4. CRASHING WITH THE STOCK MARKET

Guardianship, allowances: Patrick Reynolds and Shachtman, *The Gilded Leaf*; Robert Erwin, "Dick Reynolds," *State Magazine*, August 16, 1941.

College Adventures: Muriel Reynolds papers.

The aviator: Z. Smith Reynolds, *Log of Aeroplane NR-898W: Experiences, Comments, Impressions of a Flight from England to China* (Winston-Salem: Reynolda House Museum of Art/Wake Forest University, 2003); "Golden Isles Begins Feeder Service," *Darien News*, November 5, 1959; Robert Erwin; Muriel Reynolds papers; "Curtiss Field Saved as Aviation Centre: Big Airline

Planned," *New York Times*, August 14, 1927; "Curtiss Service Adds to Airports," *New York Times*, January 15, 1929; Patrick Reynolds and Shachtman, *The Gilded Leaf*; Howett, *A World of Her Own Making*.

A taste for alcohol: "Seek R. J. Reynolds, Tobacco Man's Heir, Missing 11 Days," *New York Times*, September 27, 1927; "Friend Reluctant to Talk," *New York Times*, September 28, 1927; "Reported Seen in Florida," *New York Times*, September 28, 1927; "Reynolds Located: Found in St. Louis Restaurant," *Los Angeles Times*, September 28, 1927; "Reynolds Is Found in St. Louis Cafe: Surprised at Hunt," *New York Times*, September 28, 1927; "Reynolds Explains Hiding," *Los Angeles Times*, September 29, 1927; "Reynolds on Way Here After 'Jaunt,'" *New York Times*, September 29, 1927; "Seeks Reynolds Award," *New York Times*, October 2, 1927; "Reynolds Absent: Friends Unworried," *New York Times*, October 3, 1927.

Dick in Paris and London: Muriel Reynolds papers; "R. J. Reynolds Is Sued," *New York Times*, March 31, 1933; Robert Erwin, "Dick Reynolds," *State Magazine*, August 16, 1941; "Millionaire's Son Sent to Prison," *Daily Chronicle*, August 1, 1929.

Drunken night in London, 1929: Suit, *Rex v. Richard Joshua Reynolds– Manslaughter,* 1929, Metropolitan Police 3/330/Old Bailey–London records; "Fatal Motor Accident," *The Times* (London), July 24, 1929.

Prison time in Wormwood Scrubs: Suit, *Rex v. Richard Joshua Reynolds*; "Reynolds on Trial for Manslaughter," *New York Times*, July 23, 1929, p. 21; "Reynolds on Witness Stand," *Winston-Salem Journal*, July 24, 1929; "Reynolds on Stand in Motor Killing," *New York Times*, July 25, 1929, p. 18; "Mistrial Ordered in Reynolds Case," *New York Times*, July 26, 1929, p. 6; "Reynolds Retrial Opens," *New York Times*, July 27, 1929, p. 5; "Reynolds Case in New Turn," *Winston-Salem Journal*, July 30, 1929; "Reynolds Gets 5-Month Term," *Winston-Salem Journal*, July 31, 1929; "Millionaire's Son Sent to Prison," *Daily Chronicle,* August 1, 1929; "American Sent to Prison," *The Times* (London), August 1, 1929; "Reynolds Guilty; Gets Five Months," *New York Times*, August 1, 1929, p. 2; "Drunkenness," *Time*, August 12, 1929.

Release and escape: "To Sue for $1,300,000 for Airplane Crash," *New York Times*, August 21, 1929; "Air Crash Suits Shifted," *New York Times*, October 19, 1929; "Miss Mary Reynolds Wed," *New York Times*, December 17, 1929; Howett, *A World of Her Own Making*; Mayer, *Reynolda*.

5. TRAGEDY AT REYNOLDA

The *Harpoon*: Robert Erwin, "Dick Reynolds," *State Magazine,* August 16, 1941; Muriel Reynolds papers.

Slain brother: "Reynolds Inquiry Awaits Brother," *New York Times,* July 15, 1932; Robert Erwin, "Dick Reynolds," *State Magazine,* August 16, 1941; Muriel Reynolds papers; "Young Reynolds Arrives Here Following 12,000 Mile Trip from Africa," *Winston-Salem Journal,* August 24, 1932.

Maddening journey home: "Reynolds Brother Leaves Brazil," *New York Times,* August 6, 1932; "Reynolds Will Fly to Miami," *New York Times,* August 16, 1932; "Expect Holman Trial to Be Held in 6 Weeks," *New York Times,* August 16, 1932; "Reynolds Reported Near Home," *Los Angeles Times,* August 21, 1932; "R. J. Reynolds Jr. Arrives," *New York Times,* August 22, 1932; "Brazil Revolt Gains Ground," *Los Angeles Times,* August 25, 1932; "Young Reynolds Arrives Here Following 12,000 Mile Trip from Africa," *Winston-Salem Journal,* August 24, 1932.

Smith's tumultuous life: Z. Smith Reynolds, *Log of Aeroplane NR-898W*; Emily Herring Wilson, *For the People of North Carolina: The Z. Smith Reynolds Foundation at Half-Century, 1936–1986* (Chapel Hill: University of North Carolina Press, 1988); Howett, *A World of Her Own Making*; Hamilton Darby Perry, *Libby Holman: Body and Soul* (Boston: Little, Brown, 1983); "Reynolds vs. Reynolds," *Time,* January 23, 1933; Tursi, *Winston-Salem*; "Couple Wedded November 29," *Twin-City Sentinel,* 1932.

A party and a gun: Wilson, *For the People of North Carolina*; Jon Bradshaw, *Dreams That Money Can Buy: The Tragic Life of Libby Holman* (New York: William Morrow, 1985); Francis H. Casstevens, *Death in North Carolina's Piedmont: Tales of Murder, Suicide and Causes Unknown* (Charleston: History Press, 2006); "R. J. Reynolds Heir Commits Suicide," *New York Times,* July 7, 1932; "Widow's Parents Mystified," *New York Times,* July 7, 1932.

The questions begin: Bradshaw, *Dreams That Money Can Buy*; Casstevens, *Death in North Carolina's Piedmont*; Perry, *Libby Holman*; "Reynolds a Suicide, His Guardian Holds," *New York Times,* July 8, 1932; "Reynolds Case Has a New Turn," *Los Angeles Times,* July 11, 1932; "To Fingerprint Guests," *New York Times,* July 11, 1932; "Sheriff Continuing Reynolds Inquiry," *New York Times,* July 13, 1932; "Reynolds Inquiry Awaits Brother," *New York Times,* July 15, 1932; "Finds New Evidence in Reynolds Death," *New York Times,*

August 11, 1929; "Widow Believed at Former Retreat," *New York Times*, August 11, 1929; "Reynolds Trial Oct. 3 Expected by Defense," *New York Times*, August 21, 1932; "Dick Reynolds Thinks Smith Was Murdered," *Florence Morning News*, August 25, 1932; "Brother Thinks Young Reynolds Was Murdered," *Los Angeles Times*, August 25, 1932; "Reynolds Desires to See 'Justice' Done Regarding Tragic Death of Brother," *Winston-Salem Journal*, August 25, 1932; "Dick Reynolds Is in Winston-Salem," *The Landmark*, August 26, 1932; "Midnight Autopsy Made on Reynolds," *New York Times*, September 2, 1932; "Reynolds Case Inquiry Revived," *New York Times*, September 2, 1932; "Libby Holman Reynolds Asks Full Exoneration," *New York Times*, October 20, 1932; "Libby Holman Asks Trial to Clear Her," *New York Times*, October 20, 1932.

Emotional aftermath: Bradshaw, *Dreams that Money Can Buy*; "Reynolds Left Suspect Cash," *New York Times*, October 8, 1932; "Sues to Apportion Reynolds Estate," *New York Times*, March 25, 1933; "Family Proposes Reynolds Division," *New York Times*, November 17, 1934; *Anne Cannon Reynolds et al. v. Zachary Smith Reynolds et al.*, 208 N.C. 578; 182 S.E. 341; "Reynolds Settlement Overruled," *Los Angeles Times*, March 22, 1934; "Family Threatens New Reynolds Suit," *New York Times*, March 12, 1935; "Miss Holman Wins in Reynolds Fight," *New York Times*, March 16, 1935; "House by Reynolds," *Time*, September 2, 1935; "Libby Holman Wins on Estate Appeal," *New York Times*, November 2, 1935; "Names Make the News," *Time*, March 23, 1936; Wilson, *For the People of North Carolina*.

6. LOVE, YACHTS, AND POLITICS

Ella Cannon: Muriel Reynolds papers; "Milestones," *Time*, June 11, 1934.

Wedding bells: Muriel Reynolds papers; "R. J. Reynolds to Wed: Heir of Tobacco Man to Marry Miss Dillard Tomorrow," *New York Times*, December 31, 1932, p. 8; "R. J. Reynolds to Wed Miss Dillard," *New York Times*, December 26, 1932; "R. J. Reynolds Weds Miss Dillard," *New York Times*, January 2, 1933; "Milestones," *Time*, January 9, 1933; Elliot, *Winston-Salem's Historic West End*.

The era of Blitz: "Dick Reynolds Given $25,000,000," *Daily-Times News*, April 4, 1934; "So They Took the $25,000,000," *Los Angeles Times*, April 9, 1934; "R. J. Reynolds Is Sued," *New York Times*, March 31, 1933; "R. J.

Reynolds Fights Suit," *New York Times*, October 31, 1933; "Reynolds Loses Point," *New York Times*, December 17, 1933; "Reynolds Answers Dancer's $140,000 Suit," *New York Times*, September 8, 1934; "$1,475,000 Suit Settled," *New York Times*, May 8, 1934; "Son to R. J. Reynolds Jr.," *New York Times*, December 8, 1933; "Pacing Stake Won by Dick Reynolds," *New York Times*, July 7, 1933; "Hambletonian Won by Mary Reynolds," *New York Times*, August 17, 1933; "Taffy Volo Takes Trot," *New York Times*, September 14, 1933; "Mrs. Harriman Wins Special Trot for Amateur Drivers at Goshen," *New York Times*, July 23, 1936; "3-Heat World Trot Record Set by Calumet Dilworthy at Goshen," *New York Times*, July 24, 1936; Ross Mactaggart, *The Golden Century: Classic Motor Yachts, 1830–1930* (New York: W. W. Norton, 2001); "Island to R. J. Reynolds," *New York Times*, April 19, 1934; "Reynolds Leases Sapelo Island," *New York Times*, April 19, 1934; "Island Fad Hits South," *New York Times*, February 7, 1937; Garraty et al., *American National Biography*; Buddy Sullivan, *Sapelo: A History* (Darien: Darien News, 1988); "R. J. Reynoldses Jr. Hosts," *New York Times*, February 11, 1938; "Sloop Blitzen Launched," *New York Times*, June 3, 1938; "30 Craft Ready to Start Today in Bayside's Block Island Race," *New York Times*, July 29, 1938; "Blitzen Sails on to Early Lead," *New York Times*, July 30, 1938; "38 Yachts Start in Vineyard Race," *New York Times*, September 3, 1938; James Robbins, "Baruna's Victory a Feature of the Year," *New York Times*, December 25, 1938; "Yawl Crosses Ocean, Ruled out of Race," *New York Times*, August 8, 1937; "American Yacht Disqualified in Race," *Los Angeles Times*, August 8, 1937; "American Yawl Is Fifth," *New York Times*, August 13, 1937; "Lead Poured at City Island Yard for Keel of New Schafer Yawl," *New York Times*, December 30, 1937.

Dreams chased: "Blitzen from the East," *Oakland Tribune*, July 2, 1939; "Miami Women Watch Yachts from Plane," *New York Times*, February 16, 1939; "Small Boats Race Today at Newport," *New York Times*, March 26, 1939; "Wakiva Takes Lead in Race to Havana," *New York Times*, March 5, 1939; "Wakiva Sets Pace for Racing Fleet," *New York Times*, March 6, 1939; "Small Yachts Take the Lead," *New York Times*, July 6, 1939; "Blitzen Is Victor in Key West Race," *New York Times*, March 12, 1939; "Blitzen Triumphs on Corrected Time," *New York Times*, March 7, 1939.

Kid Carolina strikes again: "Threatened Wife of R. J. Reynolds," *New York Times*, November 4, 1933; "Faces Extortion Trial," *New York Times*, November 5, 1933; "Extortion Defendant Sentenced," *New York Times*, November

21, 1933; Wilson, *For the People of North Carolina*; "Reynolds Fund Aids
Warfare on Syphilis," *New York Times*, December 19, 1937; Tilley, *The
R. J. Reynolds Tobacco Company*; Muriel Reynolds papers; "Chatterbox,"
Los Angeles Times, August 10, 1939; "Hawaii Yacht Race Winner at Mat-
sonia," *Los Angeles Times*, August 10, 1939; "Gossip and Smart Talk," *Los
Angeles Times*, August 20, 1939; "For First Place," *Fresno Bee*, July 17, 1939;
"Chatterbox," *Los Angeles Times*, May 24, 1939; "Chubasco Fails to Report
in Honolulu Race Yacht Race," *Los Angeles Times*, July 16, 1939; "Fan-
dango 2 Miles Ahead," *New York Times*, July 17, 1939; "Yacht Race Vic-
tor in Doubt," *Los Angeles Times*, July 21, 1939; James Robbins and Morris
Rosenfield, "Nation's Yachtsmen and Speed Boat Pilots Enjoyed a Record-
Breaking Year," *New York Times*, December 24, 1939.

Political ventures: "Democrats Report Outlay," *New York Times*, October
31, 1936; "Democratic National Group Reorganization Disclosed," *Los
Angeles Times*, January 5, 1941; "Democratic Shift Committee Posts," *New
York Times*, January 5, 1941; Letter, Franklin D. Roosevelt to Mr. Reyn-
olds, February 5, 1941, PPF 7370, Franklin D. Roosevelt Library; "Reyn-
olds Gets Call in Inquiry," *Los Angeles Times*, January 14, 1941; "Tobey
Demands Hague Inquiry," *New York Times*, March 8, 1941, p. 10; "Senate
Seat Declared Won by Illegal Methods," *New York Times*, February 21, 1941;
"Milestones," *Time*, April 14, 1941; "The Controversial Princess," *Time*,
April 11, 1960; Erwin, "Dick Reynolds," *State Magazine*, August 16, 1941;
Robert C. Albright, "'Boss Away,' Democrats Call off $100 Feast," *Wash-
ington Post*, March 28, 1941, p. 1; "Both Parties Evaded Law, Says Gillette,"
Washington Post, January 12, 1941, p. 11; "Jackson Day Dinner Set," *New
York Times*, February 24, 1941; "Roosevelt to Make Jackson Day Speech,"
New York Times, March 24, 1941; "Democrats Report $414,617 Unpaid,"
New York Times, March 13, 1941, p. 17; Arthur Sears Henning, "Find Campaign Was History's Most Expensive," *Chicago Daily Tribune*, January 24,
1941; "Jersey Democrats Got Reynolds Loan," *New York Times*, January 9,
1941, p. 46; "More Party Loans Told at Inquiry," *New York Times*, January
10, 1941, p. 20; "Quayle Decides Loan Testimony Was a 'Mistake,'" *Chicago Daily Tribune*, January 12, 1941, p. 13; "Roosevelt Radio Loan Questioned," *Los Angeles Times*, January 9, 1941, p. 8; "Says Both Parties 'Evaded'
Hatch Act," *New York Times*, January 12, 1941, p. 42; Unpublished U.S.
Senate Committee Hearings, 18th Congress–88th Congress, 1823–1964
(18) SJ-T.1–(82) SSM-T.23; Tursi, *Winston-Salem*; Patrick Reynolds and

Shachtman, *The Gilded Leaf*; Roy Thompson, "R. J. Reynolds Dies at 58 in Swiss Clinic: Cause Not Determined," *Winston-Salem Journal*, December 16, 1964; Charles Osolin, "Career as Mayor: Brief, Distinctive," *Winston-Salem Journal*, December 17, 1964; "Tom Davis: Entrepreneur of the Air," *News and Observer*, June 23, 2004.

Breakdown ahead: Letter, Richard J. Reynolds to Franklin D. Roosevelt, December 2, 1941, Franklin D. Roosevelt Library; Letter, Franklin D. Roosevelt to Dick Reynolds, December 5, 1941, PPF 1069, Franklin D. Roosevelt Library; "Women Invite Men to Parley," *Los Angeles Times*, August 7, 1941; "Radio Today," *New York Times*, August 28, 1941; "Young Democrats Back All Out Aid," *New York Times*, August 24, 1941; "Flynn Sees Slap at Foreign Policy," *Los Angeles Times*, September 12, 1941; "Victory Seen by Secretary," *Los Angeles Times*, September 13, 1941; Linda Lee Reynolds, interview with Joan Maltese, February 2009; "Ship Construction Ahead of Schedule," *New York Times*, May 18, 1941; "Seattle Mail Ship Launched in East," *Los Angeles Times*, May 25, 1941; "New Line to Orient Approved by U.S.," *New York Times*, October 6, 1940; Rene De La Pedraja, *A Historical Dictionary of the U.S. Merchant Marine and Shipping Industry: Since the Introduction of Steam* (Santa Barbara: Greenwood, 1994); "Expanded Service of Line Approved," *New York Times*, November 7, 1940; Divorce suit, *Elizabeth Dillard Reynolds v. Richard Joshua Reynolds*, 1946, Forsyth County records.

7. LOVE AND WAR

Political resignations, family trouble: Gene Whitman, "Mayor Reynolds Hit Apathy," *Twin City Sentinel*, December 16, 1964; Letter, Franklin D. Roosevelt to Dick Reynolds, July 30, 1942, PPF 7370, Franklin D. Roosevelt Library; Letter, Richard J. Reynolds, Treasurer, DNC to Franklin D. Roosevelt, June 4, 1942, Franklin D. Roosevelt Library; Memorandum, Edward J. Flynn to Franklin D. Roosevelt, June 17, 1942, Franklin D. Roosevelt Library; Reynolds family member (anonymous), interview with Joan Maltese, February 2009; Patrick Reynolds and Shachtman, *The Gilded Leaf*.

Marriage abandoned: Muriel Reynolds papers, Patrick Reynolds and Shachtman, *The Gilded Leaf*; "R. J. Reynolds to Marry: Son of Tobacco Firm Founder to Marian Byrne, Actress," *New York Times*, August 7, 1946, p. 19; "R. J. Reynolds Weds," *New York Times*, August 8, 1946.

San Diego, California, 1944: Muriel Reynolds papers; Patrick Reynolds and Shachtman, *The Gilded Leaf*; "Dick Reynolds Weds an Actress," *The Landmark*, August 8, 1946.

Active service: Muriel Reynolds papers; Patrick Reynolds and Shachtman, *The Gilded Leaf*; Wilson, *For the People of North Carolina*; Clay Marston, interview correspondence with Joan Maltese, June 2009.

Postwar activities: Tursi, *Winston-Salem*; Divorce suit, *Elizabeth Dillard Reynolds v. Richard Joshua Reynolds,* 1946; Cornelia Walker Bailey, interview with the author, September 2008; Forsyth County records; "Reynolds Tobacco Heir Files Suit for Divorce," *New York Times*, June 1, 1946; "R. J. Reynolds Sues Wife," *New York Times*, June 1, 1946; "Divorce Granted to Mrs. R. J. Reynolds," *New York Times*, June 25, 1946, p. 23; "Mrs. Reynolds Agrees to Divorce Settlement," *Los Angeles Times*, June 15, 1946.

Enter wife no. 2: "R. J. Reynolds to Marry: Son of Tobacco Firm Founder to Marian Byrne, Actress," *New York Times*, August 7, 1946, p. 19; "R. J. Reynolds Weds," *New York Times*, August 8, 1946; "Dick Reynolds Weds an Actress," *The Landmark*, August 8, 1946; Muriel Reynolds papers; Patrick Reynolds and Shachtman, *The Gilded Leaf*; "Tobacco Tycoon Tosses Surprise Party," *The Times Recorder*, December 13, 1947; Divorce Suit, *Richard J. Reynolds v. Marianne O'Brien Reynolds,* 1952, Dade County records; Suit, *Marianne O'Brien Reynolds v. Estate of Richard J. Reynolds*, 1975, McIntosh County records; "National Aid Given State Democrats," *New York Times*, October 30, 1946; Cornelia Walker Bailey and Christena Bledsoe, *God, Dr. Buzzard, and the Bolito Man: A Saltwater Geechee Talks About Life on Sapelo Island, Georgia* (New York: Anchor, 2001); Sullivan, *Sapelo: A History*; "President's Wartime Aide Heads Caribou Mines," *New York Times*, March 2, 1950; "Parties List Funds in State Campaign," *New York Times*, December 1, 1944; R. E. G. Davies, *Delta: An Airline and Its Aircraft* (McLean, VA: Paladwr, 1990); Pony Duke and Jason Thomas, *Too Rich: The Family Secrets of Doris Duke* (New York: HarperCollins, 1995); Isabella Wall, Marty Wall, and Robert Bruce Woodcox, *Chasing Rubi: The Truth About Porfirio Rubirosa, the Last Playboy* (Newport Beach, CA: Literary Press, 2005).

The Knickerbocker Ball: Muriel Laurence, "Letters to the Times," *New York Times*, December 15, 1941; Muriel Laurence, "London," *New York Times*, December 20, 1941; "Marriages: Mr. R. D. A. Greenough and Mrs. M. Allison-Laurence," *The Times* (London), October 10, 1946; Clay Marston, interview correspondence with Joan Maltese, June 2009; "Mrs. M. A. Laurence Married in Prague," *New York Times*, October 15, 1946; Marriage certificate for Richard Greenough and Muriel Laurence, 1946, City of Westminster General Register Office, London; Muriel Laurence, "Shortage of Food Weakening the French," *New York Times*, November 15, 1943; Muriel Reynolds papers; Divorce suit, *Richard J. Reynolds v. Marianne O'Brien Reynolds,* 1952.

8. DESTINY CALLS

Going-away party: Muriel Reynolds papers.

Muriel and Eleanor: Muriel Reynolds papers.

The Ritz: Muriel Reynolds papers; Divorce suit, *Richard J. Reynolds v. Marianne O'Brien Reynolds,* 1952; Duke and Thomas, *Too Rich*; Wall et al., *Chasing Rubi*; Patrick Reynolds and Shachtman, *The Gilded Leaf*; Erwin, "Dick Reynolds," *State Magazine*, August 16, 1941; "Tobacco Heir Divorced," *New York Times*, August 8, 1952.

9. DICK AND MURIEL'S SECRET AFFAIR

The courtship: Muriel Reynolds papers; Divorce suit, *Richard J. Reynolds v. Marianne O'Brien Reynolds,* 1952; Divorce suit, *Richard J. Reynolds v. Muriel M. Reynolds,* 1960, McIntosh County records (including motions, depositions, testimony); Divorce suit *Richard J. Reynolds v. Muriel M. Reynolds,* 1962.

The Italian idyll: Muriel Reynolds papers.

10. ON THE RUN

Dick's code name: Muriel Reynolds papers.

Return to America: Jay Te Winburn, "Mary K. Babcock Married in South," *New York Times,* September 2, 1951; Tursi, *Winston-Salem*; Thomas K. Hearn III, *Wake Forest University* (Charleston: Arcadia, 2003); Muriel Reynolds papers.

Trouble at One Beekman Place: Suit, *Marianne O'Brien Reynolds v. Chemical Bank & Trust Company,* 1951–1952, New York County records; Divorce suit, *Richard J. Reynolds v. Marianne O'Brien Reynolds,* 1952; Muriel Reynolds papers; "A Spell of Unemployment," *Time*, December 21, 1953.

Journey to Mexico: Muriel Reynolds papers.

11. RETURN TO SAPELO ISLAND

Christmas 1952: Muriel Reynolds papers.

Sapelo Island, 1952: Sullivan, *Sapelo: A History*; Burnette Lightle Vanstory, *Georgia's Land of Golden Isles* (Athens, GA: University of Georgia Press, 1982); Buddy Sullivan, *Darien and McIntosh County: Images of America* (Charleston: Arcadia, 2000); "President Vacationing on Island in Georgia," *New York Times*, April 14, 1939; William S. McFeely, *Sapelo's People: A Long Walk into Freedom* (New York: W. W. Norton, 1995); Bailey and Bledsoe, *God, Dr. Buzzard, and the Bolito Man*; Cornelia Walker Bailey, interview with the author, September 2008; Yvonne Grosvenor, Island tour information, September 2008; Muriel Reynolds papers; Patrick Reynolds and Shachtman, *The Gilded Leaf*; Michele Nicole Johnson, *Sapelo Island's Hog Hammock, GA* (Charleston: Arcadia, 2009); "Works of Art from 40 Tiny Islands," *New York Times*, January 23, 1971; Divorce suit, *Richard J. Reynolds v. Muriel M. Reynolds*, 1960; Divorce suit, *Richard J. Reynolds v. Muriel M. Reynolds*, 1962; Clay Marston, interview correspondence with Joan Maltese, June 2009.

Jamaican adventures: Divorce suit, *Richard J. Reynolds v. Muriel M. Reynolds*, 1960; Divorce suit, *Richard J. Reynolds v. Muriel M. Reynolds*, 1962; Muriel Reynolds papers; Garraty and Carnes, *American National Biography*; "Reynolds' Second Wife to Get $2,000,000," *Los Angeles Times*, July 29, 1952.

Building the *Aries*, March 1952: Divorce suit, *Richard J. Reynolds v. Marianne O'Brien Reynolds*, 1952; Divorce suit, *Richard J. Reynolds v. Muriel M. Reynolds*, 1960; Divorce suit, *Richard J. Reynolds v. Muriel M. Reynolds*, 1962; "Reynolds' Second Wife to Get $2,000,000," *Los Angeles Times*, July 29, 1952; Suit, *Marianne O'Brien Reynolds v. Chemical Bank & Trust Company*, 1951–1952; Muriel Reynolds papers; "Concessions Charged on Party Loans," *Los Angeles Times*, April 30, 1952; "Olson's Spending Put Above Income," *New York Times*, May 1, 1952; "U.S. Official Defends Political Loan Rule," *New York Times*, May 28, 1952.

12. CRACKS IN THE ROMANCE

Naming Rubirosa: Divorce suit, *Richard J. Reynolds v. Marianne O'Brien Reynolds*, 1952; "A Spell of Unemployment," *Time*, December 21, 1953; "Tobacco Heir Divorced," *New York Times*, August 8, 1952; Wall et al., *Chasing Rubi*.

Trouble at Hôtel du Nord: Muriel Reynolds papers. Divorce suit, *Richard J. Reynolds v. Muriel M. Reynolds*, 1960; Divorce suit, *Richard J. Reynolds v. Muriel M. Reynolds*, 1962.

At Marianne's: Divorce suit, *Richard J. Reynolds v. Marianne O'Brien Reynolds*, 1952; Patrick Reynolds and Shachtman, *The Gilded Leaf*; Divorce suit, *Richard J. Reynolds v. Muriel M. Reynolds*, 1960; Divorce suit, *Richard J. Reynolds v. Muriel M. Reynolds*, 1962.

13. LE DIVORCE

Taking care of Josh, settlement agreement: Muriel Reynolds papers; Reynolds family member (anonymous), interview with Joan Maltese, February 2009; Fambrough Brownlee, interview with Joan Maltese, February 2009; "Tobacco Heir Divorced," *New York Times*, August 8, 1952; "Reynolds' Second Wife to Get $2,000,000," *Los Angeles Times*, July 29, 1952; Divorce suit, *Richard J. Reynolds v. Marianne O'Brien Reynolds*, 1952.

Holy matrimony, August 1952: "Tobacco Heir Divorced," *New York Times*, August 8, 1952; "R. J. Reynolds Married," *New York Times*, August 10, 1952; "Marriages: Mr. R. J. Reynolds and Mrs. M. M. Greenough," *The Times* (London), August 18, 1952; "Reynolds on Honeymoon in 60-Room Home," *Los Angeles Times*, August 11, 1952; Muriel Reynolds papers; Divorce suit, *Richard J. Reynolds v. Muriel M. Reynolds*, 1960; Divorce suit, *Richard J. Reynolds v. Muriel M. Reynolds*, 1962; Patrick Reynolds and Shachtman, *The Gilded Leaf*.

14. WINSTON-SALEM SOCIETY

Roaring Gap: Muriel Reynolds papers; Mayer, *Reynolda*; Howett, *A World of Her Own Making*.

Devotion drama: Muriel Reynolds papers; Roy Thompson, "Reynolds Had Many Sides: Wealth, Generosity, Flash," *Winston-Salem Journal*, December 17, 1964; Patrick Reynolds and Shachtman, *The Gilded Leaf*; Mayer, *Reynolda*; Smith, *The Reynolda House Aeolian Organ*.

15. SMITH

Going down Memory Lane: Muriel Reynolds papers; "R. J. Reynolds ...ullu Brother Was Slain," *New York Times*, August 25, 1932; Wilson, *For the People of North Carolina*; Fambrough Brownlee, interview with Joan Maltese, February 2009; Molly Grogan Rawls, *Winston-Salem: From the Collection of Frank B. Jones Jr.* (Charleston: Arcadia, 2006); Roy Thompson, "Reynolds Had Many Sides: Wealth, Generosity, Flash," *Winston-Salem Journal*, December 17, 1964.

The Launch at Gosport: Rawls, *Winston-Salem*; Muriel Reynolds papers; Clay Marston, interview correspondence with Joan Maltese, June 2009.

16. THINGS FALL APART

Dick's health, family: "Gone Are the Days When Tobacco Brought Only Wealth," *New York Times*, February 26, 1995; Divorce suit, *Richard J. Reynolds v. Muriel M. Reynolds*, 1960, and divorce suit, *Richard J. Reynolds v. Muriel M. Reynolds*, 1962; Clay Marston, interview correspondence with Joan Maltese, June 2009.

The Copenhagn Debacle: "Co-op Apartment Sold," *New York Times*, October 21, 1953; Divorce suit, *Richard J. Reynolds v. Muriel M. Reynolds*, 1960, and divorce suit, *Richard J. Reynolds v. Muriel M. Reynolds*, 1962; McFeely, *Sapelo's People*; "Mrs. Mann Married," *New York Times*, October 19, 1954; Marriage certificate for Richard Greenough and Ileana Mann, 1954, City of Westminster General Register Office, London; "Tobacco Heir Safe After Yacht Blast," *New York Times*, February 25, 1955; Hearn, *Wake Forest University*; Muriel Reynolds papers; Reynolds family member (anonymous), interview with Joan Maltese, February 2009; Bailey and Bledsoe, *God, Dr. Buzzard, and the Bolito Man*; Cornelia Walker Bailey, interview with the author, September 2008; "Stevenson Names 50 Business Aids," *New York Times*, October 11, 1956; "Political Gifts by 12 Wealthy Families Listed," *Los Angeles Times*, February 3, 1957; Linda Lee Reynolds, interview with Joan Maltese, February 2009.

Dick's rapid decline: Divorce suit, *Richard J. Reynolds v. Muriel M. Reynolds*, 1960, and divorce suit, *Richard J. Reynolds v. Muriel M. Reynolds*, 1962; Muriel Reynolds papers; "Co-op Apartment Sold," *New York Times*, October 21, 1953; Roy Thompson, Cornelia Walker Bailey, interview with the author, September 2008; "Golden Isles Begins Feeder Service," *Darien News*, November 5, 1959; "Reynolds Is President New Airlines Company Located at Sapelo Island," *Darien News*, November 5, 1959; Robert Erwin, "Dick Reynolds," *State Magazine*, August 16, 1941; Yvonne Grosvenor, Island tour information, September 2008; Bailey and Bledsoe, *God, Dr. Buzzard, and the Bolito Man*; "R. J. Reynolds Jr., Tobacco Heir, Dies: Financier and Ex-Politician Was a Former Playboy," *New York Times*, December 16, 1964, p. 43; Mickey Olson, interview with Joan Maltese, October 2008; "Richard J. Reynolds Gym Dedication Set for Dec. 29," *Darien News*.

Summer 1959: Divorce suit, *Richard J. Reynolds v. Muriel M. Reynolds*, 1960, and divorce suit, *Richard J. Reynolds v. Muriel M. Reynolds*, 1962.

17. DARIEN

Pretrial activity, opening statements: Divorce suit, *Richard J. Reynolds v. Muriel M. Reynolds*, 1960, and divorce suit, *Richard J. Reynolds v. Muriel M. Reynolds*, 1962; Clay Marston, interview correspondence with Joan Maltese, June 2009; Patrick Reynolds and Shachtman, *The Gilded Leaf*; Celestine Sibley, Richard Eldredge, and Fleming Sibley, *Celestine Sibley Reporter* (Athens, GA: Hill Street, 2006); Bailey and Bledsoe, *God, Dr. Buzzard, and the Bolito Man*; Roy Thompson, "Reynolds Had Many Sides: Wealth, Generosity, Flash," *Winston-Salem Journal*, December 17, 1964.

Muriel takes the stand: Divorce suit, *Richard J. Reynolds v. Muriel M. Reynolds*, 1960, and divorce suit, *Richard J. Reynolds v. Muriel M. Reynolds*, 1962; Sullivan, *Darien and McIntosh County*; "Reynolds Gets Divorce," *New York Times*, May 17, 1960; "Milestones," *Time*, May 30, 1960.

A new love: "Tobacco Heir Wed: Ex-Wife Shocked," *New York Times*, April 5, 1961; "Ex-Spouse Protests New Marriage by Reynolds," *Pasadena Independent*, April 6, 1961; Divorce suit, *Richard J. Reynolds v. Muriel M. Reynolds*, 1960, and divorce suit, *Richard J. Reynolds v. Muriel M. Reynolds*, 1962.

The appeal: "New Reynolds Trial," *New York Times*, September 9, 1961; Divorce suit, *Richard J. Reynolds v. Muriel M. Reynolds*, 1960, and divorce suit, *Richard J. Reynolds v. Muriel M. Reynolds*, 1962; Divorce suit, *Richard J. Reynolds v. Muriel M. Reynolds*, 1962, U.S. Court of Appeals.

Dick and Annemarie: Divorce suit, *Richard J. Reynolds v. Muriel M. Reynolds*, 1960, and divorce suit, *Richard J. Reynolds v. Muriel M. Reynolds*, 1962.

The second trial: "Gifts Made by Reynolds to Projects Here Are Cited in Opening Hours of Retrial," *Darien News*, May 10, 1962; Divorce suit, *Richard J. Reynolds v. Muriel M. Reynolds*, 1960, and divorce suit, *Richard J. Reynolds v.*

Muriel M. Reynolds, 1962; Tim Pat Coogan, *The IRA* (New York: Palgrave Macmillan, 2002); "Reynolds Inventory Filed," *New York Times*, December 20, 1961.

Dick takes the stand: Divorce suit, *Richard J. Reynolds v. Muriel M. Reynolds*, 1960, and divorce suit, *Richard J. Reynolds v. Muriel M. Reynolds*, 1962; Tilley, *The R.J. Reynolds Tobacco Company.*

Adultery with Annemarie: Divorce suit, *Richard J. Reynolds v. Muriel M. Reynolds*, 1960, and divorce suit, *Richard J. Reynolds v. Muriel M. Reynolds*, 1962.

Closing arguments: Divorce suit, *Richard J. Reynolds v. Muriel M. Reynolds*, 1960, and divorce suit, *Richard J. Reynolds v. Muriel M. Reynolds*, 1962; "Tobacco Heir Settles: $2 Million Alimony," *New York Mirror*, April 28, 1963; "Tobacco Heir's Ex-wife Gets $2 Million Alimony," *Los Angeles Times*, April 28, 1963; "R. J. Reynolds Divorce Pact Gives 3rd Wife $2 Million," *New York Times*, April 28, 1963; Suit, *Muriel M. Reynolds v. Richard J. Reynolds*, 1963, New York County records; Suit, *Muriel M. Reynolds v. Richard J. Reynolds*, 1963, McIntosh County records; "The Marriage-Go-Round," *Time*, January 25, 1963; "Mrs. E. D. Reynolds," *New York Times*, December 11, 1961; Dow, *Business Leader Profiles for Students.*

18. NORTH CAROLINA'S PRINCE OF WALES: THE MYSTERY

Death, aftermath: Death Certificate of Richard Joshua Reynolds, 1964, Confederation Suisse, Lucerne, Switzerland; "R. J. Reynolds Is Buried in Cemetery in Lucerne," *New York Times*, December 18, 1964, p. 64; Roy Thompson, "Reynolds Heir Is Dead at 58," *News and Observer*, December 16, 1964; "Reynolds Heir Born 36 Hours After He Died," *Charleston Gazette*, December 17, 1964; "Reynolds Baby Born," *Twin City Sentinel*, December 16, 1964; "R. J. Reynolds Is Dead: Stricken in Switzerland," *Twin City Sentinel*, December 15, 1964; "Reynolds Buried at Church in Village Near Swiss Home," *Twin City Sentinel*, December 17, 1964; "Widow of R. J. Reynolds Gives Birth to Daughter," *New York Times*, December 16, 1964; Maria Coffey, *Explorers of the Infinite* (New York: Tarcher, 2008); "R. J. Reynolds Jr., Tobacco Heir, Dies: Financier and Ex-Politician Was a

Former Playboy," *New York Times*, December 16, 1964, p. 43; Fambrough Brownlee, interview with Joan Maltese, February 2009; "A New Planetarium," *New York Times*, July 8, 1956; Charles Osolin, "Career as Mayor: Brief, Distinctive," *Winston-Salem Journal*, December 17, 1964; "Tobacco Heir Reynolds Dies in Swiss Clinic," *Los Angeles Times*, December 16, 1964; Roy Thompson, "R. J. Reynolds Dies at 58 in Swiss Clinic: Cause Not Determined," *Winston-Salem Journal,* December 16, 1964; "Amerikanischer Zigarettenfabrikant in Luzern Gestorben," *Luzerner Tagblatt,* December 17, 1964; Roy Thompson, "Reynolds' Flag to Fly at Half Staff," *Winston-Salem Journal*, December 17, 1964; Wilson, *For the People of North Carolina*; Dow, *Business Leader Profiles for Students*; "Reynolds Leaves Entire Estate to 4th Wife," *Twin City Sentinel*, January 20, 1965; Estate papers of R. J. Reynolds Jr., 1965, McIntosh County Courthouse, Probate section; Patrick Reynolds and Shachtman, *The Gilded Leaf*; "Infant Girl Ruled an Heiress of Reynolds Tobacco Millions," *New York Times*, November 5, 1965; "Trust Set Up for Reynolds Is Dissolved," *Twin City Sentinel*, November 5, 1965; Muriel Reynolds papers; Private investigation materials, courtesy Jeanette Scotton; H. W. Hutchins, personal papers; "Reynolds' Ex-Wife Files Suit," *Twin City Sentinel*, April 29, 1966; Tursi, *Winston-Salem*; Bailey and Bledsoe, *God, Dr. Buzzard, and the Bolito Man*; Linda Lee Reynolds, interview with Joan Maltese, February 2009; Reynolds family member (anonymous), interview with Joan Maltese, February 2009.

EPILOGUE

Suit, *Marianne O'Brien Reynolds v. Estate of Richard J. Reynolds,* 1975; Estate papers of R. J. Reynolds Jr., 1965, McIntosh County Courthouse, Probate section; "Suit Filed," *Daily Times News*, January 1, 1976; Gene Whitman, "Reynolds Lawsuit Comes as a Surprise," *Twin City Sentinel*, January 2, 1976; Gene Whitman, "Where Did He Die? Reynolds Lawsuit Raises Bizarre Questions," *Twin City Sentinel*, January 5, 1976; *Marianne O'Brien Reynolds v. Nancy S. Reynolds,* 238 Ga. 1, 230 S.E. 2d 842; Suit, *Marianne O'Brien Reynolds v. the State of Georgia,* 1981, U.S. Court of Appeals, 5th Circuit; Patrick Reynolds and Shachtman, *The Gilded Leaf*; H. W. Hutchins, personal papers; Fambrough Brownlee, interview with Joan Maltese, February 2009; "A Reynolds Takes on Cigarette Industry," *New York Times*, October 25, 1986; Reynolds family member (anonymous), interview with

Joan Maltese, February 2009; "Georgia Buys Island," *New York Times*, June 23, 1968; Terrence Smith, "President, Vacationing on Island in Georgia, to 'Read, Sleep, Fish,'" *New York Times*, April 13, 1979; Burrough and Helyar, *Barbarians at the Gate*; Bilder Georg Anderhub, "Die Erinnerung der Eideschsen," *Tages-Anzeiger*, August 21, 1998; Peter Hagmann, "Ein Haus fur die Zukunft der Musik," *Neue Zurcher Zeitung*, August 30, 2007; "KKL-Finanzierung," *Neue Luzerner Zeitung*, April 10, 2000; Gunther Jungnickl, "Benz-Band Ludwigsburg," *Stuttgarter Nachrichten*, January 26, 2005; Gret Heer, "Mit Mazenen in die Salzburg-Klasse," *Handelszeitung*, August 20, 2008; Jim Vickers, "Cigarettes, Whiskey and Wild, Wild Women," *The Spectator*, May 4, 1989; Jo Leslie, "$2 Puts You on Priceless Isle," *Atlanta Journal-Constitution*, November 9, 1977, p. 18A; P. Freeman, "Patrick Reynolds Fumes About His Tobacco-Rich Clan in a Tangy, Tell-All Book," *People Weekly*, April 24, 1989; White et al., *Lost Empire*.

BIBLIOGRAPHY

BOOKS

Bailey, Cornelia Walker, and Christena Bledsoe. *God, Dr. Buzzard, and the Bolito Man: A Saltwater Geechee Talks About Life on Sapelo Island, Georgia.* New York: Anchor, 2001.

Berendt, John. *Midnight in the Garden of Good and Evil.* New York: Vintage, 1994.

Bradshaw, Jon. *Dreams That Money Can Buy: The Tragic Life of Libby Holman.* New York: William Morrow, 1985.

Broeske, Pat H., and Peter Harry Brown. *Howard Hughes: The Untold Story.* Cambridge: Da Capo, 2004.

Burrough, Bryan, and John Helyar. *Barbarians at the Gate: The Fall of RJR Nabisco.* New York: HarperCollins, 1990.

Casstevens, Francis H. *Death in North Carolina's Piedmont: Tales of Murder, Suicide and Causes Unknown.* Charleston: History Press, 2006.

Coffey, Maria. *Explorers of the Infinite.* New York: Tarcher, 2008.

Coogan, Tim Pat. *The IRA.* New York: Palgrave Macmillan, 2002.

Davies, R. E. G. *Delta: An Airline and Its Aircraft.* McLean, VA: Paladwr, 1990.

De La Pedraja, Rene. *A Historical Dictionary of the U.S. Merchant Marine and Shipping Industry: Since the Introduction of Steam.* Santa Barbara: Greenwood, 1994.

Dow, Sheila M. *Business Leader Profiles for Students*. Florence, KY: Gale Research, 1999.

Duke, Pony, and Jason Thomas. *Too Rich: The Family Secrets of Doris Duke*. New York: HarperCollins, 1995.

Elliot, Eric J. *Winston-Salem's Historic West End*. Charleston: Arcadia, 2004.

Garraty, John A., and Mark C. Cames. *American National Biography*. New York: Oxford University Press, 1999.

Gleason, Michael P., and Andrew McCutcheon. *Sarge Reynolds: In the Time of His Life*. Gwynn, VA: Gleason, 1996.

Hearn, Thomas K., III. *Wake Forest University*. Charleston: Arcadia, 2003.

Howett, Catherine. *A World of Her Own Making: Katharine Smith Reynolds and the Landscape of Reynolda*. Amherst: University of Massachusetts Press, 2007.

Johnson, Michele Nicole. *Sapelo Island's Hog Hammock, GA*. Charleston: Arcadia, 2009.

Lewis, Arnold. *The Opulent Interiors of the Gilded Age*. Mineola, NY: Dover, 1987.

Mactaggart, Ross. *The Golden Century: Classic Motor Yachts, 1830–1930*. New York: W. W. Norton, 2001.

Mayer, Barbara. *Reynolda: A History of an American House*. Winston-Salem: John F. Blair, 1997.

McFeely, William S. *Sapelo's People: A Long Walk into Freedom*. New York: W. W. Norton, 1995.

Perry, Hamilton Darby. *Libby Holman: Body and Soul*. Boston: Little, Brown, 1983.

Rawls, Molly Grogan. *Winston-Salem: From the Collection of Frank B. Jones Jr*. Charleston: Arcadia, 2006.

———. *Winston-Salem in Vintage Postcards*. Charleston: Arcadia, 2004.

Ready, Milton. *The Tar Heel State: A History of North Carolina*. Columbia: University of South Carolina Press, 2005.

"Reynolda Farm." Winston-Salem: Twin-City Sentinel, 1917.

Reynolds, Patrick, and Tom Shachtman. *The Gilded Leaf: Triumph, Tragedy, and Tobacco: Three Generations of the R.J. Reynolds Family and Fortune.* Boston: Little, Brown, 1989.

Reynolds, Z. Smith. *Log of Aeroplane NR-898W: Experiences, Comments, Impressions of a Flight from England to China.* Winston-Salem: Reynolda House Museum of Art/Wake Forest University, 2003.

Sibley, Celestine, Richard Eldredge, and Fleming Sibley. *Celstine Sibley Reporter.* Athens, GA: Hill Street, 2006.

Smith, Rollin. *The Reynolda House Aeolian Organ.* Winston-Salem: Reynolda House Museum of Art, 1997.

Sullivan, Buddy. *Darien and McIntosh County: Images of America.* Charleston: Arcadia, 2000.

———. *Sapelo: A History.* Darien: Darien News, 1988.

———. *Sapelo Island, Georgia: Images of America.* Charleston: Arcadia, 2000.

Tilley, Nannie. *The R.J. Reynolds Tobacco Company.* Chapel Hill: University of North Carolina Press, 1985.

Tursi, Frank V. *Winston-Salem: A History.* Winston-Salem: John F. Blair, 1994.

Vanderbilt, Arthur T., II. *Fortune's Children.* New York: William Morrow, 1989.

Vanstory, Burnette Lightle. *Georgia's Land of Golden Isles.* Athens, GA: University of Georgia Press, 1982.

Wall, Isabella, Marty Wall, and Robert Bruce Woodcox. *Chasing Rubi: The Truth About Porfirio Rubirosa the Last Playboy.* Newport Beach, CA: Literary Press, 2005.

White, Susan E., Frank V. Tursi, and Steve McQuilkin. *Lost Empire: The Fall of R.J. Reynolds Tobacco Company.* Winston-Salem: Winston-Salem Journal, 2000.

Wilson, Emily Herring. *For the People of North Carolina: The Z. Smith Reynolds Foundation at Half-Century, 1936–1986.* Chapel Hill: University of North Carolina Press, 1988.

ARTICLES

"$1,475,000 Suit Settled." *New York Times*, May 8, 1934.

"3–Heat World Trot Record Set by Calumet Dilworthy at Goshen." *New York Times*, July 24, 1936.

"30 Craft Ready to Start Today in Bayside's Block Island Race." *New York Times*, July 29, 1938.

"38 Yachts Start in Vineyard Race." *New York Times*, September 3, 1938.

"$7,500 Bracelet Found on Vagrant Returned to Wife of Tobacco Heir." *New York Times*, December 16, 1952.

"Air Crash Suits Shifted." *New York Times*, October 19, 1929.

Albright, Robert C. "'Boss Away,' Democrats Call Off $100 Feast." *Washington Post*, March 28, 1941, p. 1.

"American Sent to Prison." *The Times* (London), August 1, 1929.

"American Yacht Disqualified in Race." *Los Angeles Times*, August 8, 1937.

"American Yawl Is Fifth." *New York Times*, August 13, 1937.

"Amerikanischer Zigarettenfabrikant in Luzern Gestorben." *Luzerner Tagblatt*, December 17, 1964.

Anderhub, Bilder Georg. "Die Erinnerung der Eideschsen." *Tages-Anzeiger*, August 21, 1998.

"Blitzen from the East." *Oakland Tribune*, July 2, 1939.

"Blitzen Is Victor in Key West Race." *New York Times*, March 12, 1939.

"Blitzen Sails On to Early Lead." *New York Times*, July 30, 1938.

"Blitzen Triumphs on Corrected Time." *New York Times*, March 7, 1939.

"Both Major Parties Report 1941 Deficits." *New York Times*, January 4, 1942.

"Both Parties Evaded Law, Says Gillette." *Washington Post*, January 12, 1941, p. 11.

"Brazil Revolt Gains Ground." *Los Angeles Times*, August 25, 1932.

"Brother Thinks Young Reynolds Was Murdered." *Los Angeles Times*, August 25, 1932.

"Chatterbox." *Los Angeles Times*, May 24, 1939.

"Chatterbox." *Los Angeles Times*, August 10, 1939.

"Chubasco Fails to Report in Honolulu Race Yacht Race." *Los Angeles Times*, July 16, 1939.

"Concessions Charged on Party Loans." *Los Angeles Times*, April 30, 1952.

"The Controversial Princess." *Time*, April 11, 1960.

"Co-op Apartment Sold." *New York Times*, October 21, 1953.

"Couple Wedded November 29." *Twin City Sentinel*, 1932.

"Curtiss Field Saved as Aviation Centre: Big Airline Planned." *New York Times*, August 14, 1927.

"Curtiss Service Adds to Airports." *New York Times*, January 15, 1929.

"Democratic National Group Reorganization Disclosed." *Los Angeles Times*, January 5, 1941.

"Democratic Shift Committee Posts." *New York Times*, January 5, 1941.

"Democrats Report $414,617 Unpaid." *New York Times*, March 13, 1941, p. 17.

"Democrats Report Outlay." *New York Times*, October 31, 1936.

"Dick Reynolds Given $25,000,000." *Daily-Times News*, April 4, 1934.

"Dick Reynolds Is in Winston-Salem." *The Landmark*, August 26, 1932.

"Dick Reynolds Thinks Smith Was Murdered." *Florence Morning News*, August 25, 1932.

"Dick Reynolds Weds an Actress." *The Landmark*, August 8, 1946.

"Divorce Granted to Mrs. R. J. Reynolds." *New York Times*, June 25, 1946, p. 23.

"Double Win Registered by Fleming." *New York Times*, July 4, 1936.

"Drunkenness." *Time*, August 12, 1929.

East, Bill. "Young Reynolds' Newspaper Was Neighborhood Success." *Twin City Sentinel*, December 16, 1964.

"Eloquent Milk Man." *Time*, May 18, 1931.

Erwin, Robert. "Dick Reynolds." *State Magazine*, August 16, 1941.

"Expanded Service of Line Approved." *New York Times*, November 7, 1940.

"Expect Holman Trial to Be Held in 6 Weeks." *New York Times*, August 16, 1932.

"Ex-Spouse Protests New Marriage by Reynolds." *Pasadena Independent*, April 6, 1961.

"Extortion Defendant Sentenced." *New York Times*, November 21, 1933.

"Faces Extortion Trial." *New York Times*, November 5, 1933.

"Family Proposes Reynolds Division." *New York Times*, November 17, 1934.

"Family Threatens New Reynolds Suit." *New York Times*, March 12, 1935.

"Fandango 2 Miles Ahead." *New York Times*, July 17, 1939.

"Fastest Quarter by Static." *New York Times*, January 17, 1937.

"Fatal Motor Accident." *The Times* (London), July 24, 1929.

"Finds New Evidence in Reynolds Death." *New York Times*, August 11, 1929.

"Flynn Sees Slap at Foreign Policy." *Los Angeles Times*, September 12, 1941.

"For First Place." *Fresno Bee*, July 17, 1939.

Freeman, P. "Patrick Reynolds Fumes About His Tobacco-Rich Clan in a Tangy, Tell-All Book." *People Weekly*, April 24, 1989.

"Friend Reluctant to Talk." *New York Times*, September 28, 1927.

"Georgia Buys Island." *New York Times*, June 23, 1968.

"Georgians Mourn Reynolds' Death." *Winston-Salem Journal*, December 17, 1964.

"Gifts Made by Reynolds to Projects Here Are Cited in Opening Hours of Retrial." *Darien News,* May 10, 1962.

"Golden Isles Begins Feeder Service." *Darien News*, November 5, 1959.

"Gone Are the Days When Tobacco Brought Only Wealth." *New York Times*, February 26, 1995.

"Gossip and Smart Talk." *Los Angeles Times*, August 20, 1939.

Hagmann, Peter. "Ein Haus fur die Zukunft der Musik." *Neue Zurcher Zeitung,* August 30, 2007.

"Hambletonian Won by Mary Reynolds." *New York Times*, August 17, 1933.

"Hawaii Yacht Race Winner at Matsonia." *Los Angeles Times*, August 10, 1939.

Heer, Gret. "Mit Mazenen in die Salzburg-Klasse." *Handelszeitung*, August 20, 2008.

Henning, Arthur Sears. "Find Campaign Was History's Most Expensive." *Chicago Daily Tribune*, January 24, 1941.

"House by Reynolds." *Time*, September 2, 1935.

"Infant Girl Ruled an Heiress of Reynolds Tobacco Millions." *New York Times*, November 5, 1965.

"Island Fad Hits South." *New York Times*, February 7, 1937.

"Island to R. J. Reynolds." *New York Times*, April 19, 1934.

"Jackson Day Dinner Set." *New York Times*, February 24, 1941.

"Jersey Democrats Got Reynolds Loan." *New York Times*, January 9, 1941, p. 46.

Jungnickl, Gunther. "Benz-Band Ludwigsburg." *Stuttgarter Nachrichten*, January 26, 2005.

"KKL-Finanzierung." *Neue Luzerner Zeitung*, April 10, 2000.

Laurence, Muriel. "Letters to the Times." *New York Times*, December 15, 1941.

———. "London." *New York Times*, December 20, 1941.

———. "Shortage of Food Weakening the French." *New York Times*, November 15, 1943.

"Lead Poured at City Island Yard for Keel of New Schafer Yawl." *New York Times*, December 30, 1937.

Leslie, Jo. "$2 Puts You on Priceless Isle." *Atlanta Journal-Constitution*, November 9, 1977, p. 18A.

"Libby Holman Asks Trial to Clear Her." *New York Times*, October 20, 1932.

"Libby Holman Reynolds Asks Full Exoneration." *New York Times*, October 20, 1932.

"Libby Holman Wins on Estate Appeal." *New York Times*, November 2, 1935.

"Long Island Trotting on Big Scale Planned." *New York Times*, April 1, 1937.

"The Marriage-Go-Round." *Time*, January 25, 1963.

"Marriages: Mr. R. D. A. Greenough and Mrs. M. Allison-Laurence." *The Times* (London), October 10, 1946.

"Marriages: Mr. R. J. Reynolds and Mrs. M. M. Greenough." *The Times* (London), August 18, 1952.

"Miami Women Watch Yachts from Plane." *New York Times*, February 16, 1939.

"Midnight Autopsy Made on Reynolds." *New York Times*, September 2, 1932.

"Millionaire's Son Sent to Prison." *Daily Chronicle*, August 1, 1929.

"Milestones." *Time*, January 9, 1933.

"Milestones." *Time*, June 11, 1934.

"Milestones." *Time*, April 14, 1941.

"Milestones." *Time*, May 30, 1960.

"Miss Holman Wins in Reynolds Fight." *New York Times*, March 16, 1935.

"Miss Mary Reynolds Wed." *New York Times*, December 17, 1929.

"Mistrial Ordered in Reynolds Case." *New York Times*, July 26, 1929, p. 6.

"More Party Loans Told at Inquiry." *New York Times*, January 10, 1941, p. 20.

"Mrs. E. D. Reynolds." *New York Times*, December 11, 1961.

"Mrs. Harriman Wins Special Trot for Amateur Drivers at Goshen." *New York Times*, July 23, 1936.

"Mrs. M. A. Laurence Married in Prague." *New York Times*, October 15, 1946.

"Mrs. Mann Married." *New York Times*, October 19, 1954.

"Mrs. Reynolds Agrees to Divorce Settlement." *Los Angeles Times*, June 15, 1946.

"Names Make the News." *Time*, March 23, 1936.

"National Aid Given State Democrats." *New York Times*, October 30, 1946.

Nelson, Godfrey N. "U.S. Rule Reversed on Basis for Tax." *New York Times*, October 20, 1940.

"New Line to Orient Approved by U.S." *New York Times*, October 6, 1940.

"A New Planetarium." *New York Times*, July 8, 1956.

"New Reynolds Trial." *New York Times*, September 9, 1961.

"Olson's Spending Put Above Income." *New York Times*, May 1, 1952.

Osolin, Charles. "Career as Mayor: Brief, Distinctive." *Winston-Salem Journal*, December 17, 1964.

"Pacing Stake Won by Dick Reynolds." *New York Times*, July 7, 1933.

"Parties List Funds in State Campaign." *New York Times*, December 1, 1944.

"Political Gifts by 12 Wealthy Families Listed." *Los Angeles Times*, February 3, 1957.

"President's Wartime Aide Heads Caribou Mines." *New York Times*, March 2, 1950.

"President Vacationing on Island in Georgia." *New York Times*, April 14, 1939.

"Publicity Aide; Mrs. Reynolds Wed in Monaco." *New York Times,* July 31, 1970.

"Quayle Decides Loan Testimony Was a 'Mistake.'" *Chicago Daily Tribune*, January 12, 1941, p. 13.

"Radio Today." *New York Times*, August 28, 1941.

"Reported Seen in Florida." *New York Times*, September 28, 1927.

"Reynolds Absent: Friends Unworried." *New York Times*, October 3, 1927.

"Reynolds Answers Dancer's $140,000 Suit." *New York Times*, September 8, 1934.

"Reynolds a Suicide, His Guardian Holds." *New York Times*, July 8, 1932.

"Reynolds Baby Born." *Twin City Sentinel*, December 16, 1964.

"Reynolds Brother Leaves Brazil." *New York Times*, August 6, 1932.

"Reynolds Buried at Church in Village Near Swiss Home." *Twin City Sentinel*, December 17, 1964.

"Reynolds Case Has a New Turn." *Los Angeles Times*, July 11, 1932.

"Reynolds Case in New Turn." *Winston-Salem Journal*, July 30, 1929.

"Reynolds Case Inquiry Revived." *New York Times*, September 2, 1932.

"Reynolds Desires to See 'Justice' Done Regarding Tragic Death of Brother." *Winston-Salem Journal*, August 25, 1932.

"Reynolds Explains Hiding." *Los Angeles Times*, September 29, 1927.

"Reynolds' Ex-Wife Files Suit." *Twin City Sentinel*, April 29, 1966.

"Reynolds Fund Aids Warfare on Syphilis." *New York Times*, December 19, 1937.

"Reynolds Gets 5-Month Term." *Winston-Salem Journal*, July 31, 1929.

"Reynolds Gets Call in Inquiry." *Los Angeles Times*, January 14, 1941.

"Reynolds Gets Divorce." *New York Times*, May 17, 1960.

"Reynolds Guilty; Gets Five Months." *New York Times*, August 1, 1929, p. 2.

"Reynolds Heir Born 36 Hours After He Died." *Charleston Gazette*, December 17, 1964.

"Reynolds Heir Is Dead at 58." *News and Observer*, December 16, 1964.

"Reynolds Inquiry Awaits Brother." *New York Times*, July 15, 1932.

"Reynolds Inventory Filed." *New York Times*, December 20, 1961.

"Reynolds Is Found in St. Louis Cafe: Surprised at Hunt." *New York Times*, September 28, 1927.

"Reynolds Is President New Airlines Company Located at Sapelo Island." *Darien News*, November 5, 1959.

"Reynolds Leases Sapelo Island." *New York Times*, April 19, 1934.

"Reynolds Leaves Entire Estate to 4th Wife." *Twin City Sentinel*, January 20, 1965.

"Reynolds Left Suspect Cash." *New York Times*, October 8, 1932.

"Reynolds Located: Found in St. Louis Restaurant." *Los Angeles Times*, September 28, 1927.

"Reynolds Loses Point." *New York Times*, December 17, 1933.

"Reynolds Millions Go to Heiress." *New York Times*, August 20, 1936.

"Reynolds Must Pay Nine Million Plus." *Modesto Bee*, April 28, 1963.

"Reynolds on Honeymoon in 60-Room Home." *Los Angeles Times*, August 11, 1952.

"Reynolds on Stand in Motor Killing." *New York Times*, July 25, 1929, p. 18.

"Reynolds on Trial for Manslaughter." *New York Times*, July 23, 1929, p. 21.

"Reynolds on Way Here After 'Jaunt.'" *New York Times*, September 29, 1927.

"Reynolds on Witness Stand." *Winston-Salem Journal*, July 24, 1929.

"Reynolds Reported Near Home." *Los Angeles Times*, August 21, 1932.

"Reynolds Retrial Opens." *New York Times*, July 27, 1929, p. 5.

"Reynolds' Second Wife to Get $2,000,000." *Los Angeles Times*, July 29, 1952.

"Reynolds Settlement Overruled." *Los Angeles Times*, March 22, 1934.

"A Reynolds Takes on Cigarette Industry." *New York Times*, October 25, 1986.

"Reynolds Tobacco Heir Files Suit for Divorce." *New York Times*, June 1, 1946.

"Reynolds Trial Oct. 3 Expected by Defense." *New York Times*, August 21, 1932.

"Reynolds vs. Reynolds." *Time*, January 23, 1933.

"Reynolds Will Fly to Miami." *New York Times*, August 16, 1932.

"Richard J. Reynolds Gym Dedication Set for Dec. 29." *Darien News*.

"R. J. Reynolds Asserts Brother Was Slain." *New York Times*, August 25, 1932.

"R. J. Reynolds Divorce Pact Gives 3rd Wife $2 Million." *New York Times*, April 28, 1963.

"R. J. Reynoldses Jr. Hosts." *New York Times*, February 11, 1938.

"R. J. Reynolds Fights Suit." *New York Times*, October 31, 1933.

"R. J. Reynolds Heir Commits Suicide." *New York Times*, July 7, 1932.

"R. J. Reynolds Is Buried in Cemetery in Lucerne." *New York Times*, December 18, 1964, p. 64.

"R. J. Reynolds Is Dead: Stricken in Switzerland." *Twin City Sentinel*, December 15, 1964.

"R. J. Reynolds Is Sued." *New York Times*, March 31, 1933.

"R. J. Reynolds Jr. Arrives." *New York Times*, August 22, 1932.

"R. J. Reynolds Jr., Tobacco Heir, Dies: Financier and Ex-Politician Was a Former Playboy." *New York Times*, December 16, 1964, p. 43.

"R. J. Reynolds Married." *New York Times*, August 10, 1952.

"R. J. Reynolds Seeks Divorce." *New York Times*, August 22, 1959.

"R. J. Reynolds Sues Wife." *New York Times*, June 1, 1946.

"R. J. Reynolds to Be Called in Vote Probe." *Washington Post*, January 9, 1941, p. 16.

"R. J. Reynolds to Marry: Son of Tobacco Firm Founder to Marian Byrne, Actress." *New York Times*, August 7, 1946, p. 19.

"R. J. Reynolds to Wed: Heir of Tobacco Man to Marry Miss Dillard Tomorrow." *New York Times*, December 31, 1932, p. 8.

"R. J. Reynolds to Wed Miss Dillard." *New York Times*, December 26, 1932.

"R. J. Reynolds Weds." *New York Times*, August 8, 1946.

"R. J. Reynolds Weds Miss Dillard." *New York Times*, January 2, 1933.

Robbins, James. "Baruna's Victory a Feature of the Year." *New York Times*, December 25, 1938.

———. "Vanderbilt Likely to Sail in British Regattas Next Year." *New York Times*, November 4, 1938.

Robbins, James, and Morris Rosenfield. "Nation's Yachtsmen and Speed Boat Pilots Enjoyed a Record-Breaking Year." *New York Times*, December 24, 1939.

"Roosevelt Radio Loan Questioned." *Los Angeles Times*, January 9, 1941, p. 8.

"Roosevelt to Make Jackson Day Speech." *New York Times*, March 24, 1941.

"Says Both Parties 'Evaded' Hatch Act." *New York Times*, January 12, 1941, p. 42.

"Seattle Mail Ship Launched in East." *Los Angeles Times*, May 25, 1941.

"Seek R. J. Reynolds, Tobacco Man's Heir, Missing 11 Days." *New York Times*, September 27, 1927.

"Seeks Reynolds Award." *New York Times*, October 2, 1927.

"Senate Seat Declared Won by Illegal Methods." *New York Times*, February 21, 1941.

"Sheriff Continuing Reynolds Inquiry." *New York Times*, July 13, 1932.

"Ship Construction Ahead of Schedule." *New York Times*, May 18, 1941.

"Sloop Blitzen Launched." *New York Times*, June 3, 1938.

"Small Boats Race Today at Newport." *New York Times*, March 26, 1939.

"Small Yachts Take the Lead." *New York Times*, July 6, 1939.

Smith, Terrence. "President, Vacationing on Island in Georgia, to 'Read, Sleep, Fish.'" *New York Times*, April 13, 1979.

"Son to R. J. Reynolds Jr." *New York Times,* December 8, 1933.

"So They Took the $25,000,000." *Los Angeles Times*, April 9, 1934.

"A Spell of Unemployment." *Time*, December 21, 1953.

"Stevenson Names 50 Business Aides." *New York Times*, October 11, 1956.

"Sues to Apportion Reynolds Estate." *New York Times*, March 25, 1933.

"Suit Filed." *Daily-Times News*, January 1, 1976.

"Taffy Volo Takes Trot." *New York Times*, September 14, 1933.

Thompson, Roy. "Reynolds' Flag to Fly at Half Staff." *Winston-Salem Journal*, December 17, 1964.

———. "Reynolds Had Many Sides: Wealth, Generosity, Flash." *Winston-Salem Journal*, December 17, 1964.

———. "R. J. Reynolds Dies At 58 in Swiss Clinic: Cause Not Determined." *Winston-Salem Journal*, December 16, 1964.

"Threatened Wife of R. J. Reynolds." *New York Times*, November 4, 1933.

"Three Doctors Aid Reynolds Defense." *New York Times*, July 31, 1929.

"Three Sheets in the Wind." *Time*, July 30, 1945.

"Tobacco Heir Divorced." *New York Times*, August 8, 1952.

"Tobacco Heir Reynolds Dies in Swiss Clinic." *Los Angeles Times*, December 16, 1964.

"Tobacco Heir Safe After Yacht Blast." *New York Times*, February 25, 1955.

"Tobacco Heir Settles: $2 Million Alimony." *New York Mirror*, April 28, 1963.

"Tobacco Heir's Ex-Wife Gets $2 Million Alimony." *Los Angeles Times*, April 28, 1963.

"Tobacco Heir Wed: Ex-Wife Shocked." *New York Times*, April 5, 1961.

"Tobacco Tycoon Tosses Surprise Party." *The Times Recorder*, December 13, 1947.

"Tobey Demands Hague Inquiry." *New York Times*, March 8, 1941, p. 10.

"To Fingerprint Guests." *New York Times,* July 11, 1932.

"Tom Davis: Entrepreneur of the Air." *News and Observer*, June 23, 2004.

"To Sue for $1,300,000 for Airplane Crash." *New York Times*, August 21, 1929.

"Trust Set Up for Reynolds Is Dissolved." *Twin City Sentinel*, November 5, 1965.

"U.S. Official Defends Political Loan Rule." *New York Times*, May 28, 1952.

Vickers, Jim. "Cigarettes, Whiskey and Wild, Wild Women." *The Spectator*, May 4, 1989.

"Victory Seen by Secretary." *Los Angeles Times*, September 13, 1941.

"Wakiva Sets Pace for Racing Fleet." *New York Times*, March 6, 1939.

"Wakiva Takes Lead in Race to Havana." *New York Times*, March 5, 1939.

"Wedding on July 30 is Planned by Mrs. Marianne Reynolds." *New York Times*, June 25, 1970.

Whitman, Gene. "Mayor Reynolds Hit Apathy." *Twin City Sentinel*, December 16, 1964.

———. "Reynolds Lawsuit Comes as a Surprise." *Twin City Sentinel*, January 2, 1976.

———. "Where Did He Die? Reynolds Lawsuit Raises Bizarre Questions." *Twin City Sentinel*, January 5, 1976.

"Widow Believed at Former Retreat." *New York Times*, August 11, 1929.

"Widow of R. J. Reynolds Gives Birth to Daughter." *New York Times*, December 16, 1964.

"Widow's Parents Mystified." *New York Times*, July 7, 1932.

Winburn, Jay Te. "Mary K. Babcock Married in South." *New York Times*, September 2, 1951.

"Winston-Salem Saddened by Reynolds Shift." *New York Times*, February 1, 1987.

"Witnesses at Odds in Reynolds Trial." *New York Times*, July 24, 1929, p. 7.

"Women Invite Men to Parley." *Los Angeles Times*, August 7, 1941.

"Works of Art from 40 Tiny Islands." *New York Times*, January 23, 1971.

"Yacht Race Victor in Doubt." *Los Angeles Times*, July 21, 1939.

"Yawl Crosses Ocean, Ruled out of Race." *New York Times*, August 8, 1937.

"Young Democrats Back All Out Aid." *New York Times*, August 24, 1941.

"Young Reynolds Arrives Here Following 12,000 Mile Trip from Africa." *Winston-Salem Journal*, August 24, 1932.

COURT DOCUMENTS

Anne Cannon Reynolds et al. v. Zachary Smith Reynolds et al., 208 N.C. 578, 182 S.E. 341.

Death Certificate of Richard Joshua Reynolds, 1964, Confederation Suisse, Lucerne, Switzerland.

Divorce suit, *Elizabeth Dillard Reynolds v. Richard Joshua Reynolds*, 1946, Forsyth County records.

Divorce suit, *Richard J. Reynolds v. Marianne O'Brien Reynolds*, 1952, Dade County records.

Divorce suit, *Richard J. Reynolds v. Muriel M. Reynolds*, 1960, McIntosh County records (including motions, depositions, testimony).

Divorce suit, *Richard J. Reynolds v. Muriel M. Reynolds*, 1962, McIntosh County records (including motions, depositions, testimony).

Divorce suit, *Richard J. Reynolds v. Muriel M. Reynolds*, 1962, U.S. Court of Appeals.

Estate papers of Marianne O'Brien Reynolds, 1984, New York Surrogate Court records.

Estate papers of R. J. Reynolds Jr., 1965, McIntosh County Courthouse, Probate section (including last will and testament of R. J. Reynolds, settlement agreements, investigation by Michael Reynolds).

Marianne O' Brien Reynolds v. Estate of Richard J. Reynolds, 238 Ga. 1, 230 S.E. 2d 842.

Marianne O'Brien Reynolds v. Nancy S. Reynolds, 238 Ga. 1, 230 S.E. 2d 842.

Marriage certificate for Richard Greenough and Ileana Mann, 1954, City of Westminster General Register Office, London.

Marriage certificate for Richard Greenough and Muriel Laurence, 1946, City of Westminster General Register Office, London.

Muriel M. Reynolds v. Richard J. Reynolds, 217 Ga. 234, 123 S.E. 2d 115.

Suit, *Marianne O'Brien Reynolds v. Chemical Bank & Trust Company,* 1951–1952, New York County records.

Suit, *Marianne O'Brien Reynolds v. Estate of Richard J. Reynolds,* 1975, McIntosh County records.

Suit, *Marianne O'Brien Reynolds v. the State of Georgia,* 1981, U.S. Court of Appeals, 5th Circuit.

Suit, *Muriel M. Reynolds v. Richard J. Reynolds,* 1963, McIntosh County records.

Suit, *Muriel M. Reynolds v. Richard J. Reynolds,* 1963, New York County records.

Suit, *Rex v. Richard Joshua Reynolds—Manslaughter,* 1929, Metropolitan Police 3/330/Old Bailey–London records.

UNPUBLISHED MATERIALS

Hutchins, H. W., personal papers, letters from Muriel M. Reynolds to H. W. Hutchins, courtesy Jeanette Scotton.

Letter, Franklin D. Roosevelt to Dick Reynolds, July 30, 1942, PPF 7370, Franklin D. Roosevelt Library.

Letter, Franklin D. Roosevelt to Dick Reynolds, December 5, 1941, PPF 1069, Franklin D. Roosevelt Library.

Letter, Franklin D. Roosevelt to Mr. Reynolds, February 5, 1941, PPF 7370, Franklin D. Roosevelt Library.

Letter, Richard J. Reynolds to Franklin D. Roosevelt, December 2, 1941, Franklin D. Roosevelt Library.

Letter, Richard J. Reynolds, Treasurer, DNC to Franklin D. Roosevelt, June 4, 1942, Franklin D. Roosevelt Library.

Memorandum, Edward J. Flynn to Franklin D. Roosevelt, June 17, 1942, Franklin D. Roosevelt Library.

Memorandum, "G." to Franklin D. Roosevelt, July 22, 1942, Franklin D. Roosevelt Library.

Message, W. Neale Roach to President Truman Naval Aide, July 11, 1945, Truman White House Central Files, Harry S. Truman Presidential Library.

Reynolds, Muriel, personal papers, transcripts, diaries, manuscripts, letters, and private investigation materials, courtesy Jeanette Scotton.

"Robert G. Nixon Oral History Interview, October 30, 1970," Harry S. Truman Presidential Library, http://www.trumanlibrary.org/oralhist/oral_his.htm (accessed February 7, 2009).

Telegram, R. J. Reynolds and Mrs. Clifford Long to White House Secretary William Hassett, November 24, 1948, Truman White House Central Files, Harry S. Truman Presidential Library.

Unpublished U.S. Senate Committee Hearings, 18th Congress–88th Congress, 1823–1964 (18) SJ-T.1–(82) SSM-T.23.

INDEX